HEALING WATERS

```
613.122 B935h

Bullard, Loring.

Healing waters
```

HEALING WATERS

Missouri's Historic Mineral Springs and Spas

LORING BULLARD

University of Missouri Press   Columbia and London

Copyright © 2004 by
The Curators of the University of Missouri
University of Missouri Press, Columbia, Missouri 65201
Printed and bound in the United States of America
All rights reserved
5 4 3 2 1   08 07 06 05 04

Library of Congress Cataloging-in-Publication Data

Bullard, Loring.
  Healing waters : Missouri's historic mineral springs and spas / Loring Bullard.
      p. cm.
  Includes bibliographical references and index.
  ISBN 0-8262-1554-8 (alk. paper)
  1. Mineral waters—Missouri. 2. Springs—Missouri.
3. Health resorts—Missouri. I. Title.
  RA807.M8B856 2004
  613'.122'09778—dc22   2004014983

∞™ This paper meets the requirements of the
American National Standard for Permanence of Paper
for Printed Library Materials, Z39.48, 1984.

Designer: Kristie Lee
Typesetter: Phoenix Type, Inc.
Printer and binder: The Maple-Vail Book Manufacturing Group
Typefaces: Adobe Garamond and Saloon Extended

To my father,
Rev. James W. Bullard

CONTENTS

Preface ix
Acknowledgments xiii
Introduction 1

1. Where Rocks, Water, and Life Unite 4
2. The Call of Hygieia 11
3. Springs of America 16
4. The Spice of Life 24
5. Missouri's Early Resorts 34
6. The Surveys 41
7. Spa Doctors 53
8. The Rising Tide 60
9. Social Diversions 69
10. Taking the Waters 75
11. Waters, Deep and Mysterious 83
12. Health in a Bottle 89
13. Fading toward Obscurity 99

Site Surveys and Descriptions 113

Appendix: Other Mineral Water Sites 217
Bibliography 227
Index 233

PREFACE

Winding along a Camden County highway one frigid January day, my father and I marveled at the surreal scene around us. An icy fog hung in the air, and shafts of sunlight every so often blasted through, illuminating ice-covered trees in dazzling white. More often the sun's light failed to completely penetrate the gray shroud, instead glowing through it a very pale yellowish white, like a low-watt refrigerator lightbulb. My father, gazing out across the frozen landscape, reminisced of warmer times, long ago but not so far away. As a kid, he spent glorious summer days in the mineral water swimming pool at McAllister Springs, near his boyhood home of Houstonia, Missouri, about eighty miles from here. In its heyday, McAllister was widely billed as a medicinal spring resort, but sixty years ago, my father was looking for fun, not a cure. Now, on our quest to relocate some of the old mineral springs, spas, and health resorts of Missouri, his boyhood memories gained a new perspective.

We turned north and descended into a broad valley toward the old section of Climax Springs. Stopping to inquire at the community center, we were told how to find the spring, the site of the town's genesis, but were forewarned, "there's really not much to see there anymore." Yet in the small park near the mostly abandoned storefronts of downtown, there really *was* something to see. The old spring, surging into its concrete trough from a low, mossy bluff, appeared as molten steel under the gray fog. A second, denser layer of vapor hovered above the little stream as it exited the trough and tumbled through the park toward its meeting with some creek and, eventually, the Lake of the Ozarks.

Guided by Paul Schweitzer's century-old book on Missouri's spas and mineral waters, we located a small, steep-sided sinkhole several hundred feet southeast of the spring. As we neared its rim, leaning to see into the darkness of its

Trough at Climax Springs, Camden County, 1998.
Photo by author

depths, we felt we might be standing at the very spot where Mr. Hockman stood more than a hundred years ago when he exclaimed, "that caps the climax!" or words to that effect, giving birth to an idea, a resort, and ultimately a town. The experience at Climax Springs put the notion of "not much to see" in perspective for us, for there was certainly more to see here than at many of the mineral water locations we had already visited. Very few of them had as much to offer as McAllister Springs, where the greenish ruins of the old bathhouse and swimming pool stirred my father's six-decade-old memories.

Contemplating that Climax Springs sinkhole, where wooden stairs once descended into the coolness, we found it almost inconceivable that people actually had bathed in its frigid, subterranean pool in a quest for better health. In the hot summer, the experience might have been tolerable, though it must have been gloomy. But since the underground lake remains at a nearly constant temperature year-round, it was also used for winter bathing, a prospect that brought goose bumps to our pampered flesh. What we had no trouble accepting is the fact that people went to great lengths in their search for better health, and they were willing to believe it might be found in these "medicinal" springwaters. It also occurred to us that in many ways things today are not really that different, when one considers the hordes of people jogging, drinking bottled waters, and taking vitamins in an eternal quest to hold on to the precious vigor of youth.

Later, sitting comfortably at home, I had time to reflect on my travels across the state to learn more about its old mineral springs and health spas. Largely, it was a journey into the obscure—visits to many end-of-the-road towns and the sites of places vanished. Though largely forgotten, these mineral water towns and resorts were once high points on the cultural landscape. My quest to learn more about them brought a sense of loss but also raised haunting questions: What happened to them? Why did once-vibrant, bustling enterprises fade and decay? Why were they so popular for a while? Did people really believe that the waters could heal?

My peculiar interest in mineral waters really began as a fascination with the springs themselves—in particular, those near my home in Greene County, Missouri. A short foray into the intriguing history of these local springs spawned an attempt to capture and popularize that information in a short report for the Missouri Department of Natural Resources. That work, in turn, involved an inquiry into the history of human use and development of springs, including an examination of springs in southwest Missouri that were used medicinally in the late nineteenth century—places with promising or perhaps hopeful names such as El Dorado Springs, Jerico Springs, Ponce de Leon, Reno, and Eau de Vie.

Finally, my quest led me to an obscure mineral water site back in Greene County itself; at this location today virtually no signs exist of the town that once drew breath there. Here, people came to be relieved of their afflictions as promised by the promoters of their day. Prominently marked on the 1904 county plat map, it is a place where cows now idly graze and a spring, once proudly framed and protected by neat-fitted stones, trickles unnoticed into the Little Sac River. It was a place called "Bethesda," after a sacred spring mentioned in the Bible. Like its counterparts across the state, it hoped to attract those people thirsting for healing waters.

ACKNOWLEDGMENTS

As with many such efforts, what was intended as a relatively short-lived project grew into something very time-consuming and complicated. Such, I suppose, is the nature of historical research. The work, however, was rewarding in many ways, providing an opportunity to meet scores of interesting people and see parts of Missouri I never before had an occasion to visit. If nothing more, such an undertaking certainly fosters a greater appreciation of the rich diversity of Missouri and its citizens.

An attempt has been made to bring together in this volume a wide assortment of historical tidbits and weave them into a coherent story of Missouri's mineral water past. In doing so, information was drawn from a large number of documents of admittedly varying reliability. An effort was made to be as historically correct as possible. Nevertheless, some inaccuracies probably exist in accounts given here. Readers are encouraged to point these out and to provide additional information.

The production of this book depended upon a large number of people who resonate with Missouri history. I am especially indebted to the patient and generous people who took time out of their busy lives to show me the sites of long-gone mineral spa facilities. Without their help, that curious history might remain largely a dusty relic. I would like to express my sincere gratitude to Chuck and Chris Ahlemann, Sweet Springs; Diane Boucher Ayotte, Western Historical Manuscript Collection–Columbia; Dorothy Bartram, Versailles; Phyllis Basnett, Lebanon; Vicki Bates, Excelsior Springs; Mark Bellwood, Marshall; Margaret Block, Huntsville; Rosie Boden, Montrose; Loretta Boemler, Kimmswick Historical Society; Dave Boutros, Western Historical Manuscript Collection–Columbia; John Bradbury, Western Historical Manuscript Collection–Rolla;

Thelma Brinkley, LaGrange; Pat Brophy, Nevada; Tom Carneal, Maryville; Pauline Carnell, Jane; Cedar County Historical Society; Kelly Chambers, Jackson County Historical Society; Barbara Chilcott, Missouri Department of Health, Jefferson City; William Claycomb, Hughesville; La Dora Combs, Denver; Louise Coutts, Fayette; Merle Cross, Camdenton; Mrs. Wallace Cruce, Chariton County Historical Society, Salisbury; Susan Dunn, Missouri Department of Natural Resources, Rolla; Lee Eckerson, Bethany; Trish Erzfeld, Perryville; Paul Eye, Appleton City; John Finley, State Library, Jefferson City; Kevin Fisher, Liberty; Gentry County Historical Society, Albany; Michael Glenn, Springfield–Greene County Library, Springfield; Greg Gramaud, Missouri Department of Conservation; Roberta and Hurley Hagood, Hannibal; Esley Hamilton, St. Louis Department of Parks and Recreation; Denise Haskamp, Glasgow; Calvin Hawkins, Clay County Archives, Liberty; Marie Heinemann, Stockton; Dorothy Heinze, Imperial; Bill Holman, Fayette; Jo Ann Holman, Plattsburg; Orville Holt, Bear Creek; Jim Hourigan, Rocheport; Jackson County Historical Society; Corbyn Jacobs, Hannibal; Clayton Jenkins, Tuscumbia; Sybil Jobe, Newton County Historical Society, Neosho; Willis Johnson, Ash Grove; Leola Jones, Greensfield; Brenton Karhoff, Knox County Historical Society, Edina; Walter Keith, Nodaway County Heritage Collection; Mary Ann Kempf, Boonville; Robert King, Louisiana; Wayne Koopman, Drexel; Carolyn Larson, Weston; Joyce L. Beals Lee, Neosho; Susan Littleton, Keytesville; Grace Mainprize, Thayer; Pat Manring, Albany; Julie March, Springfield; Jason McCormick, Leasburg; John McElroy, Bowling Green; Marie McNarie, Boone County Historical Society, Columbia; Mary McNary, Hamilton; Marjorie Miller, Montgomery City; Denise Morrison, Kansas City Museum; Letha Marie Mowry, Nodaway County Historical Society; Sharol Neely, Springfield–Greene County Library, Springfield; Dennis Northcott, Missouri Historical Society, St. Louis; Catherine Marcum Phelps, Henry County Museum, Clinton; Nan Poage-Prater, Spalding; Polk County Historical Society; Gilbert Powers, Warrensburg; Mary Rainey, Johnson County Historical Society, Warrensburg; Bob Ravenscratt, Palmyra; Ted Roller, Purdy; Steve Sadler, Windsor; Donna Sager, Middle Grove; Larry Schlict, Imperial; Jonathan Selsor, Hillsboro; Ruby Shirk, St. Clair Historical Society, Osceola; Anna Mae Sims, Spokane; John Paul Skaggs, Historic Madison County, Fredericktown; Louie Smith, Warsaw; Rhonda Smith, Springfield–Greene County Library, Springfield; Thomas Sneed; John Sparks, Kirksville; Pat Stambaugh, LaGrange; Frank Stark, Chillicothe; Byron Stewart, Southwest Missouri State University, Springfield; St. Louis Historical Society; Jason Stratman, Missouri

Office of the Gasconade Hotel, Lebanon Magnetic Well. *State Historical Society of Missouri, Columbia*

Historical Society, St. Louis; Geraldine Stroemer, Brunswick; Earl Taubold, Sulphur Springs; Don Troutman, Houston; Jim Vandike, Missouri Department of Natural Resources, Rolla; Jennie Vertries, Princeton; Otis Vickers, Stockton; Lois Watkins, Stone County Historical Society, Galena; Dwight Weaver, Missouri Department of Natural Resources, Rolla; Mike Weaver, Hannibal; Pat Wiles, Jamesport; Mr. and Mrs. James B. Willingham, Madison; and Margaret Wooderson, Jefferson City.

HEALING WATERS

INTRODUCTION

Most Missourians have heard of Excelsior Springs and El Dorado Springs. They probably know that special springs formed the centerpieces of those communities. Ask about Randolph Springs, Jerico Springs, Siloam Springs, Aurora Springs, or Climax Springs, and some people would know of these places, depending on what part of the state they were from. They might also guess that if the word "spring" is in the name, there must be a spring connected to the town's founding. But mention the names of Zodiac, Reno, Lithium, Radium, Blankenship, or Elk Lick, and you will probably get a blank stare or puzzled look, unless, of course, you have stumbled upon a local historian. Though now obscure and mostly forgotten, these last mentioned sites at one time had the potential of an Excelsior or an El Dorado, at least to their founders and promoters. Each of these places, along with scores of others, fought hard to capture the attention of Missourians who were seeking better health, relaxation, or good times at mineral water spas in the late 1800s and early 1900s.

The history of natural medicinal waters in Missouri is unexpectedly rich and replete with stories of ordinary and extraordinary cures, climbs to fame, days of glory and splendor, booms and busts. Few people realize how many places in the state medicinal waters were found, used, bottled, and promoted. Very few are aware of how profoundly the golden age of springs and spas influenced the cultural development of Missouri.

Many people today might dismiss the mineral water boom of the past as a craze or fad. However, the historical context for such patterns of use and their accompanying beliefs should be more fully appreciated. Missourians were not unique in their widespread faith in the curative powers of mineral waters. At the time spas blossomed in this state, "taking the waters" remained a strong national

Stone wash basin at El Dorado Springs, Cedar County.
Photo by author

tradition. Though the custom derived from colonial America, it had before that been transported across the Atlantic from Europe. To label such a long-lived, pervasive social practice as a fad does not accurately describe the phenomenon, nor does it do justice to the generations that embraced it.

The centuries old and slowly evolving patterns of human mineral water use fall within the overlapping spheres of science, medicine, recreation, and even religion. Roots of the tradition extend far into antiquity. The persistent, hopeful relationship between people and medicinal waters acted as a flywheel for recurring cycles of interest that extended over many centuries. Even well into the twentieth century, when modern medicine had seemingly taken hold, many physicians and scientists continued to proclaim the medicinal virtues of mineral waters.

For the most part, however, by the second quarter of the twentieth century medical science and popular opinion had discounted the immediate medical usefulness of mineral waters. As the sciences of microbiology and biochemistry progressed, and with the inherent promise of drug cures, orthodox medicine began to turn a cold shoulder on mineral water treatments and nontraditional medical sects in general. Americans, who always seemed to be in a hurry, were quick to embrace new medical breakthroughs that produced rapid results. Spa treatments, with their methodical, ritualized regimens extending over several weeks or months, did not fit well with fast-paced lifestyles.

It is into this long history of use and belief in mineral springs and spas that this volume delves. The people and places of Missouri's mineral water past are fascinating and deserve more than a fleeting footnote in modern historical treatments. Many sites have significant remains that, if preserved, could help to tell a story remembered by too few. Although people might consider the mineral water story itself a dusty relic, of no immediate value, there is benefit to be gleaned from the telling. If nothing else, it may prevent us from too easily dismissing what we consider the unenlightened views of our predecessors. For if we pause to reflect, we may discover that we are really not that different from them. Basically, they wanted the same things that we want—health and happiness—and their attempts to get what they wanted are no more peculiar or unworthy than our own.

→ 1 ←

WHERE ROCKS, WATER, AND LIFE UNITE

Missouri is certainly not unique in possessing mineral waters, although the state has its fair share of them. Natural mineral waters, the primary subject of this book, occur worldwide, anywhere that marine sediments have been deposited or where groundwater has been in contact with minerals for a sufficient period of time. But the natural history of mineral waters is much more complicated than that. Many interrelated physical, chemical, and biological factors determine the unique type of mineral water found at any given location. Mineral waters may be hot or cold. Although Missouri has only the latter variety, within the realm of cold mineralized springs and groundwater the state boasts a variety of mineral water types.

To understand why Missouri's mineralized waters are found where they are, or look, smell, and taste the way they do, one must examine the geologic conditions that give rise to them. The thick layers of bedrock that underlay the Ozarks of southern Missouri render the groundwater there "hard" with dissolved minerals like calcium carbonate and calcium magnesium carbonate, the primary mineral constituents of limestone and dolomite. But these waters are relatively low in dissolved solids compared to the very mineralized groundwater in the western and northern portions of the state. Where Ozark springs typically contain dissolved solids in the range of a few hundred milligrams per liter (parts per million), the salty springs in Saline County in north-central Missouri may contain solids in the range of several thousand milligrams per liter.

This heavily mineralized groundwater contains many kinds of dissolved materials such as chlorides, sulfates, carbonates, bicarbonates, sodium, calcium, magnesium, and iron. These chemical constituents were originally dissolved from the native bedrock, especially shales, which frequently contain higher concentrations of such minerals. In fact, much of the mineralized groundwater in the state occurs in areas overlain by Pennsylvanian-age shales, which prevent the downward percolation of water that would otherwise "flush out the old seawater trapped in the underlying beds."[1] Mineralized springs often contain gases, seen as the characteristic bubbles or "belches" erupting from the source. Hydrogen sulfide, nitrogen, argon, hydrogen, and carbon dioxide are often present.[2]

Scientists have long debated the sources and derivation of minerals and salt in the groundwaters of Missouri, as elsewhere. Some geologists suggested that the state's mineral waters were strictly connate, meaning that they represent seawater trapped within the marine sediments that settled on the ocean floor eons ago, before these sediments were further buried and eventually turned to rock. *Connate,* in fact, literally means "born with." Others felt just as strongly that the opposite was true, that rainwater, percolating down through the various beds of rock, dissolved and carried away minerals as it went, resulting in the mineralized water making its way to springs and wells. Some geologists recognized very early that several interrelated processes could be at work.

Missouri's mineral waters evoked great curiosity from early explorers and scientists. Edwin James of Major Stephen Long's expedition, examining a sulfur spring on River des Peres near St. Louis in 1818, speculated that "it probably derives its mineral impregnation from some decomposition in the alluvial substances through which it rises to the surface." The geologist George Featherstonhaugh believed that groundwater, moving through the bedrock, dissolved minerals along the way, a view he expressed in 1835: "it is probable that a great many mineral waters acquire some of their properties in transitu." Paul Schweitzer's later and more synoptic view, found in his *Report on the Mineral Waters of Missouri,* was expressed thus: "muriatic and alkaline waters are the products of a simple process of solution; sulphatic and chalybeate, as also sulphur waters, those of a process of chemical action and solution combined." More recently,

---

1. A. G. Unklesbay and Jerry D. Vineyard, *Missouri Geology: Three Billion Years of Volcanoes, Seas, Sediments, and Erosion,* 168.
2. John C. Miller, *Groundwater Resources of Saline County,* 26.

White mineral deposit at Camp Creek Springs, Saline County, 1999.
Photo by author

Missouri geologists have speculated about the origins of some of the state's most mineralized groundwater. The chemical composition of mineral springwaters and well waters in Saline County has been found to differ greatly from that of seawater. If it does represent the original seawater trapped in sediment as the rocks formed, the chemical composition has been radically altered. In view of these facts, the term *connate* is still used to describe these fossil waters that, if not originally derived from seawater, have been in the ground for at least thousands, if not millions of years.[3]

The presence or absence of mineralized waters in a given location is controlled by geologic factors operating at scales from local to continental. The bedrock to the north and west of the Ozark plateaus, for example, represents huge sheets of buried sandstones, limestones, shales, and coal that extend over much of the Great Plains and under the once-glaciated plains of northern Missouri. Ground-

---

3. Edwin James, *Account of an Expedition from Pittsburgh to the Rocky Mountains...*, 170; George W. Featherstonhaugh, *Geologic Report of an Examination Made in 1834, of the Elevated Country between the Missouri and Red Rivers*, 67; Paul A. Schweitzer, *A Report on the Mineral Waters of Missouri*, 2; Miller, *Groundwater Resources*, 31.

water moves very slowly through this thick sequence of rocks, resulting in very old (in terms of its time underground) and heavily mineralized water, especially in wells that penetrate the deep levels of nearly stagnant groundwater. Missouri wells producing this highly mineralized water can be found in places like Nevada and El Dorado Springs, on Missouri's western border, where very high levels of dissolved solids present serious challenges to the production of good-tasting drinking water. These wells, in fact, contain water very similar in character to some of the medicinal wells that formerly served resorts such as the Nevada artesian well. The public's expectation has changed; purity and good taste, rather than medicine, is what we demand today of our drinking water.

Between the fresh groundwater of the Ozarks and the mineralized water of the plains is what hydrogeologists refer to as the saltwater/freshwater interface, a zone of transitional groundwater quality snaking diagonally across Missouri from southwest to northeast. It is interesting to note how many of the mineral water locations referenced in this book fall near the interface zone (Figure 1). It is in this zone, where mineralized and fresh waters are in close proximity, where many of the state's mineral springs occur. In some cases, the springs represent freshwater recharge flushing the mineral waters toward the surface. The result is a mixture of water types from springs in fairly close proximity, from nearly fresh springs, such as the "sweet" spring at Sweet Springs, to the very heavily mineralized Great Salt Spring in the same county. This marked variety of water types appearing so near one another amazed and baffled the early settlers.

There are also more localized controls on groundwater quality. In Saline County, for instance, which contains some of the most heavily mineralized springs in the state, there are areas of relatively fresh water interspersed with regions of salty water. In this case, the major controlling factors are structural, primarily faults in the earth's crust and an associated warping, up or down, of many square miles of landscape between them. In upwardly arched areas, called anticlines, the groundwater drains more readily away and is recharged by rapidly moving freshwater. The result is that wells and springs here are relatively low in dissolved solids. In the troughs, or synclines, groundwater sits as in a giant bowl, moving very slowly and dissolving large amounts of minerals over long periods of time. The faults, which have occurred as blocks of crust moved up and down or side to side relative to each other, can provide paths of increased groundwater movement and may allow mineralized groundwater to access the surface as springs.

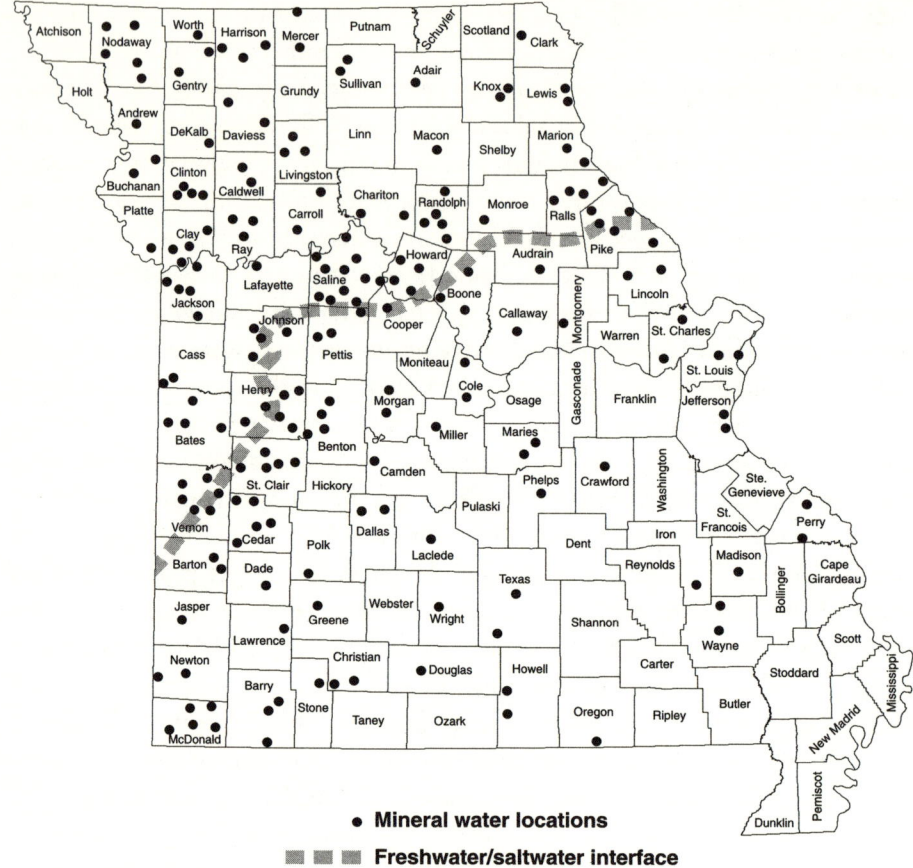

Figure 1. Mineral Water Locations in Missouri.

The mineralized artesian wells that were drilled in some areas resulted from a "head" of pressure, or area of groundwater recharge higher in elevation than the well. The artesian condition is produced by a downward dip in the deeply buried bedrock containing the mineralized waters. When this inclined bed has impermeable layers, such as shale, above and below it, the pressure is contained within the water-bearing layer until a hole is punched through the barrier, allowing the artesian water to rise in the well bore. Where enough pressure existed to force the water above the ground surface, a flowing or even a spectacular spouting artesian well resulted.

Geology is not the only factor affecting the quality of groundwater. Much of the variety in taste and smell among mineral springs may actually be the result of biological activity, largely the kinds and amounts of bacteria that live in the water, sometimes hundreds or thousands of feet underground.[4] The types and numbers of bacteria that live in different springs can accentuate subtle differences in mineral constituents between them. Water that moves along or through shale, for example, picks up minute amounts of the original, organically rich sea-bottom mud that gave birth to that rock type. With this relatively rich food source, a kind of very weak mineral broth, a proliferation of bacteria can occur, producing in turn a water very highly charged with hydrogen sulfide and other gases and exhibiting an altered mineral base. The work of bacteria may be an even greater factor than geology in creating the subtle differences in taste and smell between springs located very close to each other.

The bacteria and algae that live in the surface flow of Missouri's mineral springs can become their most striking and conspicuous features. Some early geologists were confounded by the green or white masses growing in mineral spring branches that appeared to be mineralized, yet in some ways seemed to be organic. George Featherstonhaugh, for example, described in 1834 such deposits at the "Washita Hot Springs," which had a "vitreo-gelatinous appearance, somewhat of the consistency of those glairy substances produced in stagnant water in very hot weather." Amos Woodward of the Missouri Geological Survey, impressed with the "purplish mounds" that built up around the orifice of Boone's Lick Spring, postulated that they formed from "algae, clay, and slime."[5]

These organisms play important roles in the chemistry and ecology of mineral springs. Such life-forms may represent descendants of some of the earliest life on the planet. Unlike almost all other life on earth, they subsist upon mineral matter dissolved in the water, instead of depending (at some level) on the photosynthesis of green plants. Some bacteria, for example, can strip oxygen off of mineral sulfates as a source of energy, a kind of food. In this process, the sulfates are reduced to sulfides. And it is hydrogen sulfide that gives many mineral springs their characteristic rotten-egg aromas.

Mineral springs also influence the chemistry and biology of surface streams and lakes that receive their flow. A good example of this is found at Boone's Lick, where salt springs greatly increase the salinity of the nearby stream. This habitat contains a suite of uniquely adapted life forms, such as the plains killifish and saltwater mosquito, which can tolerate saline conditions. Another example is

---

4. Miller, *Groundwater Resources*, 30.
5. Featherstonhaugh, *Geologic Report*, 68; Woodward quoted in Schweitzer, *Report*, 50.

Tile and spring at Spalding Springs, Ralls County, 1998. *Photo by author*

found at Elk Lick Springs in Saline County, where the botanist Julian Steyermark discovered the only location in Missouri where a coastal plant, seashore salt grass, was known to be found.[6] These unique ecological niches only add to the variety and wonder of Missouri's mineral springs.

---

6. Julian A. Steyermark, *Flora of Missouri*, 114.

→ 2 ←

THE CALL OF HYGIEIA

Mineral waters have been consumed, bathed in, valued, and even prized since the dawn of human civilization, if not before. Long volumes have been written on the sources, natures, and uses of these waters, testifying to mankind's fascination and preoccupation with them. Many ancient people considered springs to be sacred manifestations. To the Greeks, springs, especially thermal springs, were highly revered. Hippocrates, Homer, and Aristotle wrote of them. Worshipers built temples to Aesculapius, the god of healing, near curative springs, and for centuries the Greek goddess of health, Hygieia, symbolically adorned springhouses and pavilions, a tradition that survived to modern times.

Following the Greeks, the Romans erected their own temples, many at healing springs. This culture perfected spa bathing, building immense, opulent bathhouses. Near the end of the Roman Empire, around A.D. 300, some eight hundred thermae, or bathhouses, serviced Rome, the largest accommodating three thousand people.[1] As Roman armies vanquished neighboring and far-flung empires of Europe and Asia, they developed springs in those lands as well. At Bath, in England, for example, the Romans built a magnificent bathhouse in about A.D. 54. A few centuries earlier, legend maintains, Prince Blaudad found his miraculous cure for leprosy there, wallowing in the mud of the hot spring after observing hogs cured of the same disease.[2]

---

1. Vladimir Krizek, "History of Balneology," 31.
2. Alev Lytle Croutier, *Taking the Waters: Spirit, Art, Sensuality,* 116.

In biblical times, springs acquired spiritual significance, symbolizing renewal and purification. The Bible references Siloam's pool, a healing spring and part of Jerusalem's water supply, where Jesus gave a blind man sight, and the pool at Bethesda, with its five porches (columned porticoes) where the waters would heal when "troubled" by angels ("troubled" could mean the water became roiled by escaping gases). Later, these biblical notations played into the hands of medicinal spring promoters. The profusion of American mineral water sites with names like Bethesda and Siloam, including at least five in Missouri, show this connection.

Bible scholars and religious leaders also underscored the spiritual connotations for contemporary medicinal springs. Reverend Claudius Buchanan, preaching at Buxton Wells in England in 1811, said, "the same power, which gave virtue to the well of Bethesda, hath opened the fountain of health in this place." Physicians also forged this link, as when Dr. John Bell said of mineral springs in 1855: "duly elaborated and refined, and fitted for immediate use by an all wise and beneficent Creator, these waters constitute a large and important addition to our materia medica."[3]

In this view, the materia medica consisted of the body of natural substances that God had created for mankind to find and use. Theology supported the notion that God would provide, in each region, medicines appropriate to cure that area's particular diseases. To some extent, this was a departure from earlier dogma, which held that diseases derived from supernatural, diabolical influences, linked to the "wages of sin" and thus not curable by any earthly means. Buchanan, attempting to resolve this dilemma, explained that some people were not healed after going "from place to place to drink the waters" because they "retain their sin."

Theology and mineral water use remained tightly linked at many early resorts, where bathers also read scriptures and sang hymns. On Midsummer's Day, also known as St. John the Baptist Day, people made a point to visit holy medicinal springs. At one German spa, an entrance sign reminded people that "one bath on St. John's Day equals nine baths at other times."[4]

Through the first millennium, people no doubt used mineral waters, though records of this are scarce. By the time Columbus sailed toward North America,

---

3. Claudius Buchanan, *The Healing Waters of Bethesda; a Sermon, Preached at Buxton Wells, to the Company Assembled There for the Benefit of the Medicinal Waters, on Whitsunday, June 2, 1811*, 4; John Bell, *The Mineral and Thermal Springs of the U.S. and Canada*, vi.

4. Croutier, *Taking the Waters*, 78.

Bathing at Chouteau Springs. *State Historical Society of Missouri, Columbia*

however, entrepreneurs had established a vigorous trade in mineral waters and resorts were in business. The word *spa*, in fact, derived from the name of a town in Belgium where a resort flourished after 1326. Some European spa traditions from the Middle Ages, such as nude public bathing, enjoyed popularity for a while. But negative reaction, especially from the church, resulted in the closing of many public bathing establishments. The lewd and licentious behavior commonly seen at spas, clergymen warned, characterized the fall of the Roman Empire centuries earlier. And physicians noted a correlation of nude bathing with the spread of disease, especially syphilis.

The unsanitary conditions alone discouraged some spa goers. In 1648, the court gossip Pepys, describing life at Bath, England, scowled, "me thinks it cannot be clean to get so many bodies together in the same water."[5] For the most part, however, European writers extolled the virtues of mineral waters for drinking and bathing, with many books on the subject published from about 1500 onward.

By the late sixteenth century, important research with implications for medicine emerged from the field of chemistry. Leonhard Thurneysser, a Swiss physician, produced a detailed treatise on the examination of mineral waters in 1572,

---

5. Joseph Wechsberg, *The Lost World of the Great Spas*, 13.

describing many of the common chemical constituents. By 1685, when the English natural philosopher Robert Boyle wrote his *Memoirs of a Natural History of Mineral Waters,* many of the basic, qualitative techniques for isolating and identifying chemical constituents in mineral waters were in place.[6] This was important because physicians by then were looking for mineral waters with known constituents to prescribe for specific ailments. Commercial interests also wanted ingredient information that would allow them to produce medicinal waters artificially, obviating the need to locate and procure supplies from natural springs.

Geologic sciences also contributed to the understanding of mineral waters, although seventeenth-century scientists often merely elaborated on basic ideas espoused by Aristotle and his contemporaries. The German scholar Athanasius Kircher, for example, produced in 1664 a treatise called *Mundus Subterraneous* dealing with the origins of springs and mineral waters.[7] Kircher articulated a conceptual model in which water entered holes at the bottoms of the oceans, from which it flowed through subterranean passageways to mountaintops. The water reappeared as springs and rivers, flowing back downhill to the sea to complete the cycle. High tides acted as bellows to pump the water to higher elevations. Kircher explained mineral springs by assuming that some of these subterranean routes intersected beds of salt, or sulfur, or whatever mineral might end up in the water that emerged into daylight. Within a century, however, empirical evidence cast doubt on such theories. Men boring deep into the earth could not help but notice widespread dripping water, plainly illustrating the diffuse nature of groundwater recharge.

After the early 1700s, the use of mineral waters and the development of resorts in Europe surged markedly. The famous pump room at Bath, England, constructed in 1706, supported that city's claim to fame as the first truly international resort.[8] By the close of the eighteenth century, resorts all across Europe rode upon a high tide of popularity. With such a solid base of public interest and support, it is little wonder that colonists to the New World harbored an intimate knowledge and appreciation of mineral waters. After they crossed the Atlantic, it did not take long for these immigrants to find their own special watering holes.

6. Ferenc Szabadvary, *History of Analytical Chemistry,* 29, 30.
7. Frank Dawson Adams, *The Birth and Development of Geological Sciences,* 433.
8. Wechsberg, *Lost World,* 16.

El Dorado Springs, Cedar County, ca. 1930. *From* A Century of Progress of Missouri in Pictures *(official souvenir of Missouri exhibit at the Century of Progress Exposition, Chicago, 1933)*

3

SPRINGS OF AMERICA

Preoccupied as they were with the harsh realities of subsistence, the first colonists to the New World enjoyed few luxuries. Until food could be obtained to last through long winters, Native Americans pushed aside or befriended, and basic necessities otherwise procured, the first settlers had little time to cultivate their new home's natural amenities, including mineral springs. Before long, however, colonists discovered that Indians were living around and using mineral springs, especially warm ones. Even warring tribes enjoyed a sort of mutual truce around the springs.

By about 1669, Pilgrims and "Boston gentlefolk" were making their way to the sulfurous waters of Lynn Springs in Massachusetts, noted for their qualities in relieving scorbutic diseases (caused by a lack of vitamin C).[1] In 1747, Thomas and Phineas Bond produced for the *Philadelphia Gazette* the first scientific survey of American healing springs.[2] Some locations, such as Stafford Springs in Connecticut, already enjoyed reputations as society resorts by this time. However, resort development faced uphill struggles in some areas of the New World where Puritanical beliefs clashed with the "immoral" or leisure elements.

Mineral spring resorts in the colonies came more prominently into fashion in about 1760. By then, there were sufficient numbers of well-to-do colonists to support resort-based diversions like cotillions and gambling. Some people

---

1. Marshall W. Fishwick, *Springlore in Virginia*, 30.
2. Jonathan Paul de Vierville, "American Healing Waters: A Chronology (1513–1946) and Historical Survey of America's Major Springs, Spas, and Health Resorts," 61.

still sought out resorts for medical benefits, but others just liked to travel, flaunt their wealth, and rub shoulders with other affluent colonists. For many, the sheer adventure of it was irresistible. Additional stagecoach lines, better roads, and regular packet sailings made the springs more accessible, and traveling in any form was considered good therapy for invalids and stimulating for the healthy.

In spite of the early emphasis on leisure, the medicinal potency of mineral springs provided the underpinnings of promotion. Colonial newspapers, especially in Boston and Philadelphia, heralded the discoveries of new healing springs and provided details of successful treatments. Stafford Spring, advertised in the front pages of Boston newspapers, became a "Mecca of New England's hypochondriacs."[3] George Washington, bothered by rheumatism as a young colonel, took to the warm waters of Bath, Virginia (now Berkeley Springs, West Virginia), named for the famous English resort. In spite of the documented medical successes at these colonial resorts, ties across the Atlantic remained strong, and many people believed that resorts on this side of the ocean could never measure up to the centuries-old, tried-and-true European spas.

Along with their health benefits, colonial springs provided important social functions. By 1770, Warm Springs had become known as a great intercolonial resort where "planting aristocracy and backwood democrats mingle."[4] It has even been claimed that by attracting far-flung colonial patriots, spas became nuclei of agitation for the Revolutionary War.[5] In any case, many medicinal spring resort facilities served as infirmaries and hospitals during that war. Later spa promoters claimed that soldiers became very attached to the mineral water at Saratoga Springs in New York, and thus there were "fewer instances of drunkenness."[6]

The nineteenth century ushered in what could rightfully be called the golden age of mineral springs and spas in America. By 1803, investors had constructed the first large hotel at Saratoga Springs. Into a later version of this grand and luxurious scene writer Edna Ferber projected her characters in the 1941 novel *Saratoga Trunk*. Arriving at the springs, the heroine, dizzied by the constant

---

3. Carl Bridenbaugh, "Baths and Watering Places in Colonial America," 152.

4. Ibid., 161.

5. William Back, Edward Landa, and Linda Meek, "Bottled Water, Spas, and the Early Years of Water Chemistry," 606.

6. Stanley W. Davis and Augusta Davis, "Saratoga Springs and Early Hydrogeochemistry in the United States," 351.

hubbub around the immense hotel, observed: "Up and down, up and down the length of the enormous piazza moved a mass of people, slowly, solemnly, almost treading on each other's heels. The guests of the United States Hotel were digesting their gargantuan midday meal. Carriages and horses had already disgorged the passengers who had arrived on the half-past-two train, and these had been duly viewed, criticized, and docketed by the promenaders. It was part of the daily program."[7]

By 1800, many American resorts had successfully cultivated an aristocratic aura. The *Salmagundi Papers,* published in 1807, included a tongue-in-cheek observation that "the worthy, fashionable, dashing, good-for-nothing people of every state... flock to the springs." But "taking the waters" had also become part of the daily routine for a significant number of ordinary Americans. Adlard Welby, visiting Philadelphia in 1820, was amazed at the degree of mineral water use there: "during the hot season, mineral waters, sometimes mixed with syrups, are drunk in great abundance. The first thing every American who can afford five cents takes, on rising in the morning, is a glass of soda water. Many houses are open for the sale of it, and some of them are fitted up with Parisian elegance."[8]

By the 1830s, large numbers of Americans went spa touring, or "going to the springs," an annual ritual akin to our vacations of today. During the summer, in part to avoid the heat and lowland miasmas, they began lengthy pilgrimages to the resorts in the Appalachian foothills and mountains. It could be argued that many were pushed to the springs by coastal diseases, such as the great cholera epidemic that visited eastern cities in 1832. But people also went for the society and fashion, for the horse racing, theaters, and casinos.

Spa tourists knew of the "big six," a group of famous resorts clustered among the folds and ridges of the Appalachians in Virginia and West Virginia. These could all be visited during a single summer by following a looping, 170-mile route. Initially, road patterns dictated the order in which patrons visited the springs. The first turnpike penetrated the mountains near Warm Springs, which therefore became first and last on the standard tour. Later, with alternate routes, visitors could visit in any order the White, Red, or Salt Sulphur Springs as well as Warm Springs, Hot Springs, and Sweet Springs. But everyone planned to arrive

---

7. Edna Ferber, *Saratoga Trunk,* 152–53.
8. *Salmagundi Papers* quoted in Fishwick, *Springlore,* 15; Adlard Welby, *A Visit to North America and the English Settlements in Illinois, with a Winter Residence at Philadelphia...,* 172.

at Sweet Springs for the last week of August or the first week of September, like salmon "who know the time to go back up the Columbia River."[9]

By this time, mineral water enthusiasts had published comprehensive manuals on American springs and spas. Dr. John Bell, a former ship's surgeon, wrote *On Baths and Mineral Waters* in 1831, elaborating on the importance of bathing, the "hygienic and curative powers" of different types of mineral waters, and describing twenty-one of the chief mineral springs of the United States. Bell reinforced the notion that the proper use of mineral water spas was medical, not social, and that patrons should avoid abusing these natural gifts "owing to ignorance and false theory" and an "impatience to obtain decided results."[10]

Meanwhile, settlers on the nation's western frontier had discovered their own mineral springs. In fact, the locations of these springs helped to guide and induce inland settlement. Harrodsburg, Kentucky, one of the first permanent white settlements in the western country, was founded at a mineral spring. François André Michaux, traveling through Kentucky in 1801 and 1802, noted of the Mud-Lick Springs, sixty miles from Lexington (later called Olympian Springs), "they are held in great esteem, and the most distinguished personages in the county were drinking from them when I was in town." At the Blue Licks in Kentucky, Thomas Hulme remarked in 1819, "here is a sulphur and salt spring like that at French Lick, in Indiana, which makes this a place of great resort in summer for the fashionable swallowers of mineral waters; the three or four taverns are at this time completely crowded."[11]

Hot Springs, Arkansas, attracted early national attention because thermal springs have always been highly prized. Hot Springs also featured an interesting geologic setting and a long history of medicinal use, including that of the Spanish conquistador Hernando de Soto in about 1542. Developers established the first bathhouses there in 1830. George Featherstonhaugh, a geographer and geologist visiting in 1834, described the hot springs that were "so great an object of curiosity to men of science, and so little known to the rest of the world." He suspected its obscurity would soon change: "that these waters annually perform very admirable cures of chronic complaints incident to southern climates, is well known there; and that their efficacy, and the beauty and salubrity of the

---

9. Fishwick, *Springlore*, 6.
10. John Bell, *On Baths and Mineral Waters*, 17–20.
11. François André Michaux, *Travels to the West of the Alleghany Mountains, in the States of Ohio, Kentucky, Tennessee, and back to Charleston, by the Upper Carolines...*, 225; Thomas Hulme, *Journal Made during a Tour in the Western Countries of America*, 68.

Pagoda at Mineola, Montgomery County. *State Historical Society of Missouri, Columbia*

country, will soon cause the place to be resorted to from far and near, as soon as proper accommodations for visitors can be prepared, is very obvious."[12] In 1832, two years before Featherstonhaugh's visit and four years before Arkansas achieved statehood, President Jackson designated Hot Springs as the nation's first national preserve, the first time the federal government acquired land specifically for public health and made a commitment to the national interest in mineral springs. Forty years later, in 1872, this fascination with natural mineral waters provided a major impetus for the establishment of Yellowstone park.

By the 1840s and 1850s, scores of new resorts had popped up in the western Appalachians and Ohio Valley, following the tide of westward expansion. Many were accessible by steamboats, carrying throngs of southern plantation owners and northern businessmen. President Andrew Jackson frequented Beersheba Springs, between Nashville and Chattanooga. In Kentucky, spa customers could reach the famous Drennon's Lick after a short run by steamboat up the Kentucky River from the Ohio. This popular resort, visited by thirteen state governors, prospered until a cholera outbreak destroyed its business.[13] West Baden,

---

12. Featherstonhaugh, *Geologic Report*, 64, 69.
13. R. E. Banta, *The Ohio: Rivers of America Series*, 453–58.

in southern Indiana, became known as one of the most fashionable resorts in America during this time, as did nearby French Lick, where a boiled down, bottled concentrate of springwater became widely known and praised as "Pluto Water."

National prosperity in the mid-nineteenth century energized the spa business. In 1855, John Bell published a greatly expanded guide to 181 different mineral water resort sites, beginning his preface with this observation: "The want of a manual in which travelers for curiosity and pleasure, and invalids in quest of health, might learn where to go, how to go and what to find... has been generally felt."[14] Bell described several mineral springs in what is now the central United States, such as Harrodsburg in Kentucky, but he mentioned none in Missouri.

Many established resorts had expanded by the mid-nineteenth century, with Hot Springs, Arkansas, hosting seven major bathhouses. Sam Houston came here to treat his skin diseases. Major resorts advertised extensively, capitalizing on the success of prototypes such as White Sulphur Springs in Virginia, where owners invented the famed mint julep in 1858, a concoction of brandy, loaf sugar, "limestone water," ice, and native mountain mint.[15] Several of Missouri's mineral water resorts were going concerns by the 1850s, including Monegaw Springs in St. Clair County, White Sulphur Springs in Benton County, Sulphur Springs at Cheltenham near St. Louis, Elk Springs in Pike County, and Chouteau Springs in Cooper County.

The Civil War delivered a crushing blow to the spa business, with some resorts physically destroyed in the warfare. Profits at many northern resorts plummeted when wealthy plantation owners from the South stayed away. In a move to replace Southern patronage drained by the war, Saratoga, known as the "Queen of American spas," added horse racing in 1863, attracting great crowds.[16] In Missouri, the relatively few spas existing at the time suffered along with most of the state's other businesses.

Like much of the nation's infrastructure, spas began a long rebuilding process after the war. The seasons of 1868 and 1869 were described as "stunning" at Virginia's White Sulphur Springs, although it and other springs in that state

14. Bell, *Mineral and Thermal Springs*, v.
15. Leslie Dorsey and Janice Devine, *Fare Thee Well: A Backward Look at Two Centuries of Historical American Hostelries, Fashionable Spas, and Seaside Resorts*, 245.
16. Grace Maguire Swanner, *Saratoga, Queen of Spas: A History of the Saratoga Spa and the Mineral Springs of the Saratoga and Ballston Areas*, 139.

Baths at Blue Lick Springs, Saline County. *State Historical Society of Missouri, Columbia*

generally had passed their zenith by this time.[17] The 1870s and 1880s were generally progressive times, though interspersed with serious droughts and depressions, most notably the financial panic of 1873. During this period, railroads united the continent and its people, becoming within a short period of time the "great leveler." With the advent of reasonable railroad fares, the average citizen now had the means to travel. Spas across the nation were within reach of a sizable number of the nation's workers, who by then had campaigned successfully for shorter hours and better pay. With access open to wide sectors of society, once-exclusive resorts began to lose their aristocratic aura.

Missouri, following the national trend, became a state of rapidly expanding metropolitan areas and towns in the late nineteenth century. Between 1860 and 1880, the state gained almost a million people. With this expanding base of potential patrons, connected by continually improving road and railroad systems, the number of mineral water spas in the state mushroomed in the 1870s and 1880s. During this heyday, nearly eighty mineral water sites in the state

17. Fishwick, *Springlore*, 30.

operated as resorts, and in scores of locations companies bottled and sold mineral spring and well water.

Missouri did not represent an isolated instance of this boom. Baxter Springs and Bonner Springs in Kansas, Mineral Wells in Texas, and Sulphur Springs in Oklahoma were all enjoying widespread popularity. South of the Missouri border, sixty to a hundred people arrived daily in Eureka Springs, Arkansas. Siloam Springs in Arkansas also thrived, and Hot Springs, by the 1880s, boasted an international reputation, touting the slogan, "we bathe the world."[18]

The mineral spring resorts of the West also enjoyed great success. The Santa Fe Railroad constructed one of the grandest hotels in the West—the Montezuma, in Las Vegas, New Mexico—in the early 1880s. Palm Springs in California flourished, and Manitou Springs, Colorado, the "Saratoga of the West," attracted thirty thousand visitors annually by 1880 and two hundred thousand by 1890.[19] In 1886, Dr. Albert Peale of the U.S. Geological Survey counted 634 mineral water spas in the United States, an average of seventeen per state. To put this number in perspective, however, one should realize that by this date there were thousands of spas operating in Europe. Taking the waters was not just popular in Missouri—it was the thing to do over much of the globe.

---

18. De Vierville, "American Healing Waters," 61.
19. Janet Mace Valenza, "Places Lived, Places Lost: Taking the Waters in Texas," 42.

→ 4 ←

THE SPICE OF LIFE

Mineral water use in Missouri began not with healing, but with spicing—with curing meat, not people. Pioneers relied heavily upon salt, especially for preserving food; settlers moving west of the Appalachians completely depended on the procurement of adequate local supplies of salt. It is little wonder that salt making constitutes one of the nation's oldest commercial enterprises, and that the search for and procurement of salt springs captured the interest of federal and state governments.

Early settlers noticed animals, particularly deer, elk, and buffalo, congregating at "licks," where salt and other minerals precipitated upon the ground surface around springs and seeps. Areas around the licks became trampled, wallowed, and denuded of vegetation. In his 1687 journal, Henri Joutel, who traveled with the French explorer La Salle, noted a salt spring in what is now Ste. Genevieve County, where "the ground about it was much beaten by bullocks feet, and it is likely they love the salt water." Fortescue Cuming, in his 1807–1809 tour of what was then the western United States, observed at the Blue Licks of Kentucky that large herds of buffalo had "pressed down and destroyed the soil to a depth of three or four feet," although the animals had since been "destroyed or terrified from the country." In the 1837 *Gazetteer of the State of Missouri*, Alphonso Wetmore mentioned that early inhabitants of Cooper County observed a single, aged buffalo "pursuing the trace that had long ceased to be trodden by his race, toward one of the salt springs, his old stomping grounds, on the banks of the Lamine."[1]

---

1. Joutel quoted in Louis Houck, *A History of Missouri, from the Earliest Explorations and*

The curious remains of more ancient animals littered the ground at some salt licks. Big Bone Lick, in Kentucky, earned early fame as a wonder of the western country because it contained gigantic bones, which were later identified as those of extinct mastodons and giant ground sloths. Spring sediments near Kimmswick, in Jefferson County, Missouri, yielded the skeletons of mastodons and other animals that lived more than ten thousand years ago, which had probably been attracted to the mineral waters there.

Luckily for its settlers, the western country had a fair sprinkling of salt springs and licks. Cuming marveled of these salt deposits: "What a subject of admiration does it not afford to the moralizing philosopher, that such a provision should be made by an all bountiful nature, or rather by Nature's God, for supplying both the intellectual and brute creation, with an article so necessary to both, in the heart of an immense continent, so remote from any ocean."[2]

Missouri's salt springs attracted some of the state's earliest entrepreneurs. Lead mines and saltworks, along with fur trapping, supported the state's first business enterprises, and the products of these industries even served for a time as currency. In 1700, Jesuit missionaries commented on the rich lead mines and saltworks near the Mississippi River, at the mouth of the Meramec. One of the region's earliest saltworks operated near the junction of Saline and Little Saline creeks, in what is now Ste. Genevieve County. These saline watercourses show up on a 1775 map of the area, with Saline Creek labeled as "Salt Pan's River."[3]

These early salt-making camps were crude affairs. Iron kettles of springwater were boiled in firepits, usually by just a few workers who spent most of their time cutting firewood. In this way, saltworks could produce at most one pound of salt for every five gallons of springwater boiled away.

Of course, the salt licks had attracted humans long before the Europeans arrived. Early settlers saw Indians carrying basket loads of caked salt to their villages, and French salt makers near the Mississippi River reported that Indians were working the springs there when they arrived. Wetmore wrote in the 1830s that Indians produced salt near Ste. Genevieve, where the "remains of their kettles strew the ground to the present day."[4] In fact, the plentiful shards of earthen

---

Settlements until the Admission of the State into the Union, 1:238; Fortescue Cuming, *Sketches of a Tour to the Western Country, through the States of Ohio and Kentucky...*, 178; Alphonso Wetmore, *Gazetteer of the State of Missouri*, 68.
2. Cuming, *Sketches*, 165.
3. Houck, *A History*, 1:191, 277.
4. Wetmore, *Gazetteer*, 171.

Iron kettle used for salt making at Boone's Lick State Historic Site, Howard County, 1998. *Photo by author*

vessels around salt springs may have given European settlers the idea to set up production. Later salt makers, who were excavating for fire pits near saline springs, were surprised to find that such artifacts lay at considerable depths below the surface, indicating their ancient origins.

In what would become the state's interior, settlers claimed that saltworks burned near the mouth of the Lamine River in Saline County by 1720 or 1725. At the beginning of their expedition to the west in 1803, Meriwether Lewis and William Clark reported saline springs at the mouth of the Lamine, and Manuel Lisa and the travel writer H. M. Brackenridge, traveling independently up the Missouri River in 1811, both noted valuable salt-making camps. At the Lamine saltworks, Brackenridge described a village barely a year old yet "already considerable, and increasing rapidly." Major Stephen Long's 1819 expedition visited a saltworks on the "Le Mine," reporting that "here, at one estimate, one hundred bushels of salt are manufactured per week; eight men are employed, and 180 gallons of water are evaporated to produce a bushel of salt."[5]

---

5. Henry Marie Brackenridge, *Journal of a Voyage up the Missouri River, Performed in 1811*, 48; James, *Account of an Expedition*, 162.

Mathurin Bouvet, a Frenchman, made salt in the 1790s at a site that later became known as Spalding, in Ralls County. While exploring the upper Mississippi River, Bouvet claimed that he could taste salt in a river discharging from the west. With some skepticism, his party ascended the river, later called the Salt, and Bouvet located the buffalo lick and salt springs. He claimed eighty-four arpents of land around the spring, although nearby settlers later contested the claim. Because it was difficult to navigate the shallow Salt River by boat, Bouvet established a warehouse on the Mississippi River near the plantation of Bay de Charles, about two miles above present-day Hannibal, and hauled his salt overland to this point. Indians may have killed Bouvet near his salt warehouse in about 1805.[6]

Charles De Lauriere of St. Louis, in about 1800, operated another early saltworks of Ralls County. Reportedly, an Indian guided him to the site, near the Salt River about four miles below Bouvet's claim. De Lauriere experienced serious problems at his saltworks. Indians harassed him, and he lost a load of salt once when his boat overturned in the Mississippi River. Many years later, Missouri State Geologist Garland Broadhead reported that settlers made salt at this site, now called Freemore's Lick, but that they were frightened by Indians and threw their kettles in a well, "the works abandoned."[7]

In spite of such common setbacks, the salt trade attracted numerous businessmen and settlers westward across the Mississippi River. Much of the salt produced found its way back east. The saltworks of François Vallé, located on the Saline River with several others, by 1797 shipped salt down the Mississippi, up the Ohio, and eastward into the Cumberland River. At a place called Heath's Lick in Saline County, workers shipped salt to St. Louis in hollow logs sealed on either end with plugs of wood and chunks of clay. The Spanish government, which kept some records on salt production in the French districts, estimated that by 1800 over fourteen thousand bushels of salt were being produced annually in the area of Missouri.

At about this time, one of Missouri's frontier heroes entered the picture. Nathan Boone, the youngest son of Daniel, spotted a salt spring in 1804 while retreating from hostile Osage Indians about 150 miles from his family's home near St. Charles. Boone knew about salt springs, having watched his father make salt near their home in Boonsborough, Kentucky. Keenly aware of the difficulty

---

6. Walter Roland, Vivian Roland, J. Hurley, and Roberta Hagood, *Spalding Springs*, 3–5.
7. Garland C. Broadhead, "Mineral Springs of Missouri," 101.

of supporting himself and his family by hunting and trapping, Nathan decided to supplement his income with summer salt production. During the spring or summer of 1805, he and his brother Morgan headed west with a few other men, leading packhorses laden with heavy iron kettles. They built rock furnaces at the salt springs and began cutting firewood. Consuming huge amounts of wood, they boiled away kettle after kettle of springwater, producing about thirty bushels of salt a day. They hauled the salt to the nearby Missouri River and sent it downstream in canoes, later in keelboats, to St. Louis, where it fetched about two dollars a bushel.[8]

The site became widely known as Boone's Lick (Booneslick), although Nathan had turned the operation over to others by 1808. For several years, Boone's salt supplied most of the settlements in the region north of the Missouri River and provided an impetus for the opening of the Booneslick Road. This, the state's first major east-west route, served as a conduit for westward flowing settlers for over fifty years. Access to the state's interior afforded by this road also led to the opening of one of the Missouri territory's first land offices at Franklin. Glowingly described in promotional literature, the Booneslick Road piqued the interests of German immigrants even before they arrived on the continent. Similarly, the Salt River Road, from St. Charles to Palmyra, connected settlements to the salt springs of Ralls and Pike counties.

In some locations, the scarcity of readily obtainable fuel and construction materials hindered the development of saltworks. Alphonso Wetmore noted that at a spring in Saline County, "the insufficient amount of timber for construction of reservoirs or vats, rendered the enterprise of Mr. Jones, the projector, fruitless." Other sites had everything needed for production close at hand. Wetmore observed, "it is known to few of the inhabitants of Cooper County that their saline springs and coal banks are so situated, as to their relative localities, that this fuel may be extensively employed in the manufacture of salt." Where saltworks consumed wood for fuel, the wholesale leveling of forests sometimes alarmed the local citizens. A geologist preparing a report on Saline County, for example, charged that "there are some persons who contend that [salt springs] have already done to the country more injury by the consumption of fuel than the value of all that ever can be manufactured from them would repay."[9]

---

8. R. Douglas Hurt, *Nathan Boone and the American Frontier*, 147–50.
9. Wetmore, *Gazetteer*, 214, 67; Garland Broadhead, F. B. Meek, and B. F. Shumard, *Report of the Geological Survey of the State of Missouri, 1855–1871*, 187.

Wooden surface casing for brine well at Boone's Lick, Howard County, 1998.
Photo by author

By providing an essential mineral, salt springs also helped the settlers to raise healthy livestock. Wetmore noted that salt springs "suitable for stock-raising" occurred in Pike and Ray counties. Just as wild animals sought out salt and other minerals at salt licks, livestock benefited from these essential minerals as well. In Rives County (now Henry County), brine springs were too weak to justify salt making, but were well suited to the "fattening of stock." Salt springs in Johnson County contributed "largely to the interest of stock raisers." Wetmore added that "even hogs grow larger and fatten faster when allowed free access to salt water."[10]

The government, as well as settlers, recognized the commercial value of salt springs and salt manufacturing. One section of the 1820 federal legislation allowing the state of Missouri to form provided that "all salt springs, not exceeding twelve in number, with six sections of land adjoining each, shall be granted to the said state for the use of the state."[11] The state legislature had to select

---

10. Wetmore, *Gazetteer*, 102.
11. American State Papers, *Documents, Legislative and Executive of the Congress of the United States*, 660.

Spring at Boone's Lick, Howard County, ca. 1890. Schweitzer, *Report*

Saline spring at Boone's Lick, ca. 2000. *Photo by author*

these springs by 1825 and would agree never to sell or lease them, for a period not exceeding ten years, without the consent of Congress. Missouri's saline provisions were very similar to those included in the enabling legislation for other "western" states, such as Ohio, Indiana, and Illinois.

The *Arkansas Gazette* noted in 1822 that some of the granted springs in Missouri were being worked and marveled at the "proverbial" quantity of saltwater in the state. By 1826, records at the St. Louis land office show that the government had recorded salt spring landholdings for six sections around Spalding Spring in Ralls County and parts of two sections at the Saline Creek works near the Meramec River in Jefferson County. At the Franklin land office, the state recorded holdings in Boone County (one quarter section near Callahan Creek), Howard County (two sections at a lick on Moniteau Creek, two and one-half sections near Fayette, parts of two sections near Franklin, parts of two sections near Glasgow, and one quarter section near Boone's Lick), and Saline County (three sections near Wilton Springs, one section at McAllister Springs, one section northwest of Marshall on Straddle Creek, five sections around the Great Salt Springs, and sixteen hundred acres in five sections on the Salt Fork Creek southeast of Malta Bend).[12]

Of course, state ownership did not guarantee a lucrative trade. By the time of the state's formation, salt prices had already started to fall, a result of better inland transportation and competition from massive production areas elsewhere. One early western saltworks operated near the Wabash River at Shawneetown, a trading post on the Ohio River in what is now Illinois. Congress appropriated three thousand dollars in 1802 for the establishment of saltworks at these springs, and in 1818, to ensure production, it set aside the antislavery clause and 180,000 acres of fuel timber in this little corner of the Northwest Territory. John Bradbury, the naturalist, reported in 1810 that these springs at the "Ohio Saline" were "several acres in extent" and "six to ten feet deep."[13] By that time, workers produced 130,000 bushels of salt per year there.

New York State hosted another important production area at Onondaga. Jesuit missionaries wrote of salines here in 1646, and large-scale manufacturing of salt began by 1788. The Erie Canal, the "ditch that salt made," provided a major inland transportation route for the product. By 1810, three hundred thousand bushels per year were made at Onondaga and transported throughout the west.

12. Ibid., 857–58.
13. John Bradbury, *Travels in the Interior of America in the Years 1809, 1810, and 1811*, 276.

Even larger facilities occurred near the Kanawha River, in what is now West Virginia, where furnaces burned from 1797. Production boomed here in 1812, when English salt became unavailable and shortages threatened the colonies. By 1820, saltworks on the Kanawha produced over six hundred thousand bushels annually.[14]

Even these numbers pale in comparison to the fact that the United States imported over three million bushels of salt annually by 1810. This dependence on European salt, in fact, spurred funding to study the feasibility of the Erie Canal.[15] All of these sources dwarfed the meager production in Missouri and depressed the price of its salt. By 1822, the *Arkansas Gazette* reported that Boone's Lick salt brought only 50 to 62½ cents per bushel, one-fourth to one-third the price of fifteen years earlier. However, salt prices were known to fluctuate wildly. It was not uncommon for prices to reach four dollars or more per bushel, especially at locations far from the rivers or when water levels were too low to float salt-carrying flatboats.

In spite of fluctuating and generally falling prices, salt production continued in Missouri for many years in places like Randolph Springs, Sweet Springs, Blue Lick, McAllister Springs, and Camp Creek in Saline County, most of it to supply local markets. In 1823, the state directed the drilling of a three-hundred-foot brine well at Spalding, one of the earliest drilled wells in the state. Wetmore predicted in 1836 that "at some future time, in all probability, this salt will be quarried and brought forth from its bed, to supply the surrounding country."[16] Randolph Springs, where salt production started in the 1820s, by 1840 manufactured six thousand bushels annually, roughly 84 percent of the state's total. And in 1869, workers tried new groundwater production methods at Boone's Lick. A salt company sank a well there over a thousand feet deep, but the enterprise failed because of the weak nature of the brine pumped.

Missouri's commercial advocates hoped that the trade in salt would provide a boost to the state's economy. At the time of the Civil War, salt manufacturing remained a big business nationally, with some three thousand workers producing 225,000 tons annually. Recognizing the strategic importance of saltworks, Union troops destroyed them all over the South.[17]

---

14. Mark Kurlansky, *Salt: A World History,* 250–51.
15. Ibid., 244.
16. Wetmore, *Gazetteer,* 117.
17. Kurlansky, *Salt,* 260.

Though production had by then fallen in Missouri, some held out hope for the financial future of the state's salt springs. Garland Broadhead, speaking in 1864 before the St. Louis Academy of Science, promoted central Missouri's salt springs: "these brines are near the navigable waters of the Missouri, in the midst of an abundance of wood and coal, and might furnish salt enough to supply all the market of the continent." As late as 1873, the state geologist's report on the brine springs of Saline County forecasted, "we can not avoid the conclusion that they must ultimately become an important source of wealth to the county." As far as the capacity for production, the report continued, "the climate of central Missouri is probably better adapted to the manufacture of salt by solar radiation than at Onondaga, New York."[18] The geologists were perhaps unaware that many years earlier this method had been tried in Saline County with little success. And in spite of their rosy forecasts, salt production in Missouri would continue slipping downward, a trend from which it would never recover.

18. Broadhead, "Mineral Springs," 60; Broadhead, Meek, and Shumard, *Report,* 187.

→ 5 ←

MISSOURI'S EARLY RESORTS

There is no evidence of the existence of mineral water resorts, per se, in the Missouri territory before 1800. At that time, Missouri's mineral springs were used primarily for salt making. However, it is reasonable to assume that some of the early salt makers and nearby settlers drank the mineral waters, and some springs may have been considered "medicinal." Many pioneers had probably heard of the famous mineral water spas of the eastern states and some may have visited them. There may even have been some improvements—such as wooden baths, shelters, or simple buildings—at some of the frontier springs. No records of such appurtenances have been found, however, and even if such facilities existed then, they could hardly have been considered resorts.

In the region that would become Missouri, a very limited population base in 1800 constrained resort patronage. Only about seven thousand people lived in the whole territory at that time, with most of them concentrated in narrow swaths along the Mississippi and Missouri rivers. This situation changed rapidly in the ensuing few decades. By 1815, treaties had been signed with most of the region's major Indian tribes, opening up large tracts of land for occupation by whites. Immigration into the territory expanded greatly by 1818, with many citizens trying their hand at land speculation. New towns were enthusiastically platted and vigorously promoted.

By 1820, the year before statehood, fifteen counties had been carved from the territory. St. Louis boasted a population of 5,000, Ste. Genevieve contained 1,500, and Franklin, at the western fringe of "civilization," had a population of

1,000. Jackson, Potosi, and St. Charles each exceeded 500. For the first time, population centers were large enough to support vigorous commerce and provide sufficient clienteles for businesses such as resorts.

Probably the earliest mineral water location that could be categorized as a resort was Loutre Lick, fifty miles west of St. Louis in what is now Montgomery County. Here, a man named Isaac Van Bibber, a close family friend of Daniel Boone, settled in about 1815. Major Stephen Long's government-sponsored expedition, traveling westward in 1818, paused at Van Bibber's settlement, and the expedition's biologist and geologist, Edwin James, described the "lick," a large brine spring in the middle of the creek. Van Bibber tried, without success, to manufacture salt here. But he built a tavern and boarding house near the spring that in the 1820s became a nationally recognized landmark on the Booneslick Road. Senator Thomas Hart Benton frequented the place and later bragged about the virtues of the medicinal spring in Washington, D.C. Henry Clay of Kentucky spoke of the Missouri senator's "Bethesda" on the floor of Congress in 1824.[1]

By the 1830s, the population of St. Louis had swelled to ten thousand, and the city had become the center of commerce for the western United States. A significant portion of this commerce revolved around the Rocky Mountain fur trade, and some of Missouri's early mineral water resorts were connected with giants of that industry. William Sublette, a mountain man and trapper who helped to open the Oregon Trail, founded one of the earliest resorts in the St. Louis area. In 1831, he paid three thousand dollars for 446 acres on the River des Peres, six miles southwest of St. Louis. This, plus an additional 333 acres purchased a few weeks later, became known as the Sulphur Spring tract. It contained an odoriferous spring gushing out of the riverbank in a stream "as big as your arm." Edwin James of the Long expedition described this "large hepatic spring" when the expedition passed through in 1818, noticing that it "diffuses a strong sulphurous odor, perceptible at one-hundred yards." He recognized its unique nature from the fact that "cattle and horses, which range here throughout the season, prefer the waters of this spring to those of the creek in whose bed it rises, and may be seen daily coming in great numbers, from distant parts of the prairies, to drink it."[2]

---

1. James, *Account of an Expedition,* 170; Floyd Calvin Shoemaker, *Missouri and Missourians,* 503.
2. John E. Sunder, *Bill Sublette, Mountain Man,* 94; James, *Account of an Expedition,* 112.

Van Bibber Tavern at Mineola, Montgomery County. *State Historical Society of Missouri, Columbia*

In the summer of 1835, Sublette began construction of a large guesthouse near the spring. The imposing, two-story stone structure, with walls two feet thick, topped a hill surrounded by a lovely grove of trees. A volunteer militia organization, the St. Louis Grays, spent summer encampment there and spread word of the medicinal nature of the spring. Sublette sent samples of the water to St. Louis for examination and was delighted to learn of their chemical resemblance to the White Sulphur Springs of Virginia. The travel writer Edmund Flagg, visiting in 1836, observed that the spring water, "when taken in any quantity, throws out an eruption over the whole body."[3] By 1838, Sulphur Springs had earned a reputation as a fine resort and watering place, accommodating sixty boarders. To provide diversions for his patrons, Sublette built a ninepins alley and a racetrack, both of which were illegal in St. Louis at the time.

Sublette had difficulty retaining good managers at Sulphur Springs; he even had to forcibly evict one. A lease signed in 1842 named Dr. Thomas Hereford of Tuscumbia, Alabama, as manager. Sublette's partner, Robert Campbell, in a

---

3. Edmund Flagg, *The Far West; or, A Tour beyond the Mountains...*, 179.

letter to Sublette, described terms of the five-year lease with Dr. Hereford and the management of the resort, "together with the large stone house and all other houses, stables, offices, nine pin alley, meadows, pastures, etc., and also the use of coal near the springs, for fuel; to use and enjoy the premises with all the grounds, enclosures, houses, privileges and appurtenances necessary and convenient for the enjoyment and occupation of the same as a boarding house, tavern and watering place."[4] Analyses of the water were published in St. Louis newspapers and the resort enjoyed modest success, but Sublette eventually broke down physically from the lingering effects of consumption. He died in Cincinnati in 1845, after traveling there to consult a physician, and he was buried near his old house at Sulphur Springs.

In 1848, the property sold and new owners subdivided the land. By 1851, the resort had resumed operation. The 1851 diary of Samuel Custis contains entries based upon his acceptance of an invitation to visit Sulphur Springs, a "pleasant hour's drive" west from St. Louis on the Manchester Road. Leaving the macadamized road and winding through a beautiful grove, he reached the springs, where he found that he was "fond of the water and drank it freely," though it had the "peculiar smell of the washings of a gun barrel." Custis added, "for a day in the country, this ride is certainly the most agreeable I have found about St. Louis; and I look forward to the day when thousands will follow my few remarks in search of a few hours' relief from the toil and bustle of city life."[5]

In 1853, the resort sold again. By this time, the railroad had reached nearby Cheltenham, providing a ready clientele from St. Louis. But in 1858, the property sold once more, this time to representatives of the Icarian community, followers of the French communist Etienne Cabet. From here, the story of Sulphur Springs continues in a downward spiral. The Icarians suffered health problems (blamed on the polluted River des Peres), which, along with internal disagreements, caused many of the utopians to abandon the enterprise. The holdouts couldn't make payments on the Sulphur Springs property and defaulted in 1864.

By the early 1870s, the old resort was near ruin. The River des Peres had degraded into a virtual sewer courtesy of the engulfing industries and neighborhoods of St. Louis. The mansion was finally destroyed by fire. Then, as if to close the lid forever on the Sulphur Springs saga, the city of St. Louis diverted

4. Robert Campbell, "Letter to William Sublette."
5. Samuel R. Custis, Personal Diary, 1852.

the River des Peres into a subterranean concrete conduit in the early 1900s in order to hide its embarrassing state and stench from the masses attending the World's Fair.[6]

Another early resort of Missouri is connected with two other St. Louis fur magnates, William Ashley and (Jean) Pierre Chouteau. Chouteau, son of St. Louis founder Pierre de Laclède, helped his family to attain dominance in the fur-trading business in French Louisiana. In appreciation of Pierre's evenhandedness in trading, Osage Indians presented him in 1792 with a thirty-thousand-arpent land grant along the Missouri River in central Missouri. Not far up the Lamine River at that location were many valuable salt springs, and the large expanse of forested land included in the grant was intended, in part, to secure timber for salt making. Chouteau naturally took an interest in this nearly forty square miles of real estate, but he did not take the time to immediately establish its boundaries. The Spanish government gave tacit approval for his grant in 1799, in spite of its lack of a precise legal description.

When settlers began to move into the Boone's Lick area in the first decade of the 1800s, across the Missouri River from Chouteau's claim, he realized he would need to secure his title to the land. He tried to move its boundaries to take in some additional salt springs being worked farther up the Lamine River. Problems with boundaries and competing claims of settlers, however, led the Board of Land Commissioners to reject Chouteau's claim in 1811, then again six years later.

In 1819, Chouteau enlisted the help of fellow St. Louisan William Ashley, who had been appointed by Congress to register preemption claims. Ashley, also a veteran fur trader, once worked the lead mines in southeast Missouri and later manufactured gunpowder. With the inflation of land prices in 1818, he entered the real estate business. Later, he brokered exchanges between the Rocky Mountain trappers and the eastern fur markets. By shepherding Chouteau's claim through Congress, which achieved the desired result in 1836 with a perfection of title, Ashley acquired one-fourth of the land. This 7,500 arpent piece contained the mineral spring, which he named in Chouteau's honor. At his death in 1838, Ashley left this huge estate to his wife and daughters.[7]

6. Tim Fox, ed., *Where We Live: A Guide to St. Louis Communities*, 131.
7. Richard M. Clokey, *William Ashley: Enterprise and Politics in the Trans-Mississippi West*, 275.

Spring flowing from tile at Chouteau Springs, Cooper County, 1998. *Photo by author*

The Chouteau Springs were known as a resort by the 1840s, but the major spa development began in the 1850s. Chouteau Springs is remarkable for its extremely long and rich history, serving as a focal point for community events clear up until the 1950s. Even after the mineral water swimming pool had closed, locals continued to hold Fourth of July picnics and other public events at the site, and people continued to drink the sulfurous waters for their health.

There were other resorts in the state operating by the late 1830s. Wetmore, in his 1837 gazetteer, reported that Elk Lick Springs in Pike County had "attained some celebrity for its medical properties" and that improvements were being made for the accommodation of visitors. Similarly, he noted that "capitalists" from St. Louis were erecting a watering place south of St. Louis in Jefferson County.[8]

By 1840, the population of Missouri had reached nearly four hundred thousand. The next two decades witnessed a blossoming of travel, immigration, and commerce. Political upheavals in Europe induced heavy immigration to the United States, including Missouri. Steamboats opened up the western part of the state to settlement, and roads and railroads began to bring the state's resorts within reach of the expanding population centers. With this impetus, a few more mineral water resorts began to appear, including Monegaw Springs and White Sulphur Springs in western Missouri and Sweet Springs in the center of the state. But the real boom time of Missouri's resorts lay ahead, well after the Civil War.

---

8. Wetmore, *Gazetteer*, 149.

→ 6 ←

THE SURVEYS

The acquisition of French Louisiana, including the real estate that would become Missouri, fired the imagination of America. This raw land promised resources and opportunities that inspired and energized the hungry nation. Expeditions such as those of Lewis and Clark in 1804, Pike in 1806, and Long and Schoolcraft in 1818–1819 hinted at the depth and breadth of the region's natural resources and their intrinsic value.

At its founding in 1821, Missouri's influential citizens were already clamoring for the government to conduct accurate surveys in order to catalog these valuable resources and position them for expeditious development. George Featherstonhaugh, an English geologist visiting Missouri in 1834, compared the utility of an accurate survey with an individual's need to know the value of his estate: "In the increasing desire manifested in the States to establish geological surveys, we have evidence of this, and of the existence of a spirit that must lead to a very great development of the mineral resources of the country, as well as the extension of its intellectual character."[1]

In a message to the Tenth General Assembly in 1833, Missouri's governor Lilburn Boggs recommended that money be appropriated for a geologic survey as part of the state's internal improvements. This had been done, he pointed out, in other states, with decided benefits. Little action was taken on his request for several years, although a Board of Internal Improvements undertook some

---

1. Featherstonhaugh, *Geologic Report,* 79.

surveys along the state's big rivers. For example, Dr. Henry King conducted a survey of the Osage River in 1839, pinpointing important salt springs.

Another request for a state survey emerged from an Internal Improvement Convention in Springfield in 1846, and in 1848 the state legislature urged Congress to appropriate funds for a survey, since the federal government still owned two-thirds of the state. Finally, in 1850, at the urging of Governor Austin A. King, the legislature set into motion the creation of the state's first Geologic Survey. When final approval came in 1853, Missouri joined eight other states with survey institutions already in place.

The legislation creating the survey directed the governor to appoint a state geologist who could, in turn, select up to four assistants. The act further directed the survey to "discover and examine" all "deposits of ore, coal, marls and such other mineral substances, and mineral waters, as may be useful and valuable."[2] To enable the survey to accomplish this task, the legislature appropriated $10,000 for two years, with the salary of the state geologist not to exceed $3,000 per year and his assistants $1,500 each. Professor George Swallow, who early in life gravitated toward the "mysterious science" of geology, was appointed the first state geologist.[3]

A dedicated professional, Swallow immediately set about the task at hand. He first hired an applied chemist, Dr. A. Litton, who had served as a professor of chemistry at St. Louis Medical College since 1842. He also worked for a time as a chemist at Belcher's sugar refinery in St. Louis, where one of the state's deepest mineral water wells was drilled (see Chapter 11). Litton would perform hundreds of examinations of mineral waters, both during and after his stint at the survey.

The survey occupied office space provided by the State University in Columbia and graciously accepted access to their "library, laboratory and apparatus." Since quality scientific instruments were scarce to nonexistent in Missouri, Swallow traveled to New York City to select his "barometers, thermometers, compasses, hydrometers, theodolite, blow-pipes, chemicals, etc." and heaved a sigh of relief when he arrived back home with all of them in working condition.[4]

The new survey developed a straightforward plan of attack. It would make a "somewhat rapid though careful" reconnaissance of parts not known—for

2. Missouri Department of Natural Resources, *A Brief History of the Missouri Geological Survey*, 5.
3. *History of Boone County, Missouri*, 959.
4. George C. Swallow, *First and Second Annual Reports of the Geological Survey*, 20.

example, along the line of the Hannibal and St. Joseph Railroad across the state's north and "from the mouth of the Kansas, or some point on the Missouri, to the southwestern counties, and thence east to the Mississippi." Along these routes workers would collect and catalog minerals, fossils, soils, plants, and trees, carefully documenting their findings, since the survey's "reputation and future prospects" depended upon the "successful completion of this great work."[5]

In December 1854, Swallow turned in his first and second annual reports. True to their charge, survey workers examined and cataloged the mineral springs they encountered. Swallow noted the success of Chouteau Springs in Cooper County, which "enjoys a fine reputation as a watering place." In admiration of its setting, he remarked, "the locality is very desirable for the invalid, who would give his native powers an opportunity to recuperate in a quiet, healthful retreat, where he may enjoy all the rational amusements of a country life." The most important chalybeate, or iron-rich, springs, he suggested, were found in St. Clair County, west of Osceola. Swallow noted that sulfur springs, in particular, had acquired "considerable reputations for their sanitary qualities."[6] The most popular resorts of this type, he observed, were Chouteau Springs, Elk Springs in Pike County, and Monegaw Springs in St. Clair County.

By 1860, geologists had completed cursory investigations in eighty counties, primarily in areas aligned along the state's major railroads and big rivers. But the Civil War brought progress to a screeching halt. The survey dissolved in June 1861 and Swallow joined the Union army. After the war, he moved west to become the state geologist of Kansas, but he would later return to Missouri, signing on as dean of the Agricultural College at Missouri University in 1870.

The second Missouri Geological Survey was established in March 1870. Garland Broadhead, appointed state geologist in July 1873 to replace Raphael Pumpelly, had made an important contribution to the study of mineral waters years before accepting this position. In 1864, he delivered a paper on the "Mineral Springs of Missouri" to the St. Louis Academy of Science. In it he mentioned the same resorts earlier described by Swallow, but he added another important watering spot, Cheltenham Springs (Sulphur Springs) in nearby St. Louis County. He considered Sweet Springs to be the "most popular and valuable" resort in the state. Broadhead added interesting personal observations, including his finding a mastodon tooth at a sulfur spring in Pike County, and his

5. Ibid., 21–22.
6. Ibid., 202, 170.

noting of a spring near Jacksonville in Randolph County, where the "surface of the spring presents an iridescent appearance" and where he "was informed that cattle, when heated, could drink large quantities with impunity."[7]

After 1870, geologists under Broadhead combed many more of Missouri's counties for mineral deposits and springs. A report published in 1873 described Goreham's Lick (later called Randolph Springs), in Randolph County, where a local doctor claimed the spring would "cure the chills if you drink it and bathe with it early in the morning." Saline County, the survey geologists predicted, would soon "furnish some of the most noted watering places west of the Mississippi." In that county, a field-worker observed a brine spring whose outflowing waters pulsed in "rather sudden, irregular ebbs and flow, independent of rain or drought." The geologist might not have believed such a story had he not witnessed the spring himself in the "act of rising," with an increase in flow "so palpable as to remove any doubts from my mind on the subject." The geologist attributed the phenomenon to a drop in barometric pressure.[8]

During fieldwork in 1873 and 1874, surveyors examined counties along Missouri's western border, where mineral waters abound. At Milford, in Barton County, two wells producing mineral waters were sampled. One had a "disagreeable taste, will act on the bowels, but is said to be healthy and cannot be used for washing." The other well, nearby, had stronger water, and, the owner claimed, "if a chicken is stewed in the water, it will be too bitter to eat." At a Mr. Wilcox's well, west of Crescent Hill in Bates County, "the water is said to wash well, but gives the clothing a yellow color unless rinsed in other water."[9]

In 1875, Broadhead resigned and the second Geological Survey disbanded. It lay dormant for several years, at least partly because the legislature refused to appropriate funds. Not until 1889 did the third survey begin operations, this time under the leadership of Arthur Winslow, previously of the Arkansas Geologic Survey. During his tenure, the most comprehensive and important work on the state's mineral waters would be undertaken. But before that happened, a similar though much broader initiative had already taken shape at the national level. This study was led by Dr. Albert Peale, who worked under the direction of John Wesley Powell, the famous Colorado River explorer and director of the U.S. Geological Survey from 1881 to 1894. Peale studied the thermal springs of

---

7. Broadhead, "Mineral Springs," 61, 101–2.
8. Broadhead, Meek, and Shumard, *Report*, 107, 182, 186.
9. Garland C. Broadhead, *Report of the Geological Survey of the State of Missouri, Including Field Work of 1873–1874*, 117.

Yellowstone in 1878 while serving as geologist for the U.S. Geological Survey's Montana Division in Bozeman, so he was acquainted with the national interest in the therapeutics of mineral waters.

Peale initiated a comprehensive tabulation of the nation's mineral waters, fifteen years in the making, compiling information from "various state geologic reports, state guides and handbooks, government geologic reports and maps, and various scientific publications." Published in 1886, his monumental survey counted 2,822 mineral water localities across the United States and territories and 8,843 individual mineral springs. Mineral waters served resorts in 634 places and were bottled for sale in 223 localities. A map showing all the mineral water locations, Peale said, would illustrate that "no state or territory in the Union is without some spring that is utilized either for commercial purposes or as a place of summer resort or a sanitarium."[10]

In state-by-state descriptions, Peale offered that Missouri was "rich in mineral springs. Nearly every county possesses mineral springs of wide local reputation, and many are known well beyond the state limits."[11] One hundred thirty-three specific mineral water locations in Missouri were listed, forty-four of which Peale classified as resorts.

Peale's high-profile work provided a sense of the magnitude and importance of the mineral water business. The impressive lists of springs and resorts in nearly every state validated the idea that spas and bottled waters contributed significantly to the nation's economy. But the thousands of natural mineral spring locations also pointed to the huge potential in undeveloped sites. The lists attracted the interest of the business-minded as well as scientists and physicians. Unfortunately for those entrepreneurs hoping to exploit some unsuspecting mineral water source, Peale's report came out near what would turn out to be the zenith of mineral water popularity. Soon, the public would turn away from the mineral water embrace, in large measure relegating works such as Peale's to the dusty bookshelves of superfluous science.

In 1889, however, mineral waters still held the attention of the newly established third Missouri Geological Survey. Under State Geologist Winslow, geologic assistants mounted a concerted effort to examine and categorize mineral waters "in an authoritative manner," an endeavor until that time "almost entirely neglected." Results of analyses and observations would be published,

10. Albert C. Peale, *Lists and Analyses of the Mineral Springs of the United States*, 138.
11. Ibid., 292.

Siloam Spring at Excelsior Springs, Clay County. *Missouri Department of Natural Resources/Geological Survey Archives*

accompanied with "such illustrations and descriptions of the surroundings as will lead to the wider use of these resorts, both for the purposes of cure as well as for recreation."[12]

According to Winslow, this inquiry into the state's mineral water resources began with three primary objectives: to determine the composition of the state's mineral waters and to compare them with waters of acknowledged medicinal value; to furnish an "exact and full" statement of the results reached, particularly for use by physicians; and to make the mineral waters more widely known in order to interest others in their "development and improvement." Winslow reminded his readers that Missouri, though "not in possession of many handsomely improved resorts whose waters are of such wide reputations as to attract

---

12. Bureau of Geology and Mines, *Biennial Report of the State Geologist for the Years 1889 and 1890,* 21.

visitors from abroad," did have many springs with "undoubted medical value." The majority of people couldn't go to those well-known yet distant places, he argued, and "hence have recourse to what is provided at home."[13]

The Geological Survey's comprehensive look at Missouri's mineral waters wrapped up in 1892 under the leadership of Paul Schweitzer. Born in Berlin in 1840, Schweitzer, the son of a mathematician, moved to America at the age of twenty-four, living in Philadelphia and New York and teaching at the school of mines at Columbia College in New York City. In 1872, he accepted a position as professor of analytical and applied chemistry at the University of Missouri. With his wavy red hair and beard and wire-rimmed spectacles, Schweitzer certainly looked the part of a university professor. He was hard of hearing and nearsighted, but his students admired him and he welcomed them at his home. Being very civic-minded, Schweitzer championed improvements in the Columbia public school system and, as the applied practical chemist for the town, he tested the waters of public and private wells. He resigned his civic position in 1879, however, because the local board of health would not heed his call to clean up contamination sources and drainage problems.[14] Apparently, some townsfolk resented the fact that a university professor would try to rid them of their outhouses and free-ranging hogs.

After leaving employment with the city of Columbia, Schweitzer took the helm of the university's Agriculture Experiment Station, a position he held for only six months. It was probably with some relief that he left the university when offered a position with the Missouri Geological Survey. He no doubt believed that his work on mineral waters would provide critical scientific information of interest and benefit to the entire state. But Schweitzer actually replaced the man originally hired to do the job—an unfortunate young man named Amos Woodward.

Woodward began his short professional career mapping sedimentary rocks in Georgia and Alabama. During the summer of 1889, he worked as a chemist and metallurgist for a mining company in the boomtown of Castle, near White Sulphur Springs, Montana. He hired on with the Missouri Geological Survey in December 1889 and State Geologist Winslow assigned him to the mineral water survey. He began pouring himself into the project, even buying some of

---

13. Arthur Winslow, "Letter of Transmittal," in Schweitzer, *Report*, v.
14. Jonas Viles, *The University of Missouri: A Centennial History,* 156.

Paul Schweitzer.
State Historical Society of Missouri, Columbia

the needed laboratory equipment out of his own pocket. In the spring of 1891, just over a year into his work with the survey, he returned to the mining business in Montana. But, according to Winslow, the long hours of work took their toll on Woodward, not to mention the fact that "the atmosphere of the lab is at no time conducive to the best of health." This, plus the "change of climate," the removal to a "high altitude, which is, in itself, injurious to some constitutions" and the "mental strain of organizing and starting new work," finally put the young man down in the fall of 1891 with a "mountain fever."[15] Tragically, on the day of his death, his fiancée was set to leave California for their intended marriage in Helena, Montana.

Schweitzer inherited Woodward's notes from his travels over about half of the state, as well as most of the photographs that were eventually used in the

15. Schweitzer, *Report*, vi–vii.

book. J. D. Robertson handled the additional fieldwork during the summer of 1891. In the field, workers described the mineral water sites they visited, especially any physical facilities such as hotels, bathhouses, and bottling works. They collected samples from springs and wells: "The bottles for holding the water were of half-gallon capacity, with common or, better still, wine corks, driven into their necks with a cork-driver. They were packed, six in a box, and safely transported to their destination."[16]

Schweitzer analyzed the samples in the laboratory and recalculated Woodward's test results. He then proceeded to "gather together the threads running through field notes and memoranda and weave them into a whole," all the while collecting his own thoughts for what would be the state's first and, as it turned out, only comprehensive treatment of its natural mineral waters. Schweitzer intended to call attention to the value and variety of the state's mineral waters without "seeming a mere advertisement" and produce a work "serviceable to the people and at least suggestive to the medical profession."[17]

The survey published the *Report on Mineral Waters* in December 1892. Schweitzer attempted to be systematic and thorough; he recognized the importance of classification systems, the "systematic arrangement of the facts or phenomena," while at the same time he astutely observed that "nature herself is a unit, a succession, an evolution without division," and "any classification system must of necessity be artificial, a means to an end, rather than the end itself." With this caveat in mind, he devised a "schedule of classification" for the state's mineral waters, containing five classes that he felt would fairly represent the types found in Missouri:

1. Muriatic waters, containing sodium chloride or common salt as their main constituent;
2. Alkaline waters, containing predominantly sodium carbonate or magnesium carbonate;
3. Sulfatic waters, containing sodium sulfate (Glauber's salt), magnesium sulfate (Epsom salts), ferrous or ferric sulfate, or aluminum sulfate;
4. Chalybeate waters, containing predominantly iron salts; and
5. Sulfur waters, containing sulfides and sulfur-containing compounds.[18]

16. Ibid., 14.
17. Ibid., xi.
18. Ibid., 24, 25–26.

When they completed their project, survey workers had visited and described ninety-four of the state's mineral water sites. Field personnel had sampled eighty-three springs and wells that were analyzed in the survey's laboratory. In the report's appendix, Schweitzer included 103 additional analyses of the state's mineral waters, many of which were not sampled by survey personnel. When he had been a professor of chemistry at the University of Missouri, Schweitzer had personally performed 62 of the 103 analyses. Naturally, he was confident in the results of those analyses, but he could not vouch for the accuracy of the other 41, which were handled by others, particularly since those samples were often "taken by the party who desired the analysis made." He even cited one example, from Climax Springs, where he suspected tampering, although he did not elaborate on his reasons for suspicion.[19]

In compliance with the charge of the study, Schweitzer included a comparison between Missouri's mineral waters and those of the famous resorts of Europe, with mixed results. Waters in Missouri's alkaline class were typically much weaker than the famous alkaline spas of Europe, notably Vichy in France and Ems in Prussia. Missouri's sulfatic waters, however, compared favorably with the noted European spas such as Karlsbad, in Bohemia, and the state's chalybeate waters matched well with famous resorts like Spa, in Belgium. Although Schweitzer noted some variations in the kinds and amounts of chemical constituents between the two continents, the implications were clear. Missouri's natural mineral waters stacked up very favorably with those of the most famous resorts in the world, providing no real reason why local waters, given sufficient development and promotion, could not enjoy equal notoriety. Schweitzer proclaimed of Missouri's mineral springs, "many of these possess virtues of a very high order, which, in time, must render them famous beyond the confines of the state."[20] For most of them, of course, that would never happen.

Schweitzer's views on the therapeutics of mineral waters, to a considerable degree, reflected the scientific and medical thinking of the day. He harbored no doubts that these therapeutic values were real, since "the effects of mineral waters upon the human organism are more accurately observed and better comprehended by most people, than are those of any other medicinal agent." Recognizing, however, the inherent complexity in the issue of mineral water efficacy,

19. Ibid., 211.
20. Ibid., 41.

Schweitzer warned, "in this, as in other popular conceptions which should be based upon an understanding of cause and effect, dissuasion and encouragement, denial and assent, are linked together."[21]

In spite of such prevalent views about the medical values of mineral waters, some professionals in Schweitzer's day asserted that the real therapeutic agents of resorts were rest and relaxation, change of atmosphere, and improved diet and exercise—not the mineral waters themselves. But Schweitzer held onto what was most likely a very popular notion of his time, that "water alone, when properly administered, is a powerful agent for the restoration of health." He hastened to add, however, that effects were enhanced when one used a mineral water "in conjunction with an enjoyable change of place and diet, two most important functions in its action."[22]

As in most mineral water books of the day, Schweitzer provided his readers with advice on proper use. He supported the "time-honored custom of rising early and taking before breakfast one to four glasses" and recognized the "beneficent action" of water on the digestive tract and the powerful effects of bathing, which induces "a greater vitality, a feeling of increased strength, courage, joyousness and mental power." Acknowledging the impatience of patients, he warned that to experience an effective cure, the period of use "should be reckoned at not less than four weeks; a shortening of this period by a greater daily consumption of water is unwise and sometimes even dangerous."[23]

It is difficult to know how the public reacted to Schweitzer's volume, since it joined the scores of other special studies the survey had produced on coal fields, petroleum geology, and iron, lead, and zinc deposits. We do know that many citizens took an active interest in things scientific during this period, so the book may have been read fairly widely. And Professor Schweitzer's name, at least, became very well known to mineral water promoters. His name, combined with a favorable analysis of one's springwater, lent a powerful credibility, if not a downright endorsement. He became the accepted authority on the state's mineral water resources.

There is little doubt that Schweitzer's book entered upon a rapidly changing, industrializing, and more scientifically oriented world. Scientists and physicians

21. Ibid., 27.
22. Ibid., 29.
23. Ibid., 30.

Nevada Artesian Well at Lake Park Springs (Radio Springs), Vernon County, ca. 1902. *State Historical Society of Missouri, Columbia*

discussed the physiological effects and values of mineral waters and debated complex chemical and medical theories. This situation would not change, but only intensify, at the dawn of the next century. In fact, important discoveries in the years just before and after the publication of Schweitzer's report would change the mineral water industry forever.

7

SPA DOCTORS

By producing favorable comparisons between Missouri's mineral springs and the famous European spas, Paul Schweitzer validated the belief in the medical benefits of the state's waters. There are two major assumptions implicit in forging this connection: first, that the famous European waters truly are medicinal, and second, that it is the particular chemical constituents Schweitzer examined that make them medicinal. Although people today might doubt both premises, those ideas were obviously taken as facts in Schweitzer's day. The question of whether mineral waters really did cure was not widely debated, either in lay or in scientific circles, until relatively modern times. Most of the available evidence supports the idea that the public, for many centuries, believed in the medicinal qualities of natural mineral waters.

The fact that so many scientists tacitly accepted as truth the curative nature of mineral water is an indication of how pervasive the notion must have been. For example, Edward Shepard, a geologist based in Springfield, Missouri, observed in 1907 that "there is no doubt that much benefit is derived from most of the health resorts connected with mineral springs or wells."[1] Although such views became increasingly challenged in the twentieth century, they were deeply ingrained and were therefore difficult to extinguish.

Chemists, from the time of Robert Boyle in the 1600s, helped to discern the chemical basis of curative mineral waters. Geologists tried to explain their occur-

---

1. Edward M. Shepard, *The Underground Waters of Missouri; Their Geology and Utilization*, 211.

rence and distribution. But it was largely physicians who observed and recorded cures, providing professional endorsement and an impetus for the continuing beliefs of succeeding generations. Through the ages, doctors were often the ones who attempted to classify mineral waters, explain proper use, discern the physiological effects of various constituents, provide guides to mineral waters, and even promote their use. It is ironic, then, that this same profession would turn out to be the most vocal opponent of the use of mineral waters in meaningful medical practice.

Very early in the history of "taking the waters," there were a few things upon which physicians generally agreed. One was that mineral waters should not be used indiscriminately and without supervision. The *Boston Gazette* in 1766 advised in the use of Stafford Spring, "these waters may do mischief, unless some able physician is on the spot to give proper advice." In his 1855 publication on mineral springs, Dr. John Bell warned, "a want of adaptation, in the time of drinking the mineral water and of using the bath, to their actual condition, is productive of injury."[2] These basic tenets would constantly be repeated by physicians, an indication of the consuming public's short attention span and lack of concern with detailed medical regimens.

Spa doctors after Bell continued to elaborate on the unique medicinal effects of different mineral waters and the role of the physician. In 1859, Dr. J. J. Moorman, longtime resident physician at the White Sulphur Springs in Virginia, published a book called *The Virginia Spas and Springs of the South and West*. Astonished that some medical practitioners directed people to the wrong springs, Moorman sent one man back home, seven hundred miles distant, where "medicine did for him what mineral waters were not calculated to do." He considered it critical to have an "intelligent resident physician at each fountain," whose responsibility was to "note the character of the various diseases submitted" and the "effects of the waters upon each case." This, he reasoned, would establish a reliable record to assist invalids in their choice of resorts, supplanting what he termed the "wild and hap-hazard empiricism in the use of mineral waters in America."[3] Although this made perfect sense, there is little evidence that many resorts actually did it.

---

2. *Boston Gazette* quoted in Bridenbaugh, "Baths and Watering Places," 154; Bell, *Mineral and Thermal Springs,* vii.

3. J. J. Moorman, *The Virginia Spas and Springs of the South and West,* 38, vii.

Like many physicians, Moorman emphasized that chemical analyses alone could not be used to accurately predict medical effects. There were still questions about which medicinal constituents were more important—salts or dissolved gases. The answer to this question had great practical value, because if gases were more important, then bottled waters had little therapeutic effect, since most gases escaped during the bottling process. This would also mean, of course, that one would need to go directly to the source, usually a resort, to achieve full benefit of the medicinal waters.

After the Civil War, efforts to describe and classify mineral springs and use systematic methods to discern their therapeutics intensified. Spa doctors, by then, had reached general agreement that mineral waters primarily helped chronic ailments, such as rheumatism, gout, dyspepsia, and scrofula. At the same time, these doctors tried to distance themselves from the loathsome promoters whose claims had not been tempered by the modern findings of medical science and were as exaggerated as ever. As in patent medicine advertising, the mineral water hucksters seemed out of control.

A distinguishing feature of the post–Civil War medical reports on mineral waters is that for the first time, Missouri's resorts hit the national radar screen. For example, Dr. George Walton, who published *The Mineral Springs of the U.S. and Canada* in 1873, described 133 springs, only one of which was in Missouri (Belcher's artesian well in St. Louis). While supporting the use of mineral waters for certain specific ailments, Walton downplayed their wider significance. "Springmania," he wrote, "has come to be accepted without challenge by multitudes of unreflecting minds," and "the unintelligent, indiscriminate flocking to watering places, going to the springs, is essentially absurd." Scorning the leisure pursuits of many resort goers, Walton noted that mineral waters would never "antidote the dissipations of enormous dinners, imbibing of spiritous liquors and continuous dancing till the morning hours." The value of spas to most visitors, he believed, was in bringing relief from the "harassing cares of business" or the "exacting demands of society."[4]

Dr. Albert Merrell published *Health Resorts and Mineral Springs in the West* in 1882. Merrell, who limped from a wound suffered in the Civil War, came to St. Louis at war's end to practice medicine. His book, written near the peak of mineral spring resort development in Missouri, echoed the frustration and disgust

---

4. George E. Walton, *The Mineral Springs of the United States and Canada,* 114, 36.

felt by many doctors toward unscrupulous promoters: "Readers of papers have no doubt noticed the frequency of announcements of the discovery of mineral springs, especially in the states west of the Mississippi River," he began. "This frequency is no more marked than the astonishing statements as to their curative virtues in healing all the diseases which afflict suffering humanity." Such revelations, he continued, resulted in "widespread excitement among the broken in health, as well as those disposed to look for wealth in providing for the wants of thousands of invalids." Merrell further recounted what physicians and others noticed for centuries, that "some rejoice in renewed health," while others "return home in disgust, characterizing all springs as frauds and the managers and promoters as robbers."[5]

Merrell explained the importance of climate and local ambient conditions for any good health resort. As a member of the St. Louis Board of Health, he also understood the value of sanitation. "Invalids can't get well in an atmosphere poisoned by their own or other's filth," he admonished, a nod to the new scientific emphasis on good ventilation, sanitation, and proper drainage in the prevention of disease.[6] Setting the tone for the arguments of spa doctors over the next half century, he attributed the skepticism of many physicians toward mineral waters to the fact that mineral water therapeutics had not been properly studied.

Being a St. Louis resident, Merrell naturally mentioned many mineral water sites in Missouri, particularly in the northern part of the state. Curiously, the medicinal springs he noted were largely different from those on lists generated by the Missouri Geological Survey. Quite possibly, Merrell consulted other doctors rather than natural scientists in generating his lists of useful mineral water locations. It is also interesting to note that one resort, "Sarnaca" (usually spelled Saranac), in Crawford County, was singled out by Merrell as "destined to be the health resort of the near future," although it never became so.[7]

Paul Schweitzer, when he began writing about mineral waters for the Missouri Geological Survey, no doubt consulted these physicians' reports. Like many scientists and doctors, he believed that mineral waters were of great value if the essential characteristics of the water were understood, the right water was selected for the intended treatment, the use was properly administered, and the

---

5. Albert Merrell, *Health Resorts and Mineral Springs in the West*, 1.
6. Ibid., 3.
7. Ibid., 27.

user did not have excessive expectations of the benefits to be derived. With these constraints in mind, Schweitzer listed in his *Report on Mineral Waters* the diseases for which the state's waters were useful, mildly complaining at the same time that the resorts themselves provided most of the information. The results of that listing, in large measure, reflect the medical reasoning of the time—that mineral waters most benefited the chronic conditions. The list also foreshadows the contemporary notion that the increasing pressures of urbanization and industrialization create multitudes of chronic ailments.

DISEASES HELPED BY MISSOURI'S MINERAL WATERS

Disease/Ailment	Number of Resorts Reporting Cures
Dyspepsia/stomach problems	16
Kidney diseases	12
Rheumatism	11
Bowel diseases	4
General disability	3
Skin diseases	2
Liver diseases	2
Bladder diseases	2
Sore eyes	2
Old sores	2
Cholera	1
Neuralgia	1
Malaria	1
Bright's disease	1
Dropsy	1
Chronic diarrhea	1
Sciatica	1
Paralysis	1
Piles	1

(*Source:* Schweitzer, *Report*)

At the end of the nineteenth century, mainstream medical practice and mineral water therapeutics had diverged considerably. Physicians prescribed mineral waters less and less and distanced themselves even more from the extravagant claims of promoters. Physicians and other professionals who still believed in

Polio pool, Excelsior Springs, 2000. *Photo by author*

mineral waters tried hard to avoid the hucksterism and to find a more credible, scientific basis for continuing use.

A good example of this struggle to find a firmer scientific footing can be found in a 1901 publication titled *A System of Physiologic Therapeutics,* in a section about health resorts and mineral springs. Compared to earlier publications, the claims of cures for mineral waters had been toned down considerably. "It is partly owing to rest and recreation," the authors explained, "that treatment by climate and health resorts often succeed when ordinary medical treatment, and sometimes every kind of treatment at home, has failed."[8]

8. F. Parker Weber, "Climatology, Health Resorts, and Mineral Springs," 260.

In decidedly cautionary tones, the authors mention several of Missouri's mineral water resorts that "may sometimes be availed of." For anemia, they advised treatment at a chalybeate spa such as Aurora Springs, with its "tonic earthy chalybeate water." For digestive disorders, one could visit one of the "alkaline, earthy, chalybeate and sulphur waters" in Saline County, such as Blue Lick Springs, Akesion Spring, or Sweet Springs.[9] In general, the authors leaned toward the view that mineral waters may help chronic conditions, but only within a larger regime of favorable climate, diet, exercise, and personal responsibility and restraint. This wider view of the context of mineral waters in human health would be echoed in modern times in many areas of the world—to a lesser extent, however, in the United States, where the popularity of mineral waters would soon wane.

9. Ibid., 153.

→ 8 ←

THE RISING TIDE

An obvious, though inherently complex question is: "Why did so many people believe in and use mineral waters?" Even the two parts of that question can be separated, with potentially several answers to each. Many people no doubt used the waters without really believing that they cured. After all, many took to the waters simply because it was the thing to do—to see and be seen, at least at the more fashionable resorts. Others bought bottled mineral waters to drink in the privacy of their homes, primarily seeking medicinal benefits. But many went to spas for drinking and bathing cures, convinced the waters could heal their bodies from both the inside and the outside.

The rise of modern medicine is often cited as the primary driving force behind the general decline in mineral water use. Therefore, it is fitting to examine the question of why people used the waters from that perspective: Just as the turning away is seen to hinge upon an increasing trust in the mainstream medical profession, the earlier attraction toward mineral waters grew, at least partly, from a pervasive mistrust of the same profession. Much of that distrust stemmed from the inability of medical practitioners to provide effective cures for a variety of human afflictions over many centuries.

Early physicians possessed only a rudimentary understanding of human physiology and disease causation. It was largely through trial and error that successful treatments were found. Procedures that brought relief were held onto, gaining wider service, and people continued to use a particular doctor as long as he seemed to be right more than he was wrong.

But doctors making their rounds, even in colonial America, were armed with some potent procedures—purging and bleeding, for example—which were interventions handed down from earlier times. Physicians commonly prescribed substances (that they often sold themselves), such as powerful narcotics and calomel, a mercury-based cure-all.[1] Unfortunately, the side effects of these drugs were often nearly as debilitating as the disease the doctor was trying to cure.

With these rough and not-so-reliable tools, organized medicine was largely powerless against the horrible epidemics of the cities. In the 1849 cholera outbreak in St. Louis, the worst the city ever experienced, almost five thousand people died, two thousand in one month at the height of the epidemic. St. Louis doctor William McPheters admitted his inadequacies in the face of this disaster: "Having no new views to present as to the nature, cause or treatment of cholera, I shall endeavor to confine myself as closely as possible to facts."[2]

Citizens in rural areas had their own scourges in fevers and ague, to the extent that fevers were considered a part of the "seasoning process" in newly settled territory. People generally knew that the medical profession had little in its arsenal to arrest the progress of such diseases, once contracted. Therefore, it is little wonder that they looked elsewhere for assistance with personal health, in many cases toward the mineral waters that promoters offered as panaceas. Huge amounts of these waters were sold in the cities, especially during the great cholera epidemics.

Doctors struggled to upgrade their profession in the first half of the nineteenth century. Only a small percentage of them had graduated from a regular medical school. Richard Shryock, in *Medicine and Society in America,* noted that legislation requiring that doctors have a medical degree may have encouraged easy schools rather than raising the standards of the profession. The president of the Wisconsin Medical Society observed in 1856, "perhaps no profession, art or even trade is looked upon with as much distrust as medicine. Even the prevailing schemes of quackery are more highly esteemed by a majority of people in some districts."[3]

The confused state of medical practice partially explains why people were drawn to patent medicines, with their promises of quick, painless, and relatively

1. Mark C. Carnes, *A History of American Life,* 306.
2. David D. March, *The History of Missouri,* 711; McPheters quoted in E. J. Goodwin, *A History of Medicine in Missouri,* 71.
3. Jan Coombs, "Rural Medical Practice in the 1880s: A View from Central Wisconsin," 60.

inexpensive cures. The patent medicine trade came early to America. The first advertisement for a patent medicine in an American newspaper appeared in 1708. The practice of self-dosing became very common and widespread. Some doctors protested the tactics of patent medicine promoters, which only fueled speculation that physicians were trying to achieve a monopoly on prescriptions for their own profit.[4]

The patent medicine business raked in huge profits by the early 1800s, and with no serious efforts in the United States to suppress the patent trade, its flamboyant promotion continued unabated through the century. In fact, with the proliferation of printing houses after the Civil War, competition among patent medicine companies intensified, leading to the employment of high-paid commercial illustrators and energizing the graphics art field.[5] In many of Missouri's newspapers from the 1870s and 1880s, a third of the advertisements pushed patent medicines, many with eye-catching artwork.

Without doubt, the patent medicine business impacted the promotion and sales of mineral waters. People became used to the sweeping, excessive claims of the patent medicine hawkers. In this context, such claims placed on mineral waters can be viewed as merely falling in line with accepted and obviously successful marketing strategies of the day. For mineral waters to compete successfully, they probably had to adopt this style.

Divergent philosophies within the medical community itself would drive many health seekers to try alternatives such as mineral waters. The 1840s and 1850s witnessed the rise of a bewildering assortment of medical sects, groups whose medical approaches were based on novel theories of disease causation and philosophies of treatment. Along with hydropaths, homeopaths, and botanics, a host of more eccentric specialties, such as phrenology, magnetic healing, and mesmerism, attracted large followings. Followers of each sect believed that they were on the true path toward personal enlightenment, health, and even perfection.

Hydropaths, one of the more interesting of the sects, ascribed to the "water cure." Hydropathists theorized that pure water was a simple yet powerful curative agent. Applied in varying contexts, it could serve as a sedative and a stimulant, an aperient, and an astringent. Dr. Russell T. Trall introduced hydropathic

---

4. See James Harvey Young, *The Medical Messiahs: A Social History of Health Quackery in Twentieth-Century America;* see also www.quackwatch.org.

5. Adelaide Hechtlinger, comp., *The Great Patent Medicine Era; or, Without Benefit of Doctor,* overleaf.

treatments into the United States at an institute he opened in New York in 1843. Between then and 1900, records indicate that over two hundred water-cure establishments operated in the United States.[6] Although Missouri had none of these, several of the state's mineral water resorts offered "hydropathic" treatments of various sorts.

Curiously, hydropathy, as originally practiced, opposed the use of mineral waters. Dr. Trall, author of the 1853 *Hydropathic Encyclopedia,* seemed incredulous that medical practitioners would accept that "impure waters were more healthful for sick persons than pure," or that "those springs of water which contain the greatest amount and variety of impurities, are the most celebrated as resorts for health-seeking invalids."[7]

One issue united most of the sects, some two dozen strong by the 1840s—that was the view that medicine as practiced by regular doctors was both futile and dangerous, referred to by Trall as "the baseless fabric we are laboring to demolish."[8] Standard medical practice mounted a mild defense by using its own statistics to show that orthodox treatments prolonged life. Regular doctors found some support among life insurance companies, which rejected sectarians and "quacks." In the middle of the nineteenth century, however, it could be said that the mainstream medical profession remained mired in confusion, its standards of practice in limbo.

At the same time, clinicians of the Paris school of medicine, performing thousands of autopsies, found little evidence that commonly applied medical treatments altered diseased organs. Therefore, they advocated "nihilism," or doing nothing, as better than most interventions then available. Even the great Dr. Wendell Holmes observed in 1860 that "if the whole materia medica, as now used, could be sunk to the bottom of the sea, it would be all the better for mankind—and all the worse for the fishes."[9]

Regular medical doctors, uncertain about what to do but favoring doing something over nothing, often fell back on the heroic practices of old, such as purging and bleeding and heavy dosing with strong drugs. By avoiding the extremes of both nihilism and heroics, alternative sects attracted a great following.

---

6. Harry B. Weiss and Howard R. Kemble, *The Great American Water-Cure Craze: A History of Hydropathy in the United States,* 44.
7. Russell T. Trall, *The Hydropathic Encyclopedia,* 36.
8. Ibid., 9.
9. Richard Harrison Shryock, *Medicine and Society in America, 1660–1860,* 31; Holmes quoted in Carnes, *History,* 155.

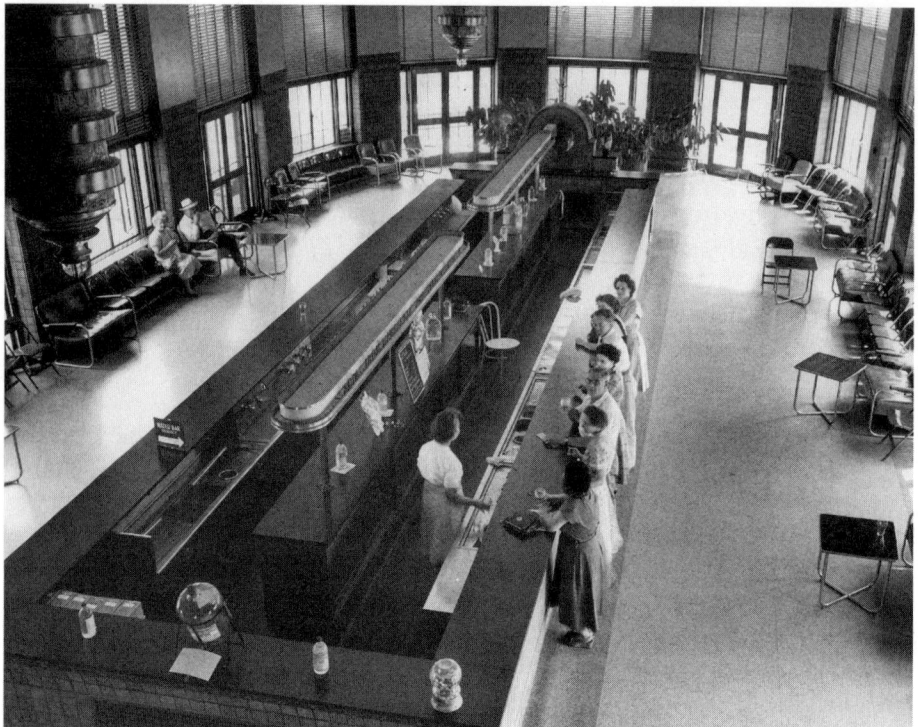

Hall of Waters, interior view, Excelsior Springs. *Massie, Missouri Resources Division, State Historical Society of Missouri, Columbia*

Mineral water treatments found a comfortable home in this setting, being natural and relatively harmless, even when overdosed. As a result, mineral water use and mineral-water-based health resorts enjoyed a rising tide of popularity.

It appears that the factors driving the development of new mineral spring resorts culminated in Missouri in the last decades of the nineteenth century. Figure 2 displays the dates of founding of the state's mineral water resorts (when they are known) in ten-year increments. From this graph, it is clear that the decade of the 1880s represented the peak time for the founding of new resorts. The decade preceding the Civil War, marked by border wars and rising unrest, and the postwar decade, when lawlessness gripped the state, witnessed the opening of few new resorts. In the 1890s, the number of start-ups dipped again, but a large number of resorts still operated profitably. Another small peak occurred in the first decade of the 1900s, when new health resorts and sanitariums surged modestly.

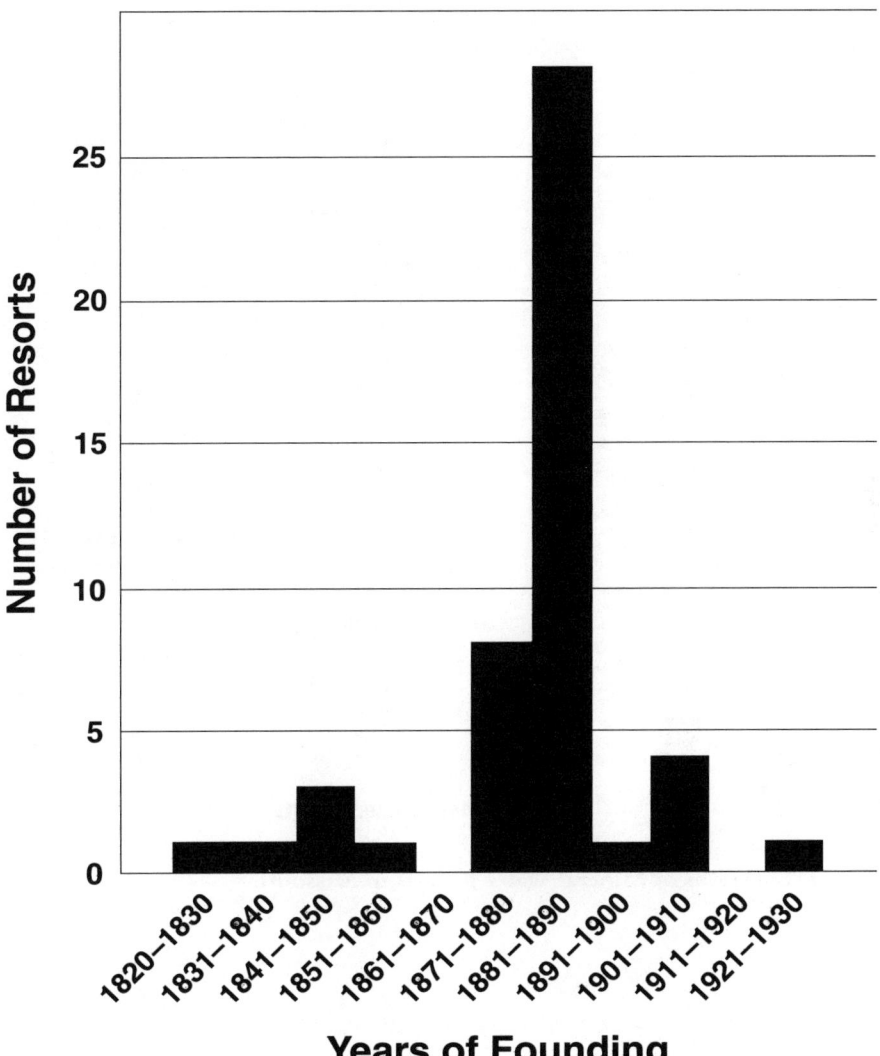

Figure 2. Founding Periods of Missouri Mineral Water Resorts.

Figure 3 lists the mineral water resorts mentioned by Paul Schweitzer, Albert Peale, and others and shows the locations of these resorts. The lives and times of these resorts span more than a century, bearing testimony to the tenacious nature of the mineral spring allure.

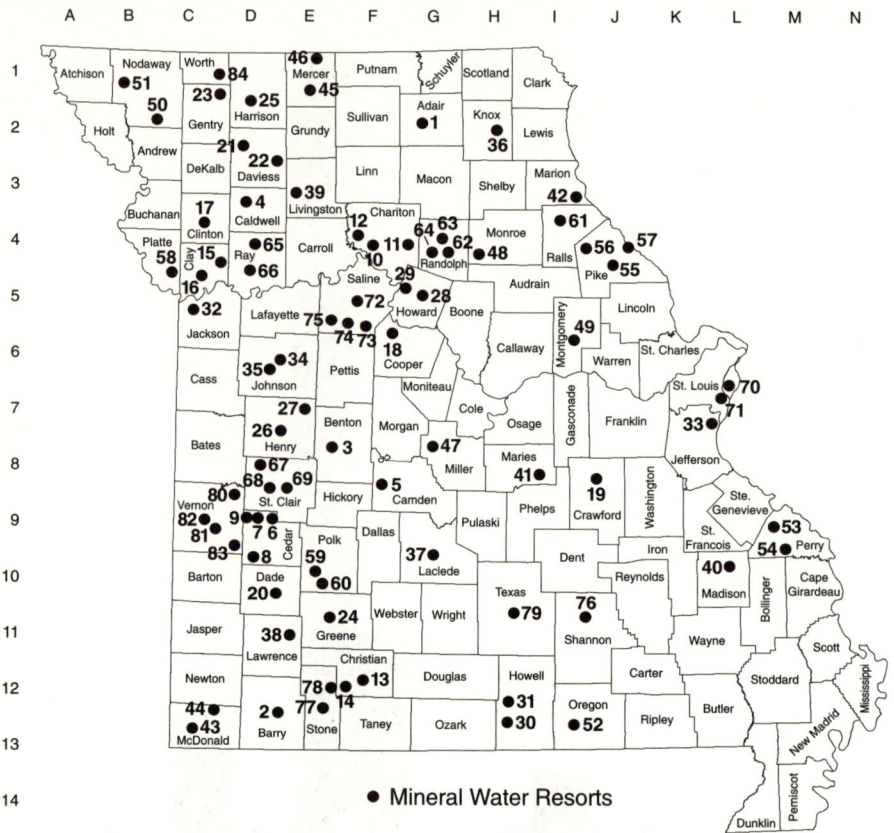

Figure 3. Locations of Mineral Water Resorts in Missouri.

MINERAL WATER RESORTS SHOWN IN FIGURE 3

Adair County (G-2)
1. New Baden (Baden Springs)

Barry County (D-13)
2. Mineral Springs (Panacea)

Benton County (E-8)
3. White Sulphur Springs

Caldwell County (D-3)
4. Bonanza Spring

Camden County (F-8)
5. Climax Springs

Cedar County (D-9)
6. Cedar Springs
7. El Dorado Springs
8. Jerico Springs
9. Nine Wonders (West El Dorado)

Chariton County (F-4)
10. Brunswick Mineral Well
11. Salisbury Well
12. Triplett Well

Christian County (E-12)
13. Eau de Vie
14. Reno

Clay County (C-4)
15. Excelsior Springs
16. Reed Springs

Clinton County (C-3)
17. Plattsburg Mineral Spring

Cooper County (F-6)
18. Chouteau Springs

Crawford County (J-8)
19. Saranac Springs

Dade County (D-10)
20. Lotus Spring

Daviess County (D-3)
21. Crystal Springs
22. Jamesport Mineral Springs

Gentry County (C-2)
23. Siloam Springs

Greene County (E-11)
24. Bethesda Springs

Harrison County (D-1)
25. Heilbron Spring

Henry County (D-7)
26. Clinton Artesian Well
27. Windsor Medical Well

Howard County (G-5)
28. Fayette Salt Spring
29. Glasgow Mineral Spring

Howell County (H-12)
30. Dixon (Cure-All) Springs
31. Siloam Springs

Jackson County (C-5)
32. Young's Medical Well

Jefferson County (K-8)
33. Montesano Springs

Johnson County (D-6)
34. Colbern (Electric) Springs
35. Pertle Springs

Knox County (H-2)
36. Forest Springs

Laclede County (G-10)
37. Lebanon Magnetic Well

Lawrence County (D-11)
38. Paris Springs

Livingston County (E-3)
39. Mooresville

Madison County (L-10)
40. White Springs
John Hahn's Spring
Mineral Well

Maries County (H-8)
41. Vichy

Marion County (I-3)
  42. Vernette Mineral Well

McDonald County (C-13)
  43. Galbraith's Medical Well
  44. Indian Springs

Mercer County (E-1)
  45. Bowsher Mineral Spring
  46. Lineville Mineral Well

Miller County (G-8)
  47. Aurora Springs

Monroe County (H-4)
  48. Harris Springs

Montgomery County (I-6)
  49. Mineola

Nodaway County (B-1)
  50. Barnard Medical Well
  51. Burlington Junction Mineral Spring

Oregon County (I-13)
  52. El Dorado Springs

Perry County (M-9)
  53. Lithium Springs
  54. Schumer Springs

Pike County (J-4)
  55. B.B. Spring
  56. Elk Lick Springs
  57. Louisiana Artesian Well

Platte County (B-4)
  58. Crystal (Tiffany) Springs

Polk County (E-10)
  59. Eudora Springs
  60. Graydon Springs

Ralls County (I-4)
  61. Spalding Springs

Randolph County (G-4)
  62. Radium Spring
  63. Randolph Spa
  64. Randolph Springs

Ray County (D-4)
  65. Mineral City
  66. St. Cloud

St. Clair County (D-8)
  67. Appleton City Well
  68. Monegaw Springs
  69. Salt Creek Spring

St. Louis County (L-7)
  70. Belcher's Artesian Well
  71. White Sulphur Springs

Saline County (F-5)
  72. Blue Lick Springs
  73. Elk Lick Springs
  74. McAllister Springs
  75. Sweet Springs

Shannon County (J-11)
  76. Welch Spring

Stone County (E-13)
  77. Galena Medical Spring
  78. Ponce de Leon

Texas County (H-11)
  79. Blankenship Medical Springs

Vernon County (C-9)
  80. Fair Haven (Conely Springs)
  81. Greene Springs
  82. Nevada Artesian Well (Lake Park White Sulphur Spring)
  83. Zodiac

Worth County (C-1)
  84. Fairview Mineral Spring (Denver Bathhouse)

9

SOCIAL DIVERSIONS

Mineral waters became the central feature of many "health resorts" around the United States and the world. These resorts catered to a variety of interests, often providing meals, lodging, and various amusements along with the required mineral waters. Patrons were encouraged to stay for several days or even weeks to receive the full benefits of the healing waters.

Most advertisers designed the promotional messages of Missouri's mineral water resorts to attract both "invalids" and "pleasure-seekers." Obviously, invalids sought specific medical benefits. But for the pleasure seeker, the resort merely provided a relaxing backdrop for fresh air, amusement, and a change of scenery, along with the required "dose" of mineral water. Increasingly, patrons came to partake of social and recreational offerings as much as elixirs drawn into tub or glass.

This happened early in the history of spas. Daniel Defoe, writing from England's Tunbridge Wells in about 1717, noted that the numbers of health seekers had dwindled in favor of the more playful, social element: "Now we may say it is the resort of the sound rather than the sick; the bathing is made more a sport and diversion rather than a physical prescription for health; and the town is taken up with raffling, gaming, visiting and, in a word, all sorts of gallantry and levity."[1] Resorts quickly discovered that to stay competitive, they had to cater to this leisure element. Mineral waters, in fact, often slipped quietly into the background behind a panoply of larger attractions. On the other hand, most

---

1. Muriel V. Searle, *Spas and Watering Places*, 93.

spas did not want to discourage the business of invalids, either. In short, owners wanted to provide something for everyone.

In the decades after the Civil War, Americans experienced rising affluence, cheaper travel, and an explosion of interest in sports and recreation. As unusual as it might seem, this indulgence in leisure pursuits came about rather slowly. Americans had been taught how to work, but not how to relax. President Garfield framed the situation well in 1880 at Lake Chautauqua, New York, when he said, "we may divide the whole struggle of the human race into two chapters; first, the fight to get leisure and then, the second fight of civilization—what shall we do with our leisure when we get it?"[2] In the last half of the nineteenth century, the expanding middle class, especially in urban centers, increasingly demanded leisure pursuits and amusements in all forms and was willing and able to pay for them.

Sports, involving organized teams or individual activities, grew in popularity. Baseball, one of the first major sports to captivate the public imagination, became established as a national pastime by the late 1860s. In 1866, *Nation* magazine announced that "of all the epidemics that have swept over our land, the swiftest and most infectious is croquet."[3] Shortly after, the velocipede made its appearance, with over a million bicycles rolling along by 1893. Progressive resorts followed and accommodated these successive fads, offering grassy lawns that were as suitable for croquet or baseball as they had been for resting in the shade of an umbrella while sipping mineral water lemonade. At many resorts, owners cut trails through the grounds for leisurely walks or bicycling.

Demands for indoor recreational and athletic amenities also increased. Some resorts, such as Excelsior Springs and Lebanon's Gasconade Hotel, provided fully equipped gymnasiums. Pin bowling, introduced in New York in 1840 and at first considered a public nuisance, soon appeared at Missouri resorts such as Electric Springs and Pertle Springs in Warrensburg, Excelsior Springs, Chouteau Springs, McAllister Springs, and Sweet Springs. Later resorts, such as Siloam Springs in Howell County, laid out golf courses, following the lead of White Sulphur Springs in Virginia, which introduced the game to the United States in 1884.

Another favorite pastime, horse racing, appeared at some of the larger mineral water resorts. Resorts built tracks in the manner of Saratoga Springs in New

---

2. Carnes, *History,* 943.
3. Marshall B. Davidson, *Life in America,* 62–63.

Old pin bowling alley, Warrensburg. *Johnson County Historical Society, Inc., Warrensburg*

York and the earlier Sulphur Springs in St. Louis. Plattsburg Mineral Springs, Clinton's Artesian Park, and McAllister Springs had tracks; Reed's Springs, in Liberty, had plans for a track but never built one.

Many resort patrons enjoyed rowing or riding in boats, peaceful and popular diversions offered on the lakes and rivers at Sweet Springs, Indian Springs, Pertle Springs, and Radio Springs. Some resorts featured the old standbys of hunting and fishing, especially those with enough acreage to provide a game preserve for the state's depleted fauna.

Bathing and swimming in mineral water pools became the main activities at several of Missouri's resorts, including Chouteau Springs, Blue Lick, Sweet Springs, McAllister Springs, and Excelsior Springs. Recreational "bathing," in fact, would tide some mineral water resorts over into nearly modern times. The 1941 *WPA Guide to Missouri*, for example, announced swimming at Chouteau Springs for twenty-five cents.[4]

Resorts saw the need to cater to the mind as well as the body. Accordingly, many resorts hired bands to play during the summer months, providing a pleasant backdrop for a game of lawn tennis or a quiet repast, sipping mineral

---

4. Works Projects Administration, *Missouri: The WPA Guide to the "Show Me" State*, 358.

Remains of modesty screens for bathers, Spalding Springs, Ralls County, 1998. *Photo by author*

water under an open-air pagoda. More stimulating were plays produced by thespian societies and especially the tent Chautauquas, or "traveling colleges," which became immensely popular by the end of the nineteenth century. The Chautauqua movement, initially intended for the training of Sunday School teachers, soon broadened into more general public education.[5] These often weeklong events, which included scientific and theological lectures by prominent scholars and orators, as well as performances by professional musicians and actors, brought a great variety of entertainment and enlightenment to Missouri. A parade of Chautauquas took center stage at resorts like Pertle and Electric Springs in Johnson County and Plattsburg Mineral Spring in Clinton County.

Camp meetings also attracted big crowds at mineral spring resorts, perhaps taking advantage of the symbolism between ever-flowing springs and everlasting life. The Reverend Sam Jones spoke in front of huge rallies at Plattsburg and Pertle Springs, for example. The pinnacle of resort social gatherings probably occurred at Pertle Springs, where huge camp meetings, free-silver conventions, teachers' meetings, temperance rallies, and Fourth of July celebrations

---

5. Carnes, *History*, 789.

consistently attracted thousands. In the 1890s, the Pertle Springs Fourth of July events occasioned full-page advertisements in Warrensburg newspapers.

By the end of the nineteenth century, some of the great mineral water resorts had essentially transformed into amusement parks. A good example of this is Montesano, south of St. Louis, where major attractions included bands, dances, and rides of all kinds, like the exciting "switchback railway"—an early kind of roller coaster. Steam-powered excursion boats made trips daily from St. Louis down the Mississippi River to Montesano Park. Traction companies provided excursions to mineral water parks in other areas, with sites like Clinton's Artesian Park accessible by horse-drawn (and, later, electric) trolleys.

Getting the masses to the resorts became progressively easier. Steamboats, in the 1830s through the 1860s, and railroads thereafter, offered cheap excursion fares and opened up travel opportunities to wide sectors of society. At the height of mineral water resort popularity in Missouri, railroads, then the primary mode of longer-distance transportation, made a wide assortment of resorts available to the state's population centers. Advertisements for railroad excursion fares to resorts like Eureka Springs, Excelsior Springs, and Montesano commonly appeared in Missouri newspapers of the late nineteenth century, and thousands bought tickets. Thirty-seven hundred people joined a single excursion from Springfield to Eureka Springs in 1900.

Eventually, the automobile brought resort customers, although the number of resorts had already declined by then. Some of the resorts that survived into the twentieth century, such as Excelsior Springs, cultivated the public's love affair with cars by designing elaborate drives for Sunday afternoon outings. Mooresville, a resort in Livingston County, advertised that it served the coast-to-coast Pike's Peak Highway, now U.S. Highway 36.

In some locations, mineral waters spawned new towns. Several resorts are associated with plats containing lots, sometimes in the hundreds, laid out around the focal mineral springs. Developers envisioned and platted towns at Chouteau Springs in Cooper County, Jackson Lithia Springs in Kansas City, Twin Springs in McDonald County, Crystal Springs in Pettis County, Mineral Springs in Ray County, McAllister Springs in Saline County, and Tiffany Springs in Platte County. In most of these locations, little evidence remains of the lots. Sometimes, areas on plats were reserved for future hotels, racetracks, and other amenities, but in many cases these facilities never materialized.

Resorts also helped to attract settlement in existing communities. Growth forced local land values up, fattening the pocketbooks of established landowners.

Family at camp meeting, Pertle Springs, Johnson County. *State Historical Society of Missouri, Columbia*

Therefore, many citizens became speculators and land boomers, trying out promotional schemes to spur immigration. Resorts and other unique local amenities helped to spark outside interest and served to distinguish a community from its neighbors. Town booster books, common in the late nineteenth and early twentieth centuries, often contained several pages enthusiastically describing local resorts.

As time progressed, social diversions came to define the character of resorts more and more. The mineral waters themselves often became secondary to the fun. Yet even with this new emphasis on leisure, Missouri's mineral water health resorts would eventually fade from the social landscape.

10

TAKING THE WATERS

By the time of Missouri's great resort boom of the 1880s, the ancient rituals of mineral water drinking and bathing had evolved through many cycles of development and refinement. The more aristocratic resorts patterned themselves after the famous watering places of the east, like the White Sulphur Springs of Virginia. At Sweet Springs, for example, white-gloved servants filled trays of glasses lowered by a windlass into the porcelain spring receptacle, while patrons waited, resting on benches under the large, ornate pagoda. Most of Missouri's resorts, however, catered more to the mainstream, and the mineral waters themselves were generally affordable and available to all classes.

If health seekers wanted to drink mineral waters at home, they could order by mail and receive delivery of a case of bottled water from their favorite sources. For the purists, or for those who believed that bottled waters lost their medicinal potency, mineral waters could usually be drawn right at the source. The water was often free or at least very inexpensive. In Excelsior Springs, one could stroll around town, pausing at one of the many little spring or well pagodas to purchase water at a penny a glass. At El Dorado Springs, a person could draw as much water as desired from politically correct spigots—one for Democrats, the other for Republicans. Or, at resorts in Clinton or Nevada, patrons could hold their cups right under the cascading fount of an artesian well.

Whatever the source, the process of drinking mineral water needed to follow certain traditional and set patterns to achieve maximum results. Paul Schweitzer, for example, provided his readers with some standard prescriptive advice:

Taking the waters at Lithium spring, Perry County. *Trish Erzfeld, Perry County Clerk's Office*

"The water should be taken slowly, glass by glass, allowing an interval of a few minutes between the first and second and between the third and fourth glasses, and from ten to twenty minutes between the second and third; this latter interval should be passed in walking and a walk of a half-mile or a mile at the end is recommended."[1]

Many accounts of mineral water drinking refer to the vile nature of the liquid imbibed. Patrons found sulfur waters particularly difficult to quaff in the recommended quantities, requiring them to hold their noses or suppress the gag reflex. Of course, a pervasive notion held that the stronger and more unpleasant the taste, the better the medicine. One eighteenth-century patron called the nauseating doses of sulfur water offered at a European spa a "good rehearsal for Purgatory."[2] In spite of the often offensive taste or aroma, and counter to the advice of most physicians, resort patrons sometimes downed prodigious

1. Schweitzer, *Report*, 30.
2. Searle, *Spas and Watering Places*, 47.

quantities of mineral waters. By some accounts, some hopeful health seekers drank as much as two hundred to three hundred ounces every morning over a period of several weeks.

Bathing in mineral waters, as in drinking them, has a long history. While George Washington soaked his rheumatism at Bath, Virginia, in the early 1760s, physicians speculated that medicinal minerals in the water somehow permeated his skin and treated his ailing body internally. Thomas Jefferson was also a mineral water bather and strongly believed in the health benefits; he described several medicinal springs in his *Notes on the State of Virginia*.[3] In 1831, John Bell, writing about mineral waters and baths in 1831, reflected on the "total regeneration" to be found by relaxing in a bath. Others responded favorably to the feel of the mineral waters, one author likening a Virginia spring to a "reservoir of Champaign," saying the water was so soft that "the roughest hide will seem smooth, as if anointed with myrrh and frankincense."[4]

Early mineral water resorts used simple wooden or metal bathtubs that were filled with water right from a spring (but often heated). Later resorts usually had enclosed bathhouses with separate bathrooms, but some early versions, such as Blankenship Springs in Texas County, featured larger tubs with room for several bathers. By the resort boom of the 1880s, most facilities offered porcelain tubs for individual baths and large bathing pools made of wood or even cement for communal bathing. Pools, which were usually square or round, came in many sizes, with the large octagonal pools at Sweet Springs being rather distinctive. Operators maintained flow rates high enough to keep the pool water "fresh," and some resorts proudly announced how often they changed the water. Several resorts featured separate pools for the sexes, but as time went on, most resorts offered coed bathing, at least during certain specified times. A Sweet Springs promotional booklet from 1884 noted that allowing men and women to bathe together advanced the "useful art of swimming among the fairer sex." At McAllister Springs, patrons could choose from a variety of new fashions in bathing suits available at the front office.

By the 1880s, many spas offered more sophisticated versions of the individual bath, such as magnetic baths, galvanic baths, mud baths, carbonic acid baths,

---

3. De Vierville, "American Healing Waters," 142.
4. Perceval Reniers, *The Springs of Virginia: Life, Love, and Death at the Waters, 1775–1900*, 107.

Swimming pools at Sweet Springs, Saline County. *State Historical Society of Missouri, Columbia*

peat baths, Russian baths, and Turkish baths, among others. Doctors prescribed particular baths for specific ailments at mineral spring sanitariums, and white-frocked attendants assisted bathers. The federal government, recognizing the value of baths in therapeutics, established the Army and Navy General Hospital at Hot Springs in 1882, where baths were integral to the medical regimen. By this time, the science of bathing for health had even acquired a specialty designation within the field of hydrotherapy and was awarded the awkward name of balneology.

In order to profit from their drinking and bathing cures, resorts depended heavily upon advertising and promotion to keep the crowds coming. In the days before television and radio, newspapers served as the primary vehicles for reaching the masses, and resorts used them extensively. In 1880, at the height of Missouri's mineral water resort boom, daily and weekly newspapers sold nearly a million subscriptions.[5] Resorts also used circulars, which they distributed

---

5. Lawrence O. Christensen and Gary R. Kremer, *A History of Missouri: Volume 4, 1875 to 1919*, 77.

to other businesses, handed to railroad passengers, or mailed to prospective patrons, often from names referred by regular clients.

In addition to basic information about the resort—location, amenities, date of opening, length of season, and proprietor's name—certain other items became standard fare in promotional literature. Testimonials—statements from people who used the water and were willing to share their glowing accounts of success—usually appeared somewhere in advertisements. These statements frequently came from prominent citizens like doctors, bankers, judges, and ministers. Of course, it didn't hurt to have the endorsement of famous personalities, either: We can be sure that the promoters of Saratoga Springs in New York seldom forgot the fact that George Washington, Alexander Hamilton, and DeWitt Clinton had frequented that resort. Likewise, in Missouri, Thomas Hart Benton had helped publicize the healing waters at Loutre Lick, and much later Harry S. Truman used the facilities at Excelsior—a tidbit used in promotions to this day.

There is no evidence that people providing testimonials received monetary compensation, but it is reasonable to assume that owners offered them some sort of perquisite—a free bath, perhaps, or an extra day at the resort. Some people may have been satisfied just seeing their name in print. Whatever the means of solicitation, almost every resort offered testimonials, whether printed within circulars, prominently displayed in local newspapers, or offered upon request by the management of the resort.

Of course, the patrons whose testimonials were printed do not represent a statistically valid sample of a resort's clientele. But the list does give some idea of the geographic scope of the service area. For example, a statement in an 1889 circular from the proprietor of Paris Springs that "there has been very little effort to advertise this now celebrated watering place," is backed up by the fact that most testimonials are from locals—a Lawrence County judge, a merchant and a pastor from Springfield, and a farmer from Lawrenceburgh, for example. In contrast, a Sweet Springs promotional flyer from 1878 included testimonials from all over the Midwest and beyond—Jefferson City; Olathe; somewhere in Virginia (this testimonial came from a woman whose brother-in-law from Harrisonville shipped her water; she found great benefit, she claimed, "after the use of three barrels"); St. Louis; Texas; Illinois; and from Dr. Thomas J. Montgomery, former president of the Missouri State Medical Association.

In addition to medical testimonials, promoters used other forms of endorse-

Promotional pamphlet for El Dorado Springs, Cedar County. *State Historical Society of Missouri, Columbia*

ment in resort pamphlets. Several major resorts issued new promotional booklets each season, often including the names of prominent citizens who had visited the previous year. At resorts such as Sweet Springs, where owners intended to project an aristocratic aura, this who's who list of resort patrons became an honor roll and a mark of distinction.

Another essential piece of information on mineral water advertisements—the chemical analysis—provided the scientific basis for promotion. This ingredient statement needed to look official. In fact, the chemical constituents present and their relative amounts may have been less important than the visual appeal of a scientific-looking analysis on the label or in the advertisement. Analysts usually reported mineral matter amounts in grains per gallon (each grain being equivalent to 17.1 parts per million), often with an accuracy down to four decimal places, or ten thousands of a grain. This made the analysis appear to be very precise.

A largely oblivious public knew or cared little about long-standing disagreements between chemists and physicians on how mineral water analyses should be reported. By the 1880s, chemists understood that most mineral constituents in solution occurred in a dissociated, or ionic form (for example, common salt or sodium chloride dissociates in water into sodium ions and chloride ions). Many scientists believed that these ionic forms actually exerted the medicinal effects. Albert Peale, among others, urged that chemical constituents be reported in this manner. Physicians, however, were used to dealing in medicinal compounds, not ions, and therefore wanted results reported in "hypothetical combinations," which is how they normally appeared.

In addition to the appearance of the analysis, it also helped if it had a recognizable name attached to it—Paul Schweitzer, Dr. Litton, or the St. Louis laboratory of Merrill and Wright. These names became marks of authenticity and authority that perhaps added more weight than the grains of the minerals themselves. The same names also appear consistently in local historical accounts, indicating the likelihood that they had become household words to many Missourians.

We must remember that the analyses that appeared on ads and labels in the late nineteenth century represented the culmination of hundreds of years of scientific inquiry, dating back at least to the sixteenth century. In fact, much of the early development of chemical methods originated in the study of mineral waters.[6] By Paul Schweitzer's time, the essential details of various analytical methods for determining the kinds and quantities of chemical constituents in mineral waters had been worked out. Some of these basic methods had been in use for centuries, although equipment and techniques had been highly refined over the years. Still, as Schweitzer explained in his *Report on Mineral Waters,* the modern laboratory work was far from a walk in the park: "The experienced chemist holds the analysis of a mineral water a problem of no mean difficulty, partly on account of the relatively small quantity of solids dissolved, and partly on the account of the necessity of bringing to bear upon each operation much knowledge and judgment in order to obtain results that can be relied upon."[7] Schweitzer and his colleagues analyzed hundreds of mineral waters using these methods, providing a basis for the comparison of springs and wells across the

---

6. Back, Landa, and Meek, "Bottled Waters," 605.
7. Schweitzer, *Report,* 11.

state. Below is given one of Schweitzer's analyses to illustrate how the mineral constituents were commonly reported:

LANDRETH'S WELL, NEAR KNOX CITY; ANALYZED JUNE 1884

silica	0.9508
alumina	0.6697
ferrous bicarbonate	2.3919
calcium bicarbonate	32.6502
calcium sulfate	18.4061
magnesium sulfate	23.5369
potassium sulfate	0.4724
sodium sulfate	30.8562
sodium chloride	1.1721
carbon dioxide gas (free)	7.5586
mineral matter	118.6649
fixed residue	99.8183

(Amounts given in grains.)

The chemical constituents were proudly listed for anyone to see. If a person believed in the medicinal efficacy of these minerals, the statements of content may have been reassuring. One must wonder, however, how many health seekers, even in Schweitzer's day, were concerned about the particular mix of chemical compounds in their mineral water. More likely, people either believed in the medicinal value of mineral waters or they did not. Not long after Schweitzer's time, the majority did not.

11

WATERS, DEEP AND MYSTERIOUS

Early mineral water resorts were, of necessity, established near mineral springs. However, with the advance of well-drilling technologies in the nineteenth century, many later resorts turned to wells as their primary means of extracting mineral waters. From that point forward, the siting of new resorts no longer depended upon the location of natural mineral springs. Many of the bottling operations in Excelsior and El Dorado Springs, for example, used wells of varying depths to obtain the desired kind of mineral water. The public's fascination with deep wells and especially with flowing artesian wells is evident from the literature describing some of Missouri's mineral water resorts.

Drillers sank one of the state's early and very deep mineral water wells with a different purpose in mind—to obtain pure water for industrial use. For its time, the well drilled to supply the Belcher Sugar Refinery in St. Louis was a true engineering marvel. Drillers began their work in 1849 using manpower alone and finally finished the well five years later, utilizing steam power, reaching nearly twenty-two hundred feet of depth. The Belcher well remained the deepest in the state until 1966.[1] Its water, which was sparkling clear but heavily mineralized and pungent with hydrogen sulfide, could not be used in refining sugar, but it eventually supplied the famous Belcher Bath House.

Many early wells in the state provided saline water for salt production. The earliest brine "wells" consisted of hollow logs placed into springs where clarified water would collect and could be dipped out. The naturalist John Bradbury

---

1. Mary McCracken, "Some Historical Aspects of Well Drilling," 67.

noted in 1810 that sections of hollow logs used in this manner were called "gums," because gum trees served the purpose particularly well.[2] When flows of saline springs were weak, or when the water was not salty enough, developers attempted to obtain stronger brines by drilling wells nearby. Drilled in 1823, the well at Spalding, one of the earliest drilled wells in Missouri, produced brine for salt making near one of the twelve salt springs originally deeded to the state at its formation. In 1869, drillers sank a well more than one thousand feet deep at Boone's Lick. Part of the square wooden surface casing (used to keep out the "quicksand") is still visible. Ironically, drillers sometimes encountered petroleum in these early wells, forcing them to go deeper in the hopes of obtaining saline groundwater. The presence of petroleum, however, came to be seen as a sign that saline water might be found below, and at some of the early salt springs in the Ohio Valley the oil itself was skimmed off and sold as a "cure-all."[3]

Like the famous well at Belcher's, other wells in Missouri used for mineral water production were originally drilled for different purposes. Mineral exploration companies drilled Clinton's artesian well and the mineral well at Brunswick in hopes of obtaining natural gas. Hopeful prospectors sank a well at La Grange for "fuel," wells at Triplett and Randolph Springs for oil, and the artesian well at Nevada for oil, coal, or anything else of value. At Mineral City, workers drilled a well in search of fresh drinking water, and at Denver they dug a well as a water supply for camp meetings.

Citizens became excited if a local well turned out to be artesian. Artesian wells, named for a flowing well sunk in 1126 in the French province of Artesia, have long captured the imagination of the public. Although the artesian condition did not impart medicinal effects, it did at least add promotional value. Mineral water promoters capitalized on the public's fascination with these curiosities. At several mineral water sites, a gushing artesian well that spouted eight or ten feet into the air became the central feature of the resort. Artesian wells had practical value as well: Pumping costs were reduced or even eliminated when groundwater reached the surface under its own power.

In Missouri, resorts used artesian mineral water wells at various times in Rolla, Louisiana, Fair Haven, Sweet Springs, and Lebanon, in addition to Nevada

---

2. Bradbury, *Travels in the Interior,* 277.
3. Banta, *The Ohio,* 481.

Clinton Artesian Well, Henry County. Schweitzer, *Report*

and Clinton. In Lebanon, promoters claimed the well water possessed magnetic properties. Even some doctors believed that the magnetism that was supposed to exist in some natural mineral waters conferred additional medicinal powers upon them. As a result, "magnetic" water showed up at mineral water resorts across the nation, perhaps in line with the magnetic healing in vogue at the time. Scientists like Schweitzer, however, believed what many experimenters reported—that water, mineral or not, could neither produce nor confer magnetism. Of course, such evidence did not seem to deter the tireless and vocal promoters.

In some areas, competing interests drilled wells near the mineral springs that provided source waters for existing resorts. There is little information available to determine if the increasing use of wells in places like Excelsior Springs or El Dorado Springs affected the output of springs in those areas. Such a problem *did* reach potentially huge economic proportions in Saratoga Springs, New York, where business interests became concerned that large numbers of wells might interfere with and threaten existing spring-based resorts. In that case, with evidence provided by the newly emerging discipline of hydrogeology, the state stepped in to purchase land, close wells, and regulate the withdrawal of mineral waters.[4] The city of Excelsior Springs also eventually interceded in the production and use of its mineral waters, a move intended more to clean up the city's image than to protect its resources.

An interesting aspect of the production of mineral waters is that during the heyday of mineral water resorts and bottling operations, promoters often made little effort, at least in written descriptions, to differentiate between wells and springs. Part of the disparity may have arisen from the fact that resort operators often modified spring outlets with tiles or vaults or dug them out to accept flow, therefore creating something more well-like. There seems to have been a greater tendency, however, to refer to sources as "springs" when they were, in fact, wells. The use of the word *spring* may have provided promotional value, in that "spring" implies a more natural source, while "well" indicates an artificial and therefore perhaps a lower-quality source.

In the first decade of the twentieth century, the promotion of mineral waters entered a more forceful and aggressive era, one that in its overzealous nature would eventually come back to haunt the promoters. Much of the hype derived from an earth-shaking event that took place at the end of the nineteenth century, in 1898, when French chemist Marie Curie isolated radium and found it to be more radioactive than any substance then known.

Within a few years of this discovery, scientists detected radioactivity almost everywhere they looked—in caves, in soil, and even in rain and snow—but in some mineral waters they found the phenomenon to be especially pronounced. Herman Schlundt, a University of Missouri graduate working with the U.S. Geological Survey, found high levels of radium emanations in mineral springs in Yellowstone Park in 1902.[5] Soon, scientists, doctors, and others began to ask questions about the possible health significance of radium and radioactivity in natural mineral waters.

Not surprisingly, many promoters quickly embraced radioactivity as the "magic bullet," the hidden curative agent that explained the hitherto unexplainable powers of mineral waters upon human health. But early praise for the medicinal importance of radioactivity also came from high scientific circles. A 1907 U.S. Surgeon General's report announced that with the discovery of radium emanations, "the question of the curative agency of a great number of

---

4. Davis and Davis, "Saratoga Springs," 350.
5. De Vierville, "American Healing Waters," 442–43.

mineral springs" had been solved.⁶ Further scientific studies seemed to add credence to this claim; researchers, for instance, found that radioactive waters inhibited the growth of bacteria and increased cell metabolism. Spa doctors reported cures for hypertension and impotence from the use of these waters.

It did not take long for mineral springs around the world to be analyzed for radioactivity and when positive results were obtained, the proliferation of "radium" and "radio" springs and wells was assured. At least two "Radium Springs" occurred in Missouri, in Randolph County and Barry County. The owner of Radio Springs in Nevada may have also named it for these newly found emanations.

With the magic genie of radioactivity in their bottles, the mineral water promoters entered a forceful new era of advertising. The aggressive nature of these promotions, along with exaggerated claims about the effects of lithium in water, led to a targeting of mineral water advertising by the federal government in the Pure Food and Drug Act of 1906. This law forever changed the way mineral waters could be promoted, and the associated public discourse led to their diminished credibility. For example, a 1914 article published in *Good Housekeeping* magazine warned readers about "so called radioactive waters" and asked them to consider the advertising tactics employed: "The moment a new principle is discovered, hosts of promoters fall upon it, distorting it out of all relation to the facts, and play upon the credulity of the public by the use of new terms applied in a meaningless way."⁷

In 1926, the U.S. Public Health Service questioned the efficacy of radioactivity in mineral waters, suggesting that levels normally found were below those expected to produce therapeutic effects. And by the 1930s, considerable attention focused on the harmful effects of radioactivity, especially from the ingestion of radium by the painters of luminous watch dials. In 1932, Senator Royal S. Copeland of New York—a physician himself—spoke in Congress of such concerns and recounted a story about a man who died after drinking manufactured radium water. Publicity surrounding these cases effectively quelled much of the remaining interest in radium treatments at spas in the United States.

Even then, however, radioactive waters had their vocal advocates. Dr. William Fitch, who in 1927 published the *Mineral Waters of the United States and American Spas,* considered the discovery of radium emanations in mineral waters of

---

6. Ibid., 444–45.
7. Harvey W. Wiley and Anne Lewis Pierce, "The Mineral Water Humbug," 108.

"momentous importance" and suggested that because of this and other factors, American spas were every bit as good as those of Europe. Fitch believed that the discovery of radioactivity would occasion a revival of interest on the part of the medical profession, which until then had exhibited an "apathetic attitude" toward mineral waters. Oskar Baudisch, the "father of American hydrotherapy," recalled in 1938 how the discovery of radium emanations in healing springs "kindled a tinder box" in the developing science of balneology. Of radioactivity, he cautioned, "nobody knows as yet the minimum content capable of stimulating action or the upper limit at which harm will be done instead of good."[8] Today, most doctors recommend avoiding radiation altogether, whenever possible. But radium spas are still popular, especially in Europe and Japan, and people continue to go into caves and radon mines to receive the "invisible cure" for arthritis.

8. William Edward Fitch, *Mineral Waters of the United States and American Spas,* 6; Oskar Baudisch, "Magic and Science of Natural Healing Waters," 444.

→ 12 ←

HEALTH IN A BOTTLE

Between the 1880s and World War I, the consumption of bottled waters, including mineral waters, reached gigantic proportions in this country. The U.S. Geological Survey (USGS) began tracking the production and sales of bottled waters in 1883, and in 1905 it began separating "mineral waters" and "table waters" into separate statistical categories. Sales were brisk in 1905, when Myron Fuller of the USGS commented, "on the whole, the outlook is encouraging, use of mineral waters is growing, and the number of springs furnishing waters for the market is increasing."[1] This upward trend continued through the next decade, although table waters soon outpaced mineral waters in sales. But within another decade, the use of bottled mineral waters began to decline, the result of shifting public attitudes about the quality of public water supplies and the real medicinal values of mineral waters.

The bottling of mineral waters—like the practices of bathing and drinking water at resorts—is an industry with its roots in antiquity. The colonists in America eagerly bought stocks of bottled waters shipped from Europe. But before long, homegrown labels came into prominence. In 1809, the U.S. government issued the first patent for the preparation of an artificial mineral water, and by the middle of the nineteenth century, the bottling of water was a big business nationally.[2]

---

1. Myron Fuller, "Mineral Waters: A Review of the Trade in 1905," 1287.
2. Back, Landa, and Meek, "Bottled Waters," 608.

When the USGS began gathering statistics in 1883, about 7.5 million gallons of mineral water were being produced in the country. Albert Peale, the scientist who compiled this data, admitted these figures were low, since many localities did not bother to report their production or sales. For the most part, the larger bottlers, competing in regional or national markets, were the ones that reported. Consequently, although Peale reported production from only six sites in Missouri in 1885—Mooresville, El Dorado Springs, Randolph Springs, Reiger Springs, Sweet Springs, and Montesano—dozens of sites were bottling and selling at some scale, often for local use.[3]

Between 1890 and 1900, mineral water production and sales climbed sharply (see Figure 4). Bottled waters achieved great fame in places like the Chicago World's Fair in 1893, where two waters from Excelsior Springs took home blue ribbons. On the rooftop of the Waldorf-Astoria, customers found a "literal German spa, where all the best mineral waters of the world" could be sampled. The World's Fair Commission of Missouri reported from St. Louis in 1893 that "immense quantities of spa and lithia waters are received in the city and distributed throughout the territory, which looks to the city for well-nigh everything it needs."[4] The *Springfield Republican* in 1897 commented on the brisk sales of mineral waters there, especially from nearby Paris Springs, but also from Graydon, El Dorado Springs, and Excelsior Springs. The newspaper also advised readers that "an express wagon unloading a jug or demijohn or keg in front of the residence of a good deacon need not necessarily excite suspicion, because the chances are the deacon simply is among those who are buying mineral water."

National production of mineral water had risen to almost 42 million gallons by 1904. The USGS had knowledge of twenty-six bottling operations in Missouri, with eighteen actually reporting sales. Consumers could choose from a wide variety of products by this time, including natural springwaters sold still or carbonated, as well as manufactured products such as Vichy and seltzer waters retailed in siphons. The St. Louis business directory listed thirty-three companies manufacturing mineral waters in 1904, compared to fourteen in 1898. Dr. Enno Sander of St. Louis, a household name in the mineral water business, marketed

3. Peale, *Lists and Analyses*, 137–38.
4. Dorsey and Devine, *Fare Thee Well*, 111; Missouri World's Fair Commission, *Missouri at the World's Fair: An Official Catalogue of the Resources of the State, with Special References of the Exhibits at the World's Columbian Exposition*, 124.

Bottling plant at Sweet Springs, Saline County. *State Historical Society of Missouri, Columbia*

"Carbonic, Seltzers, Vichy and Garrod Spa and Tenfold Carlsbad Water," all of which he manufactured.[5]

While people downed prodigious quantities of mineral waters of all sorts, the age-old debate about the potency of artificial versus natural mineral waters continued to rage. Dr. Titus Coan, in an 1888 issue of *Harpers* magazine, defended manufactured waters, in that the "leading ingredients of the most valuable waters are easily and accurately combined in the laboratory," so "we know precisely what they are."[6] Others remained equally convinced that artificial waters could never achieve the healthful stature of natural sources, the most medicinal constituents of which were still unknown.

Missouri, as well as bottled mineral waters, enjoyed a banner year in 1904. The St. Louis Louisiana Purchase Exposition and World's Fair attracted 20 million tourists, who admired the wonderful new inventions of mankind and the latest American technologies. In the Mines and Metallurgy Building, Albert Peale set up an exhibit portraying the great variety of American mineral waters,

5. Missouri World's Fair Commission, *Missouri at the World's Fair,* 124.
6. Titus Coan, "Home Use of Mineral Waters," 721.

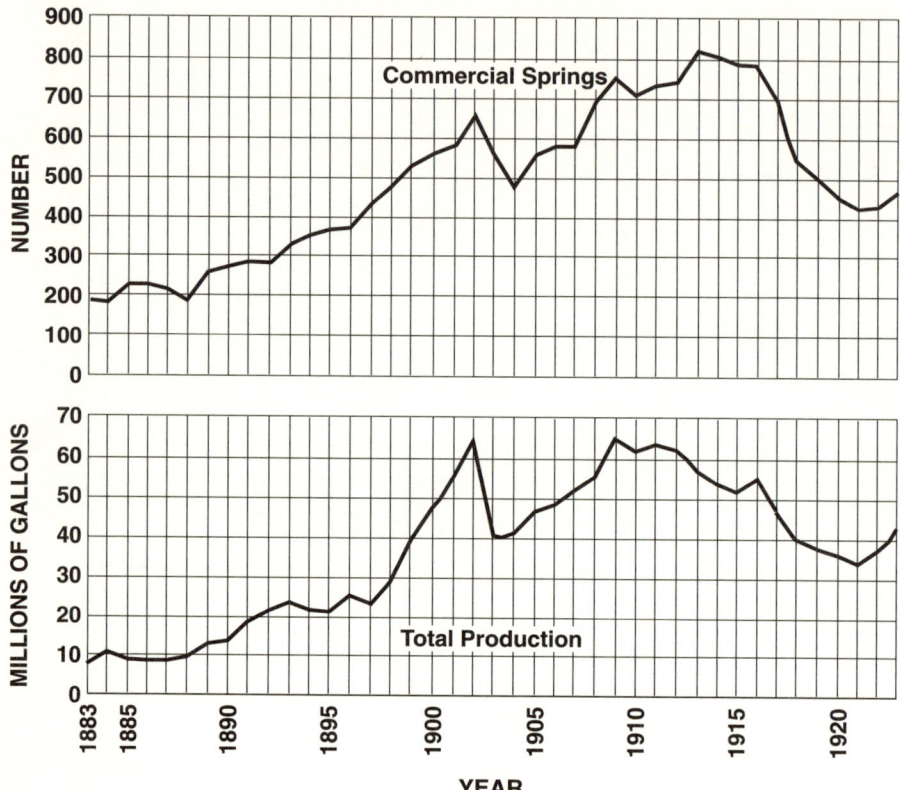

Figure 4. National Production of Mineral Waters. *Top:* number of commercially used springs; *bottom:* total production.

including 121 springs from around the country. He illustrated the chemical composition of each mineral water by using a series of jars, the largest being a gallon of the mineral water itself, with an accompanying series of smaller bottles showing the various solid ingredients in their respective proportions.

Ten of Missouri's mineral waters appeared in Peale's exhibit—B. B. Bitter Mineral Spring in Pike County; Belcher Mineral Water in St. Louis; Wyaconda Diuretic Mineral Water from La Grange in Lewis County; Windsor Water and Old Orchard Mineral Water from St. Louis; Chalybeate Spring from Mooresville in Livingston County; Regents Mineral, Sulpho-Saline, and Crystal Lithia Springs from Excelsior Springs; and Jackson Lithia Spring from Kansas City. The state of Maine's Poland Spring took home the only grand prize awarded a

Palace of Mines and Metallurgy at the St. Louis World's Fair, 1904. *State Historical Society of Missouri, Columbia*

mineral water at the fair.[7] It is interesting to note that several historical accounts in Missouri mention local mineral waters that received prizes at the World's Fair, but specific references to these in the fair's official literature could not be found.

One local mineral water, however, figured prominently in the logistics of the World's Fair. Bockert Mineral Water, produced in nearby De Soto, Missouri, was hauled into the fair by the train-car load. Fair organizers evidently intended for Bockert water to supplement, not replace, the St. Louis public water supply. For its fair, St. Louis had just upgraded its water purification system, installing additional settling basins and a new, patented coagulation process.[8] Visitors

---

7. Mark Bennett and Frank Parker Stonebridge, eds., *History of the Louisiana Purchase Exposition,* 629.
8. William B. Schworm, "History of the Water Supply in the St. Louis Area."

marveled at the clarity of city water powering the "Cascades," a focal point of the fair. But even with this emphasis on a clean, clear public supply, vendors touted mineral waters prominently at the World's Fair just as they did in the nation's marketplaces.

At the opening of the twentieth century, before the widespread adoption of filtration and chlorination for water supplies, the polluted condition of some of the nation's public drinking water sources boosted sales of bottled waters. Samuel Sanford, in a 1907 USGS report on bottled waters, predicted that the slow growth of an "effective public sentiment" against the mounting pollution of sources, along with a "rapid recognition of the necessity of pure water," would cause increasing amounts of springwater to be bought in America's cities and towns, at least while the public supply was "under suspicion."[9]

Not surprisingly, promoters of mineral waters had already capitalized on the public's fear of contagion from public water supplies. In an 1892 edition of the *Kansas City Star*, for example, the Hygeia Mineral Springs Company of Kansas City placed an ad that blared, "statistics show that bad water causes more deaths than war, whiskey or famine." The ad then purported to illustrate two drops of water "magnified 800 times," the drop of Hygeia bottled water being clear but the drop of Kansas City drinking water filled with particles, presumably microbes. The caption reads, "which would you drink?"[10]

By 1909, the traffic in bottled mineral waters had reached its peak nationally, with almost 65 million gallons sold. After this, the market followed a gradual but unmistakable decline, commented upon by a succession of USGS scientists in increasingly diminished sections of the survey's annual reports. In 1913, for example, USGS scientist R. B. Dole offered that "the installation of municipal purification plants in several large cities has been followed by marked decreases in the sales of spring waters in the immediate vicinity."[11]

In Missouri, the sales of bottled waters largely paralleled the national trend, although the production peak in this state occurred in 1916. In that year, thirty-six sites reported a total production of 1.4 million gallons of bottled waters, selling at an average of eight cents per gallon. By 1919, in the midst of World War I, production reached only 15 percent of 1916 levels, although the average price had risen to nineteen cents.[12]

9. Samuel Sanford, "Mineral Waters," 170.
10. *Kansas City Star*, June 21, 1892.
11. R. B. Dole, "Mineral Waters," 397.
12. Arthur Ellis, "Mineral Waters," 115.

Ironically, the decline in bottled water use reflected some of the same types of public concerns that had caused the previous increase in their use. The creeping pollution of public drinking water sources and the perceived purity of springs led many people to choose bottled waters in the first place. Later, an increasing confidence in the safety of public water supplies and suspicions about the quality of spring sources helped to tip the balance against the use of bottled waters.

An initial tug in this unraveling of confidence actually began in the last decade of the nineteenth century. Harvey Wiley, the chief chemist of the U.S. Department of Agriculture, became alarmed at the widespread mishandling and mislabeling of the nation's foods and beverages. He helped to organize the Pure Food and Drug Congress, which convened in March 1898. The work of the congress eventually resulted in the passage of the Pure Food and Drug Act, which became effective on January 1, 1907. This law dealt a serious blow to the advertising tactics of patent medicine and mineral water companies, which had been free for centuries to make extravagant claims. Now, they were to be held truthful in their advertising. Based on this law, the federal government seized many brands of bottled mineral waters in the 1910s and 1920s as mislabeled and adulterated products.[13]

At the same time, several high-profile legal cases exposed the exaggerated claims of mineral waters to public inquiry and ridicule. The American Medical Association, in particular, went to great lengths to expose fraud in the mineral water business. In 1918, the association's journal contained an article flatly asserting that "mineral waters possess no mysterious or occult virtues in the treatment of disease." Furthermore, it continued, "no mineral water will be accepted by the medical profession for alleged medicinal properties supported only by testimonials from bucolic statesmen and romantic old ladies."[14]

Adding to punishment dealt by the medical establishment and courts, the popular press began to jeer the mineral water business in a serious way. Two articles will serve to illustrate that point. One, "Taking the Waters: The Humbug of Hot Springs," by Woods Hutchinson, author of the popular book *Common Sense and Health,* appeared in the February 1913 issue of *Everybody's Magazine.* Hutchinson took aim at mineral water spas, admonishing his readers that the particular mineral water chosen did not really matter, because "to sluice oneself

---

13. De Vierville, "American Healing Waters," 444.
14. Harry B. Weiss and Howard R. Kemble, *They Took to the Waters: The Forgotten Mineral Spring Resorts of New Jersey and Nearby Pennsylvania and Delaware,* 217.

freely with water by the gallon, internally, externally and eternally—any old water will do." Of gulping down mineral waters with their laundry lists of chemical constituents, he observed, tongue-in-cheek, "surely anyone who would swallow such a department store or geological menagerie as that might expect some positive results."[15]

Harvey Wiley and Anne Pierce penned a similar article, titled the "Mineral Water Humbug," for the July 1914 issue of *Good Housekeeping*. This piece focused on bottled waters, particularly their bacteriological quality, but it also blasted the claims of lithia waters. Spring bottlers marketed waters containing lithium in trace amounts from the 1880s, and any spring that was found to contain this element—no matter how minutely—they proudly labeled a "lithia spring." The U.S. Bureau of Chemistry, studying lithia waters at the end of the nineteenth century, found that most contained only a trace, less than one part per million, of lithium, below what physicians considered a therapeutic dose. Based upon these findings, Dr. Enno Sander, the St. Louis–based mineral water producer, extolled the virtues of manufactured lithia waters, with their greater and more controlled lithium contents.[16]

In their article, Wiley and Pierce targeted Buffalo Lithia Water, a mineral water widely promoted in Missouri and the subject of legal action under Pure Food and Drug labeling laws. The authors sneered that "the recommendations on the label that the water be used for infant feeding, nervous disorders and all kinds of fevers, etc., etc., are, of course, only a pure flight of fancy of the patent medicine brand." Furthermore, "crude and unscientific experiments have been blindly accepted by the profession upon the statements of exploiters of these waters." The government successfully prosecuted the case against Buffalo Lithia water. In a court opinion issued in 1915, the judge mentioned that "for a person to receive a therapeutic dose of lithium by drinking Buffalo Lithia Water, he would have to drink from 150,000 to 225,000 gallons of water per day." Needless to say, popular enthusiasm for lithium waters waned after this highly publicized case.[17]

The "Mineral Water Humbugs" also reviewed sanitary analyses performed on leading brands. One of the mineral waters caught in their net, a springwater from Bowling Green in Pike County, Missouri, contained fifty-five hundred

---

15. Woods Hutchinson, "Taking the Waters: The Humbug of Hot Springs," 162.
16. Robert G. Flippen, *"Drink and Be Healed": A History of Farmville Lithia Water*, 6.
17. Wiley and Pierce, "Mineral Water Humbug," 108, 107.

"colon bacilli" per cubic centimeter, well above public health standards. Another polluted product the authors mentioned was Veronica Medicinal Spring Water, bottled in St. Louis, which originated at a spring near Santa Barbara, California. Ironically, this same spring had been praised in a 1902 St. Louis Industrial and Professional directory because it contained "most, if not all, of the ingredients for which the waters of Carlsbad and other European places are so celebrated."[18]

In 1920, W. D. Collins of the USGS rebuffed the barrage of criticism then being leveled against medicinal waters. Under the "present standards of the ethics of advertising," he said, "it might be charged that practically the whole business was built on false or mistaken representations." The charge, he asserted, was not true. "Though not successful in all claims," he continued, mineral waters were nevertheless "decidedly beneficial in the treatment of disease."[19] The USGS, it seems, may have been one of the last scientific bastions of belief in the healing nature of natural mineral waters.

Reflecting the downward trend in bottled water sales, USGS reports after 1920 no longer contained state-by-state statistics on production, and after 1924, the survey's voluminous *Mineral Resource Reports* no longer included separate sections on mineral waters. A 1923 USGS report contained a review of the mineral water trade from 1883 to date. The author noted that in those forty years, the use of medicinal waters had undergone radical change. At the beginning of the period, almost all of the bottled waters were sold as medicinal agents. In 1905, the first year that the USGS made a distinction between medicinal and table waters, sales and volumes were about equal. But after the procurement of safe public drinking water supplies in most cities, sales of medicinal waters slumped, so that in 1923 these waters accounted for only 13 percent of the total value of bottled waters.[20]

Of course, the production of mineral waters continued after 1923. In that year, according to the Missouri Geological Survey, twenty-seven springs in the state produced 147,000 gallons of mineral water valued at $38,000. By the time of the 1931 biennial report of the state geologist, the value of mineral waters produced in the state had slipped to just $12,000, with twenty-two locations reporting sales. One third of these sites were in Excelsior Springs, the leading

---

18. E. D. Kargau, *Mercantile and Professional St. Louis*, 448.
19. W. D. Collins, "Mineral Waters," 165.
20. U.S. Geological Survey, *Mineral Resources of the United States, 1923*, 114.

area of mineral water production in the state. Two sites in Kansas City still produced mineral waters, two in St. Louis, and two in Bowling Green, as well as Radium Springs in Barry County; El Dorado Springs, Chouteau Springs, Sweet Springs, Bokert Springs in Jefferson County; and Haymaker Well in Mercer County.[21]

With production dwindling, by 1939 the state geologist's report stated that "no statistics are available to indicate the production and value of mineral waters in Missouri," adding only that "much water is taken from springs and flowing wells without compensation to owners, or is sold locally."[22] The report did note an increasing use of mineralized water for swimming pools in St. Louis, where sulfo-saline well waters were pumped to bathing resorts. By this time, the gradual shift in use from "medicinal waters" to "health resorts" was nearly complete.

---

21. Missouri Geological Survey, *Biennial Reports of the State Geologist, 1921,* 74.
22. Missouri Geological Survey, *Biennial Reports of the State Geologist, 1939,* 46.

→ 13 ←

FADING TOWARD OBSCURITY

By the time bottled waters dipped below the attention of the state geologist, only one mineral water resort of note remained in Missouri. Excelsior Springs weathered the ups and downs of public perceptions and medical beliefs, emerging into the second quarter of the twentieth century as a resort town aspiring to be America's "Haven of Health." Its fabulous Hall of Waters, built in the middle 1930s, symbolized a time when the nation's attention had once again turned toward the therapeutic possibilities of natural mineral waters.

It is difficult to discern exactly why Excelsior Springs survived, and even thrived, when almost all of the other hopeful mineral water resorts had perished. Its proximity to the major metropolitan area of Kansas City and good rail and highway connections certainly helped. Excelsior also had many mineral springs and wells concentrated within a small, scenic area, which helped to induce tourism, stimulate competition, and spawn a diversity of services. The town of Excelsior Springs stepped in to promote, later even to administer, its mineral water resources, a tactic that the town of El Dorado Springs also used successfully. Excelsior Springs boasted large and impressive spa hotels and professionally staffed sanitaria.

Speculation about the source of Excelsior's success naturally leads one to consider what the other mineral spring resorts and resort towns might have done wrong, or at least to ask why the stars failed to line up properly for them. The differences between success and failure are more complicated than it might at first appear. As in most evolutionary processes, many interrelated factors determine

Hall of Waters at Excelsior Springs, 2000. *Photo by author*

the ultimate outcome of taking one path versus another, thwarting overly simplistic explanations of cause and effect.

It has been pointed out that the populace in colonial America largely acknowledged the healing virtues of mineral waters, a belief they had brought over from Europe. Meanwhile, on both continents, a significant number of people always denied any legitimate basis for these beliefs. Even notable persons who used mineral springs and wanted to believe in their healing powers harbored doubts. George Washington, for example, soaking in the warm waters at Berkeley Warm Springs with two hundred other souls, "full of all manner of diseases and complaints," could not help but notice the obvious—that some benefited while others found no relief. Washington must have been bitterly disappointed when he brought Patsy Custis to the same spring seeking relief for her epilepsy, to no avail.[1]

In spite of numerous, highly publicized accounts of success, disappointments mounted in succeeding generations, as invalids made their way toward the cures

---

1. Bridenbaugh, "Baths and Watering Places," 161.

promised by the persistent and tireless promoters. William Clark, governor of the Missouri territory, took his wife, Julia, from St. Louis to the Sweet and White Sulphur Springs in Virginia for her health, but she did not get better. In the early 1880s, a family from Spalding Springs, Missouri, traveled four hundred miles by wagon to Eureka Springs, Arkansas, seeking treatment for their child's eye disease. The springs at Eureka, especially Dr. Jackson's Eye Water, were famous for treating sore eyes. After using the water for several months, the girl's eyes did not improve and, if anything, worsened.[2] It is ironic and perhaps illustrative of the power of medical witness that while the family lived near Spalding Springs, itself considered medicinal, they traveled to Eureka Springs because physicians specifically recommended the water there for eye problems.

Such stories of failure are rarely recorded in historical accounts. What has been handed down is primarily the promotional literature from the resorts themselves, with their enthusiastic testimonials. Occasionally, one uncovers a minor bit of heresy, such as a surviving postcard mailed from Burlington Junction Mineral Springs in northern Missouri, upon which a disappointed visitor scribbled, "I think it's a swindle." Many people no doubt came away with such an opinion after visiting a particular spring, prescribed for a specific ailment, and finding no relief. For the disgruntled individuals at the time and in person, spa managers no doubt had typical explanations for a lack of success—perhaps the patron didn't use the water long enough, or the problem was not properly diagnosed to begin with. Such negative experiences must have generated a sizable if, from our present standpoint, mostly silent, body of disappointed health seekers. Common knowledge about the kinds of diseases that mineral water couldn't help must have eventually permeated the culture.

True invalids, however, were probably always a minority of spa goers over the ages. Many, if not most visitors considered accommodations, convenience, and clienteles as important as the mineral waters themselves. At the early resorts, at least, visitors frequently mentioned "scant" or "primitive" accommodations. The geologist and geographer George Featherstonhaugh, upon visiting Hot Springs, Arkansas, painted a very unbecoming picture of that resort. Staying in a "wretched-looking log cabin," where on a shelf stood a pail of mineral water "with a gourd to drink it from," he wondered, "how invalids contrive to be comfortable, who come to this ragged place, I cannot imagine." Furthering the

---

2. Roland, Roland, Hurley, and Hagood, *Spalding Springs*, 81.

misery, he was kept awake by hogs rustling and grunting under the widely spaced board floor during a rainstorm.³

This and other travel adventures, with their unflattering descriptions of backwoods resorts, may have discouraged some potential visitors. There is little specific information about the types and quality of facilities at Missouri's early resorts, however, other than that found in local histories or promotional literature, which typically painted rosy pictures of "perfect accommodations" or "the best the county has to offer." In any case, Missouri's early resorts were few and far between, so competition between them for customers may not have been a significant factor.

That situation changed, however, in the 1870s and 1880s, when new resorts began to appear in many locations across the state. These resorts invariably competed for clientele, transportation access, and advertising space, spurring even more commercialism. Missouri's resorts had to compete with the more famous out-of-state locations such as Hot Springs and Eureka Springs in Arkansas as well as a host of lesser-known regional resorts. Some of the smaller, often struggling resorts undoubtedly failed to upgrade their accommodations in a timely enough manner to suit fickle public tastes, and they went under.

The question of the type of clientele a resort wanted to attract, though rarely mentioned in connection with Missouri's resorts, certainly became an issue at spas in other areas. Did owners intend to cater primarily to invalids or to pleasure-seekers? Each group had specific needs and expectations. Several authors have pointed out the potential discomfort caused by this clash of intentions. Fashionable resorts, for obvious reasons, did not want to attract too many invalids. Likewise, invalids eventually deserted resorts that became too fashionable. Yet, at many larger resorts, there remained a dualistic milieu, a "back-street army of the genuinely desperate" lurking in the "shadows behind the gay high society."⁴ Some visitors marveled at the diversity of the mix. George Featherstonhaugh, soaking at Warm Springs, Virginia, in the 1840s, registered his disgust upon seeing "old sick men, young boys, husbands of charming wives, fathers of beautiful daughters, all in the same pickle together, mingling with the most extraordinary looking, tobacco-chewing, expectorating and villainous looking non-descripts."⁵

3. George W. Featherstonhaugh, *Excursion through the Slave States, from Washington on the Potomac to the Frontier of Mexico...*, 108.
4. Searle, *Spas and Watering Places*, 137.
5. Featherstonhaugh, *Excursion*, 19.

There is little evidence that these social or medical conflicts ever became serious issues at Missouri's resorts, even though their advertisements frequently beckoned to both invalids and pleasure-seekers. Presumably, most of the "invalid" patrons during Missouri's 1880 to 1920 resort boom suffered from chronic and noncontagious maladies such as rheumatism and dyspepsia (indigestion), conditions that would not unduly alarm other guests. However, there are a few glimpses from the promotional literature of the state's resorts into the inherent potential for tension. A Sweet Springs promotional booklet from 1885, for example, advised invalids that they would "find other seasons than mid-summer more desirable," else they would "encounter a crowd, have their rest disturbed and otherwise experience inconveniences." In spite of concerted efforts to accommodate everyone, some resorts undoubtedly lost customers because of their reputations for catering to clients of a certain medical or social status.

Although promotions of the period almost always contained information on the mineral water analysis and diseases cured, there is ample evidence that other amenities came to be more important to many resorts, as witnessed by statements about fun and exciting diversions that increasingly dominated their literature. Such activities may have proven more profitable to resort owners than the standard drinking and bathing cures. Patrons increasingly came to expect these amenities and owners felt obliged to provide. Invalids, however, may have viewed these diversions as unnecessary and expensive extras, forcing them to look elsewhere for their cures.

The growing emphasis on recreation, pleasure, and gaming may have led, indirectly, to the undoing of some mineral water resorts. Activities such as bowling, dancing, horse racing, gambling, and swimming could be had in many places, not just at mineral water resorts. When the mineral waters no longer provided the primary anchor, the fun could be moved anywhere. At least one historian speculated that the rise of seaside attractions such as Atlantic City and Long Branch, competing successfully for resort customers by the 1870s, led to the demise of the eastern seaboard's mineral water resorts.[6] In the 1880s and 1890s, pleasure resorts of all types, especially in the western United States, captured the public's attention. *Harpers* and other magazines were filled with articles about vacation getaways, urging countrymen to forgo a trip to Europe, climb aboard the trains, and "see America first."

6. Dorsey and Devine, *Fare Thee Well,* 284–97.

Some historians believe the proliferation of automobiles played a significant role in the folding of Missouri's mineral water resorts. The period of rising popularity of the automobile does roughly coincide with the decline of some of Missouri's longer-lived mineral water resorts. There were enough autos wheeling around the state by 1903 that legislators felt compelled to pass safety regulations; in 1910, the fact that 95 percent of the state's highways were unpaved did not seem to dampen the passion to drive.[7] The average family could now reach new destinations, places not even accessible by rail. Vacation getaways close to home were no longer necessary, and remarkable, unique destinations—including state and national parks, new reservoirs, and recreation areas—beckoned to family travelers.

Many of Missouri's resorts faced problems with ease of access. Then, as now, resort owners competed for convenience. Traveling long distances over rough roads became tests of endurance, rather than the "pleasant drives" promoters liked to advertise. Many descriptions of Missouri's resorts noted poor access as a deterrent to success. J. D. Robertson of the Missouri Geological Survey, for example, commented of Jerico Springs, "scant accommodations and difficulty in reaching the place retard its development." One could reach Siloam Springs, in Howell County, only "over a very rough road, especially after a season of rainy weather."[8]

In the years after the Civil War, resorts hoped to improve their financial prospects by gaining rail access. This seems to have been a make-or-break situation for many health resorts. The relatively low railroad fares, especially the popular excursion rates, helped to guarantee crowds and profitability. Unfortunately for many resorts, their bids for rail access, often in conjunction with nearby towns, ultimately failed. Missing out on the railroad was cited as a prominent factor in the decline of Plattsburg Mineral Spring in Clinton County, which eyed with envy the success of nearby Excelsior Springs when it completed a rail connection with Kansas City. Other resorts that faded when hoped-for rail connections failed to materialize include Siloam Springs in Gentry County, Aurora Springs in Miller County, and Indian Springs in McDonald County.

The rise in modern medicine is often cited as the single biggest factor in the decline of the mineral water resort business. The heightened profile of the profession actually had its roots in public health and sanitation initiatives of the

---

7. March, *History of Missouri*, 1327.
8. Schweitzer, *Report*, 106, 153.

1850s through 1870s, which laid the groundwork for the monumental advances in medicine and public works technologies that would soon follow. Even before the Civil War, health boards and agencies used quarantines and sanitary conventions fairly effectively to address epidemic diseases. New York City's first Board of Health, commissioned in 1866, enjoyed nearly immediate success in combating cholera due to its rigorous application of sanitation measures.

Even before they had direct, firsthand knowledge of disease germs, sanitarians and other health workers had convinced the public that sewage, filth, improper drainage, and foul air somehow propagated disease. Moreover, many in the scientific community already accepted the notion that unseen germs could cause disease and the idea became well infused into the public consciousness by the early 1870s. The first issue of *Popular Science,* in 1872, carried an article on sanitation, disinfection, and the germ theory of disease.[9]

Astute mineral water resorts quickly capitalized on this new public interest in sanitation and personal hygiene. Resort advertisements changed in subtle ways after the 1870s, now emphasizing "healthful settings," "perfect drainage," "complete systems of sewerage," and "well-ventilated rooms" more frequently and more prominently. Resort hotels, especially in the 1890s, proudly announced their modern "water closets" and "room ventilators." But while some resorts responded positively to the new scientific concepts, the seeds of their destruction may have been sown in this same flowering of knowledge about diseases and health.

The 1880s ushered in a golden age in medical science, with a great proliferation of discoveries in the microbiological world. In rapid succession, scientists discovered the organisms causing tuberculosis, Asiatic cholera, diphtheria, and malaria. When researchers applied the new laboratory procedures to springs and other source waters, they found tiny germs lurking there as well. Some Missouri resorts tried to incorporate this newfound knowledge, reporting satisfactory sanitary analyses of their mineral waters. By and large, however, the microbiological quality of Missouri's mineral springs never became much of an issue. Oddly, Schweitzer did not even broach the subject in his 1892 report on Missouri's mineral waters.

This seems odd because concerns about the sanitary quality of mineral waters actually have a long history. Dr. Benjamin Rush, addressing the American

---

9. Nancy Tomes, "The Private Side of Public Health: Sanitary Science, Domestic Hygiene, and the Germ Theory, 1870–1900," 521.

Philosophical Society in 1773, acknowledged a problem with a certain mineral water well in Philadelphia, which "lost its virtue" after being found to be contaminated by the "necessary"—the privy.[10] Over a hundred years later, a similar situation would arise in a small town in Vernon County, Missouri. Upon grading the streets, workers uncovered a "mineral spring." Several citizens drank the water and pronounced it to be, indeed, medicinal. But on opening up the spring to obtain more flow, the hopeful workers found it to actually be a sewer leak.[11] Both of these cases, however, reflect more directly on sanitary quality in general than on concern about specific disease organisms.

The isolation and identification of disease-causing germs in the 1880s set into motion an inevitable and inexorable push to define and conquer all of man's diseases. Medical science, for a change, found itself in a position to promise great advances in the prevention and treatment of disease in the not-too-distant future. By the 1890s, doctors graduating from the new Johns Hopkins and similar medical schools, who embraced new concepts of disease and new ideas for treatment, had begun to infiltrate medical schools and hospitals across the country. Mineral waters no longer figured in their arsenals of standard medical procedures.

Scientific understandings of disease transmission and prevention provided the underpinnings for new drinking water filtration and disinfection technologies. These treatment techniques made public water supplies markedly more safe by the first decades of the twentieth century. Such advances, in fact, are often credited with the significant decline in infectious diseases noted after the turn of the century. By the 1920s, upper- and middle-income Americans, at least, no longer lived in fear of many infectious diseases. However, the mortality rate in the United States actually fell by 10 percent between 1890 and 1900, *before* these technological advances had become widely applied. These gains may be attributable to the public's greater awareness of germs in general, and to the vigorous applications of sanitation and domestic hygiene principles in the last decade of the nineteenth century.[12]

Major breakthroughs in health and medicine may indeed have turned the tide of public opinion against the use of mineral waters. However, the mounting bad press was working hand in hand with modern medicine to loosen the

---

10. Cecil K. Drinker, *Not So Long Ago: A Chronicle of Medicine and Doctors in Colonial Philadelphia*, 25.

11. Article in *Nevada Daily Mail*, June 7, 1924, reprinted in *Bushwacker Musings* (newsletter of the Vernon County Historical Society) 25, no. 3 (1993): 14.

12. Nancy Tomes, *The Gospel of Germs: Men, Women, and the Microbe in American Life*, 16.

mineral water grip. Mineral waters always had their detractors, but attacks toward the end of the nineteenth century became more pointed, scientifically oriented, and highly publicized. For example, a New Jersey newspaper in 1878 ran a spoof on "Owatahox Spring" in New York, poking fun at those who used medicinal springs and characterizing them as exceedingly gullible.[13] Articles in major magazines from 1910 through the 1920s followed up on this theme, supporting their arguments with healthy doses of pseudoscientific "facts." Some authors delighted in exposing what they considered to be frauds and quacks. Although such skepticism about water cures had been around from early times, this effort to influence public opinion through the popular press built great momentum in the first decades of the twentieth century. The power of the press may have been an even greater force than the rise in modern medicine in the general abandonment of mineral water treatments.

Some resorts recognized that to survive, they must go with the flow—apply the newly embraced findings in health and medicine. A trend in this direction involved the establishment of sanitariums, which were basically more medically oriented health resorts. Seven sanitariums incorporated in Missouri in 1897 alone.[14] These doctor-supervised facilities frequently used mineral waters as one part of their total treatment regimes. Mineral water sanitariums, embracing new treatment concepts, were established at Schumer Springs, Siloam Springs in Gentry County, Burlington Junction, Louisiana, Mooresville, Lebanon, Bethany, and Hannibal. Some of these facilities operated profitably in the first quarter of the twentieth century and a few sanitarium doctors achieved considerable reputations. The Heilbron Sanitarium in Bethany, for example, utilized the services of Dr. Jerome Kintner, a noted hydrotherapist who studied the latest treatment methods in Germany.

One of the last mineral water sanitariums in the state, apart from Excelsior Springs, opened during the Depression. Beginning in the early 1930s, Dr. George Bilyea operated the Mineral Springs Sanitarium in Louisiana, Missouri, using a large artesian mineral well there called the "Therapeudor." This facility had an icy-blue mineral water swimming pool in the rear and a flowing mineral water fountain in the entrance sidewalk. Bilyea visited patients in the upstairs rooms. But even this facility eventually went out of business, and the building was converted into the county's first hospital.

13. Weiss and Kemble, *They Took to the Waters*, 215.
14. Secretary of State, *Official Manual of the State of Missouri* (1899 edition), 351–69.

Even with more scientific footings, easy access, plenty of amusements and diversions, and robust promotion, almost every one of Missouri's once-popular resorts eventually folded—some with a whimper, others with a bang. Nature conspired against some, catastrophically ending their dreams of success with fires and floods. Other resorts slipped quietly into obscurity as parodies of their former selves, becoming the sites of trailer parks, apartments, or poor farms. However, even after infrastructure had washed away, burned, crumbled, or decayed, many mineral water sites continued to serve the public for many years as picnic grounds and meeting places. Such is the case at White Sulphur Spring in Benton County, Peerless Springs in Clinton County, Windsor Medical Spring in Henry County, and Forest Springs in Knox County.

At many sites, popular resorts or mineral water towns seem to have simply vanished off the face of the earth, leaving very few traces of their existence. Here, a person might find a few bricks or stone blocks, humps of earth, old flower beds, or trees that once lined an entrance road. A long list of such places could be made, including Zodiac Springs in Vernon County, Blankenship Springs in Texas County, Reno Springs in Christian County, Lotus Springs in Dade County, Bethesda in Greene County, Mineral City in Ray County, Harris Springs in Monroe County, Elk Lick Springs in Saline County, El Dorado Springs in Oregon County, Schumer Springs in Perry County, and Crystal Springs in Pettis County.

Such a profound silence at sites all across the state suggests a common, underlying factor in the demise of mineral water leisure resorts. Each of the contributing elements mentioned above—stiff competition, poor access, fires and floods, seedy reputations, ineffective advertising and promotion, and the inability to keep up with public demands for more and better leisure activities—may have become single, identifiable factors in the decline of a particular resort. But the pall of shifting public perceptions became a suffocating cloud hanging over all, even after they had successfully shifted the emphasis from being healing refuges to becoming recreational destinations. To put it simply, mineral water resorts eventually succumbed to the changing times.

Like other resorts and resort towns, Excelsior Springs experienced serious downturns in its history, but unlike them it was able to rebuild and grow from the experience. By the 1920s, the town had a thriving mineral water bottling industry and a number of well-staffed sanitariums. Luckily for Excelsior, national interest in the science of spa therapy reawakened in the 1930s, spearheaded by the Simon Baruch Research Institute that opened at Saratoga Springs in 1935.

Artesian Park trolley, Clinton, ca. 1906. *Henry County Historical Society, Clinton; photo by Ellsworth Marks*

In 1938, Oskar Baudisch of the institute wrote, "mineral springs are a natural asset, and any nation which fails to make wise use of these gifts of nature causes loss and damage to the economic strength of its people."[15]

Medical hydrology had by then evolved into separate fields of research. Balneology, or bathing therapy, became widely integrated into refined therapeutic procedures at major spas and hospitals. Hydrotherapists improved whirlpool baths and experimented with electrical, mechanical, and physical therapies. Radiologists worked to understand the effects of exposure to radioactive waters. Radio talk shows on mineral waters, such as one produced at Hot Springs, Arkansas, sponsored by the Garland County Medical Society, elaborated on proper bathing procedures. There were widely publicized lectures, spa surveys, new resort publications, and even commissions on mineral waters.

Excelsior Springs followed these national trends with interest. By the 1930s, nearly two dozen mineral water clinics operated in town at any given time. Forty-six wells and springs did business within a one-mile radius of the founding

15. Baudisch, "Magic and Science," 448.

location along the Fishing River. Meanwhile, the place also suffered from an overly commercialized, "medicine-show" atmosphere. Vicki Bates, manager of the water bar at the Hall of Waters, described the scene as a sea of "snake-oil salesmen" who would latch onto potential customers as they arrived at the train station or hotel. Complaints about overly aggressive tactics must have been common, for in 1935 city leaders decided something had to be done to renew the city's image.

The changes they wrought were sweeping. They created a municipal "mineral water system," making it illegal for anyone but the city of Excelsior Springs to sell mineral waters. City leaders also approached the federal Works Progress Administration for help in financing a project that would integrate mineral water therapeutics and civic improvements. The WPA loaned the city nearly nine hundred thousand dollars, funding the construction of the elaborate and ornate Hall of Waters. The flows of four separate springs were captured and piped to the building. The impressive structure featured three swimming pools, two bathhouses, a bottling plant, and the "world's longest water bar," where patrons could sip local and exotic varieties of mineral waters. The art deco building, with its gigantic bronze doors and sleek rounded facade of enormous windows set in gleaming stone, housed a one-of-a-kind, state-of-the-art health facility when it went into service in 1937.

But even with this boost for Excelsior's reputation as a modern, scientific, and publicly owned and operated mineral water spa, there would be no easy road to success. In 1942, the Snapp Hotel in Excelsior applied for an American Medical Association certificate as a health resort, but it could not meet the new "hospital-like" rules.[16] After World War II, health insurance no longer covered stays at mineral water resorts. The government also imposed limitations on tax deductions for resort bills. For many Americans, it no longer made sense to pay for a lengthy stay at a health resort when alternative, insurance-approved treatments were available. Besides, many doctors advised their patients that essentially the same therapeutic effects could be obtained by pouring Epsom salts into one's bathtub.

Vicki Bates recalled another downturn, in the early 1960s, when the *Saturday Evening Post* published an article called "Hucksters of Pain," which made a case for prohibiting doctors from advertising. To produce an undercover story, the author posed as a patient at Excelsior Springs. His story created an impression of

---

16. De Vierville, "American Healing Waters," 664.

Snapp's Hotel, Excelsior Springs. *State Historical Society of Missouri, Columbia*

a fraudulent pseudomedical enterprise. Business at the city mineral water clinics tapered off. By the early 1970s, the last of the city's clinics were closed and many of the downtown businesses had been abandoned. Only recently, with a renewed focus on tourism, relaxation, and the city's image as a "retreat community" for Kansas Citians, has Excelsior Springs begun to forge a strong comeback.

In spite of efforts to upgrade and modernize Missouri's mineral water health resorts and sanitariums in the twentieth century, most never reattained their former days of glory. The medical community had lost interest. Henry Sigerist, in a 1942 piece titled "American Spas in Historical Perspective," lamented the fact that most physicians considered spa treatment a swindle, or, at best, a "dignified medical superstition."[17]

Public enthusiasm for mineral waters also waned. Broad societal shifts in lifestyle were reflected in dwindling numbers of patrons. For people looking specifically for medical benefits, the ordered and ritualistic culture embodied in spa therapy gave way to a desire for speed and high technology. Today, relaxation and pleasure seem to offer mineral water resorts their last vestiges of hope.

It is somewhat ironic that an opposing trend has emerged in much of the

---

17. Henry Sigerist, "American Spas in Historical Perspective," 140.

world, where the science of hydrotherapy has received massive influxes of research dollars. In many foreign countries, resorts have been highly modernized, and the use of mineral waters supported and even promoted by their governments, including coverage by nationalized health insurance. While American doctors remain skeptical, European and Japanese doctors refer patients to spas without hesitation.

For the most part, Missouri's spas are silent. Their various tales, however, are not unconnected pieces of history, but rather fluid steps in a progressive heritage. These popular places can be considered the founding impulse for the tourist camps, motels, public swimming pools, hot tubs, and vacation resorts of today. And although bottled water sales slumped after the 1920s, there has been a dramatic rise in recent years, with bottled mineral waters constituting a strengthening segment of the industry. Wellness, in addition to convenience, seems to come in a bottle once again. And on serious reflection, America's current fascination with health and fitness—with jogging, vitamins, diets, and dietary supplements—is really little different in principle from our ancestors' tuning in to the promotions of their day and attempting to achieve similar results by "taking the waters."

SITE SURVEYS AND DESCRIPTIONS

The following are county-by-county descriptions of some of the more prominent mineral water locations in the state. These descriptions illustrate that such places are scattered across the entire state. There is, however, a clustering of sites and resorts in a broad arc from the western tier of counties through Saline and Howard counties into Pike and Ralls counties, north of St. Louis. This pattern reflects the underlying geology of the state, as described in Chapter 1.

During my research for this project, I attempted to visit the mineral water locations, especially those that were once noted as resorts, to see what evidence, if any, remained to demarcate the site. I interviewed historians, postal clerks, librarians, and local residents in my search for oral and written information and for photographs. Local written histories, especially county histories, often contained the most information, but separate accounts did not always agree and could not be trusted in every detail. This information was added to that found in scientific treatments, especially the work of Paul Schweitzer and his colleagues recorded in their *Report on the Mineral Waters* published in 1892.

The results of my survey were not always gratifying. There is virtually nothing left at many of the sites to indicate their mineral water history. Information and (especially) photographs are hard to find on resorts that in most cases have been gone for over a century. Many pieces of the puzzle, such as detailed descriptions of hotels and bathhouses, personal accounts of resort users, or even the period of time a resort operated, were often difficult or impossible to locate. There is a much greater likelihood of finding flowery descriptions of a resort when it was new than information about when it finally closed, reflecting the fact that many resorts suffered a gradual and unnewsworthy decline in use and prestige.

Another aspect of the survey was to see, smell, and taste the once-noted mineral springs, when possible. This can be done at surprisingly few of the sites. The fact that many of these once-celebrated springs no longer flow is somewhat of an enigma, given the magnitude of flows mentioned in historical accounts. For example, Paul Schweitzer stated that Sweet Springs in Saline County flowed at a rate of over one thousand gallons per hour, enough to sustain a small bottling plant. As late as 1941, the WPA guide to Missouri reported flows of over four hundred gallons per hour. At the time of my visit, however, no flow was observed. I could also find no flowing springs at Harris Springs, Lotus Springs, Glasgow Mineral Spring, Aurora Springs, B.B. Spring, Bowsher Mineral Spring, Fayette Salt Spring, Randolph Springs, or either of the state's Radium springs. The Great Salt Spring in Saline County, once said to be the county's largest, cannot even be located with certainty today.

At locations such as McAllister Springs, Zodiac, Siloam Springs in Howell County, Spalding Springs, Pertle Springs, and Mineola, springs still flow, though very feebly. Schweitzer had indeed reported that flows were small at many of the mineral springs serving resorts. At some sites, such as Chouteau Springs, Jerico Springs, Climax Springs, El Dorado Springs, Reno, and Elk Lick Springs, flows seem to have remained fairly constant. There are several possible reasons for these observed inconsistencies.

For one thing, it is difficult to accurately measure flows at many locations. Schweitzer did not describe the methods his survey workers had used to determine flows, but we can surmise that where possible, they timed the filling of a container of known capacity. Seasons of the year and recent rainfall amounts obviously contribute to variations in flow. But in many cases, such as at Sweet Springs, Great Salt Spring, Glasgow Mineral Spring, Harris Springs, and Montesano Springs, where today there is virtually no flow, we must accept the fact that outputs have diminished. One possible explanation is that increased groundwater pumping, especially around cities like Kansas City and St. Louis, has depleted the springs' sources of supply. For some springs, particularly those with deeply seated sources of mineralized waters, this is certainly a plausible explanation. However, many mineral springs are thought to receive their recharge from relatively shallow depths and should thus be less influenced by pumping from much deeper wells. In urban areas, increasing amounts of impervious surfaces such as rooftops and roads may have reduced the amount of water infiltrating into the ground to provide spring recharge. This could be an explanation for the fact that the famous Manchester Spring in St. Louis no longer flows.

Another possibility offered by Jim Vandike of the Missouri Department of Natural Resources Geological Survey and Resource Assessment Division (the descendent of the Missouri Geological Survey) is that the openings of some mineral springs have become plugged. This, too, is a plausible explanation, given that site histories frequently mention that spring mouths were "opened up" or "improved" or "excavated" in an attempt to maintain or increase flows. With abandonment and disuse, the springs may have eventually reverted to their more natural antecedent condition, depositing minerals at the orifice that would eventually reduce flow to a seep or trickle. Land disturbance activities such as grading or backfilling could have eventually obliterated any sign of a spring orifice.

At Sweet Springs, Schweitzer observed that the nearby Blackwater River deposited sediment over the orifice of the spring during flooding events. In fact, the low bluff along the river, illustrated in Schweitzer's book, is no longer visible. Stream overflow sediments may have covered many low-lying mineral springs over the years, a process sometimes accelerated by man's erosion-inducing activities in the watershed. Scientists in Schweitzer's time, for example, observed that in-washing sediments from nearby farmlands were reducing the size of the Great Salt Spring.

Many mineral spring sites have disappeared due to the heavy-handed actions of man. Several, like Plattsburg Mineral Spring, White Sulphur Springs, and Monegaw Springs, are under the waters of reservoirs all or most of the time. Others, such as Jackson Lithia Spring in Kansas City and Sulphur Springs and Windsor Spring in St. Louis, were long ago gobbled up and obliterated by development.

In fact, there are very few places in the state where historic mineral springs can be observed in a natural or nearly natural state. There are a few examples in Saline County, at Elk Lick and Blue Lick springs. Blue Lick, in particular, is a unique mineral spring complex that has been protected in a state Conservation Area. It also provides a good example of a phenomenon frequently mentioned by early settlers and resort promoters that greatly intrigued them: Separate springs, often very close together, sometimes have marked differences in character. One can actually *see* the differences between the springs at Blue Lick, attesting to the wide variety of properties among natural mineral waters.

TO LEARN MORE

For those who are interested enough to delve further, there are artifacts and information illustrative of the state's mineral water history at several sites, including Excelsior Springs, El Dorado Springs, and Sweet Springs; and at local museums in Clinton, Warrensburg, Kimmswick, and Huntsville. Historical societies in several counties can produce information about local mineral springs that were popular resorts or camping and picnicking sites. One can view mineral water springs in natural or nearly natural states at places like Spalding, Boone's Lick, Chouteau, Blue Lick, and Elk Lick. Most of the sites, however, are on private property.

The interpretive facilities at Boone's Lick review important aspects of early salt making and the ecological significance of salt springs. At Blue Lick Conservation Area, along the valley of Finney Creek, one of the state's best remaining examples of mineral spring complexes, or clusters of springs, can be visited. At Excelsior Springs, one can still take a hot, relaxing mineral water bath, and El Dorado Springs glories in the loving care one city has bestowed upon its main mineral water attraction. At places like Chouteau, Randolph, Spalding, and McAllister springs, there are significant remains of that bygone era when mineral water resorts were prominent features of the local landscape. These sites represent unique and varied aspects of Missouri's mineral water past that deserve an attempt at preservation and interpretation.

Fountain Bathhouse at El Dorado Springs, Cedar County. *State Historical Society of Missouri, Columbia*

ADAIR COUNTY

New Baden (Baden Springs)

George Shaw and his wife, Ann, founded the resort of New Baden Springs in 1881 and platted a town the same year, selling lots for fifty dollars each. The Shaws' choice of names probably reflects a desired bond with the celebrated European spa, Baden, in Germany. Soon, the town had a three-story hotel along with a church, saloons, stores, blacksmith shop, and post office. Buggies and hacks frequently plied the fourteen-mile road between Kirksville and New Baden. Patrons bathed in heated springwater in outdoor tubs, and picnics and public events like temperance meetings drew crowds approaching two thousand.

Shaw advertised heavily in local papers, especially in Kirksville. Promotional efforts were in vain, however, and the town began to fade not long after its founding. A passerby in 1884 described a virtual ghost town where only a year earlier "all was life and activity." The hotel burned about 1900 (dates given vary between 1890 and 1901), people moved away, and the spa town, like so many others, ceased to exist.

The spring, of course, continued to flow. In the 1930s, an entrepreneur launched a vigorous but unsuccessful campaign to market the New Baden water through a Quincy, Illinois, radio station. Through it all, locals filled their jugs, clinging to faith in the health-giving properties of New Baden spring. A 1976 Adair County history said the spring "now bubbles up in a neatly constructed spring house" and is used as a farm water supply.

BARRY COUNTY

Mineral Springs (Panacea)

Five miles east of Cassville, in the shady recesses of a steep-sided ravine, a mineral spring still trickles into an old concrete trough. This is the site of Panacea, later renamed Mineral Springs, a town that boomed suddenly in the early 1880s with bathhouses, hotels, boardinghouses, and residences.

By the time the Panacea post office opened in about 1879, the medicinal natures of the two local mineral springs were well known. In 1880, George Parrish surveyed for a town that incorporated the following year; soon, a "convenient bathing house" and "the best hotel in the country" were built. In 1882, what would become a prominent newspaper, the *Republican,* was founded here. Many patrons arrived by train, disembarking at the Exeter depot, where they caught the stage to Mineral Springs.

In addition to bathing, health seekers drank the mineral water, ate the precipitated minerals, or applied them as a salve. Promoters claimed cures for rheumatism, kidney diseases, dyspepsia, and "bowel troubles."

In 1886, in an attempt to open up the lake thought to exist behind the main spring outlet, a man dynamited the opening, damaging the spring and the nearby bathhouse. By 1888 to 1890, the boom had taken a downturn, with several large property holders diverting their interests elsewhere. For example, one hotel moved to Cassville. Several houses remain today at Mineral Springs, but the last store closed in the early 1960s.

Radium Spring

In the rugged mountains south of Roaring River, at the foot of a steep ravine, stands an old, mossy, concrete tank. This, along with a few crumbling stone blocks and rusty lengths of pipe, is about all that remains of the lower development at Radium Spring. In the shady upper depths of the ravine is another, larger concrete tank, just below a scar of tumbled stone and soil. This could be the site of Radium Spring itself—or perhaps it is a prospecting pit, probed, like other sites in the vicinity, by hopeful uranium hunters.

In 1927, Dr. William Fitch described Radium Spring as "sulphuretted and radio-activated." The radioactivity, though strong enough to register on a Geiger counter, does not indicate economical deposits of uranium. The Missouri Geological Survey explained that the radiation is imparted to the water as it flows over the Chattanooga Shale, a slightly radioactive formation that underlies much of the southeastern United States. In the early twentieth century, many hopeful mineral water promoters touted the medicinal benefits of radioactivity.

Sometime before 1920, a man named Douglas Cloe heard about the spring from friends in Arkansas. Cloe camped at the site, drank the water, and found relief from an unspecified medical ailment. After several years, he borrowed enough money to purchase the spring property, then built a bottling works and storage tanks that he lined with beeswax. He bottled in five-gallon jugs and shipped out two wagonloads per day, which was a real feat given the rugged and steep terrain. Sometime in the late 1920s, the bottling operation shut down.

Cloe participated in a scheme to form a uranium prospecting company, but the venture turned sour. Cloe, however, continued to spend every nickel he could find in digging, searching for that new kind of gold.

BENTON COUNTY

Black Sulphur Springs

According to an 1888 Benton County history, Black Sulphur consisted of six springs with a combined flow powerful enough to "turn heavy machinery." The county history described the medicinal qualities but contained no descriptions of improvements.

Several Benton County residents cited in county histories recalled days of camping, picnicking, and courting at the Black Sulphur. Jeff Morgan, born in 1861, saved money as a boy to rent a buggy and drive girls to the springs, a regular "Beau Brummell." Mrs. Stanley Gregory remembered many campers near their home at the spring in 1913 and 1914, eager to buy "homemade bread, eggs, or any eats we had to spare." Local histories contain pictures of prominent events at the Black Sulphur, including a 1930 fish fry with gentlemen in overalls proudly displaying strings of large catfish, probably taken from the nearby Osage River. Like the White Sulphur Springs, Black Sulphur now sleeps at the bottom of Truman Reservoir.

Boling Spring

The photograph of Boling Spring in Paul Schweitzer's *Report on the Mineral Waters* shows a crude wooden structure erected over the spring, perhaps a simple lean-to designed to shelter patrons from the summer sun. The spring issued from a low-lying area and flowed about five thousand gallons per hour. Visiting in 1890, Amos Woodward noted that Boling Spring, six miles west of Warsaw, had become a summer resort, but roads leading to it remained "in poor condition."

Clark Sulphur Spring

In 1890, J. D. Robertson of the Missouri Geological Survey described these four springs, located six miles west of Warsaw in "low, marshy ground" and subject to overflow and mud from a nearby stream. In spite of this, the place served as a popular picnic site and "visitors make stays there, for their health, of

Structure at Boling Spring, Benton County. Schweitzer, *Report*

several weeks duration." The water, freely dispensed by the owners, the Clark brothers of Warsaw, benefited kidney, stomach, and blood diseases.

A 1943 Missouri history noted that Clark Sulphur Spring was also known as the Black Sulphur. Other accounts, however, describe the two springs in different locations. In any event, the site of Clark Sulphur Spring is today most likely covered by the waters of Truman Reservoir.

White Sulphur Springs

Though it now lies beneath the waves of Truman Reservoir, the White Sulphur still flows through the memories of some Benton County residents. The resort was founded at a mineral spring on a meander loop of the Osage River, about eight miles northwest of Warsaw. Long after it ceased to be a fashionable resort, the site hosted many seasons as a popular campground, with families pitching tents in the nearby pecan grove, often staying for a week. They would hold their noses and drink the healing water or disguise its foul taste in strong coffee.

To Lewis Smith of Warsaw, the White Sulphur produced a sensory smorgasbord—the pungent smell, especially strong in winter as he passed by on his way to school; the soft gurgle of the medicinal waters welling up and over their wooden receptacle; the "white moss" (sulfur-encrusted algae wafting in the current of the spring branch); and the first movie Lewis ever saw—a silent picture at the springs. Alice Farmer remembered the "great tent cities on the bottom lands." Chad Gregory recalled that the springs flowed in a slough, and after a small lake had been built around them, he had to go out in a boat to reach the little stand over the spring, where he filled cream cans with the pungent water.

The White Sulphur is rich in history, thriving as a resort even before the Civil War. The proprietor mentioned having a good season in 1852, and a Mr. Maupin's Fourth of July celebration in 1858 was especially noteworthy: "the pleasant, smiling and intelligent faces of the fair ones, who graced the joyous and happy scene, might have been seen glimmering with bright mirthfulness, in every portion of the scene, while the sterner sex were softened into admiration by the syble-like forms that flooded through the room like aerial fairies, to the harmonious cadence of the sweet music."

Hacks serviced the springs daily from Warsaw. For western Missouri, life at the hotel seemed grand and luxurious, the table furnished with the "best the country affords," the bar "well-equipped with the choicest liquors." The proprietor felt no compunction to advertise the healing virtues of the water, since the "reputation of the Springs is too well-established to require it."

No one then could have foreseen the imminent demise. The hotel burned, and the Civil War thwarted plans to rebuild it. In 1888, a county history mentioned the "once-noted" resort, the springs "now deserted." But the fame of the place didn't pass so readily. From the 1890s through the 1920s or 1930s, families camped there, drinking the medicinal springwater and carting it home in jugs.

The White Sulphur is mentioned in Vineyard and Feder's *Springs of Missouri* as having flow rates of 71,000 and 258,000 gallons per day, measured in 1963 and 1966. Attention again focused on the White Sulphur Springs when construction began on Kaysinger Dam (now called Truman Dam) in 1967. The lake began to fill by 1977, and plans were made to conduct an archaeological excavation at the springs. Mastodon bones have been found at similar sites in the nearby Pomme de Terre River basin and Native American artifacts are commonly found at springs throughout the Ozarks. But before the University of Illinois dig could begin, the waters of Truman Lake closed over the White Sulphur Springs site.

BOONE COUNTY

Bratton Spring

A mineral spring is shown on the property of J. E. Bratton in the SE 1/4 S15 T49N R12W in the 1875 *Illustrated Historical Atlas of Boone County*. Schweitzer performed an analysis of the springwater in 1874.

Columbia Chalybeate Spring

This spring, mentioned in several manuscripts, is most likely the chalybeate spring on the campus of the University of Missouri analyzed by Paul Schweitzer in 1873. The handsome springhouse is illustrated in Jonas Viles's centennial history of the university.

Rocheport Sulphur Spring

The sulfur spring site visited by the author in June 1998 is actually in Howard County, not Boone. The Sulphur Springs Church, located within the Davisdale Conservation Area, is about 3½ miles northwest of Rocheport and may be near the "Rocheport Sulphur Spring" mentioned by Albert Peale in 1886, although he records the location as Boone County. Jim Hourigan, a local historian, recalled that the springs were small and had little odor. On the day of the author's visit, they could not even be located.

At the time of Peale's report, the town of Rocheport had a population of about six hundred. Today, with about half that population, the historic settlement is a popular tourist destination along Katy Trail State Park.

Twin Springs and Stice's Spring

According to a 1994 Boone County history, several springs of medicinal value flowed in the vicinity of Dripping Spring, a small village on the Silver Fork of Perche Creek about seven miles north of Columbia. Twin and Stice's springs were probably two of these medicinal springs.

CALDWELL COUNTY

Bonanza Spring

Used medicinally from at least 1850, Bonanza Spring issues from the rocky bed of Shoal Creek in central Caldwell County. In the summer of 1881, speculators laid out a town, with eighty lots selling the first year. That fall, developers built the Bonanza Spring Hotel. During those first two summers, as many as a hundred people a day visited the spring. A well on the bank allowed the springwater to be drawn up even when the creek overflowed the spring orifice. Promoters hoped that Bonanza might rival the successful Excelsior Springs, not far to the southwest.

But the hotel burned in August 1882. The next year, partners in the venture fell out, bringing improvements to a standstill. To top it off, the anticipated Kansas City to Chicago railroad alignment through Bonanza failed to materialize. The crowds began to wane. The town developed a handsome park around the spring, but the former glory days were never regained, and by the 1920s only a church, school, and telephone office remained.

CAMDEN COUNTY

Climax Springs

Compared to the days of glory, not much is going on in the old heart of Climax Springs today. Nevertheless, it is a unique and interesting mineral water site. Not far from the small park containing the spring is a small, steep-sided sinkhole. At this spot, W. W. Hockman and his friend, a Mr. Jackson, stood on a fateful day in 1881. The two were exploring the area around the spring on their way back from a business trip to Linn Creek. As Mr. Hockman peered into the sinkhole, already outfitted with crude steps, and down into its subterranean lake, he had a eureka moment, reportedly exclaiming, "this caps the climax!"—thus, the inspiration for the town and the Climax Springs Association.

In 1882, the town was platted. Professor H. W. Wiley, the state chemist of Indiana, performed a favorable analysis of the water (Schweitzer later suspected, based on his own work, that the samples had been tampered with or mishandled). Later the same year, developers built a hotel, with a drugstore, blacksmith shop, school, church, and shoemaker soon to follow.

Promoters advertised the medicinal properties of the water far and wide. Medical consultation and baths could be obtained for two dollars a day, along with "beautiful scenery, pure air and cool nights above malaria, hay fever and mosquitoes." Patrons arrived from the Warsaw railhead, a mere four hours' drive away by hack or stage, at a nominal fee. In 1891, J. D. Robertson of the Missouri Geological Survey noted in less flattering tones that the spa was accessible over "very rough roads."

Promotionals extolled the successful treatment of a wide variety of ailments, including syphilis and skin diseases, and claimed these waters were America's "only cure for epilepsy." George Walton, a renowned spa doctor, publicly acknowledged, "I find in the ingredients of iodide and bromide of potassium and iodide and bromide of magnesium they are not equaled by any springs in the world now known."

Visitors reached the spa's most unusual attraction, its underground bathing, by descending twenty-five feet into the sinkhole, where they were shielded from "the rays of the summer sun or the inclemency of the weather in winter."

The town boomed by 1889. Huge, three-day picnics and public events were commonplace. Boosters built a larger hotel, complete with a fanlike "shoo fly" dining-room contraption operated from an adjacent room by cords. But like most other spa towns, the bubble eventually burst. Businesses moved away, and new ones located along the highway that had bypassed the old town center.

In 1970, hydrologists from the Missouri Geologic Survey verified a connection between the sinkhole and the spring nine hundred feet away by tracking fluorescein dye. They worried that minerals in the spring might be more a function of local septic tank density than of bedrock geology—or, it might be added, of divine providence. Jerry Vineyard and Gerald Feder note, in *Springs of Missouri,* that the village of Climax is growing and that the homes are on septic tanks, so that "further development of the area may be accompanied by degradation of water quality in the spring."

CARROLL COUNTY

Carrollton Mineral Waters

Schweitzer, in his *Report on the Mineral Waters,* included an analysis he performed in 1885 on the artesian well supplying the town of Carrollton with drinking water. A 1911 Carroll County history mentioned a mineral spring northwest of Carrollton that closely resembled the "famous saline waters of Excelsior Springs." Mineral wells were also located southeast of Carrollton. Had these local waters been more extensively advertised, the historian maintained, Carrollton might have become a health resort "equal to that of Excelsior Springs."

The local mineral water producers settled instead for a moderately successful bottled water trade. The USGS followed the bottling operation at "Carrollton

Mineral Spring" from 1909 through 1914, and the state Geological Survey acknowledged production at the "Carrollton Mineral Well" from 1918 through 1923.

CASS COUNTY

McLellan's Well (Springs)

In the fall of 1885, Minard McLellan and his family, of Garnett, Kansas, exchanged farms with a Mr. Farmer residing in Cass County, Missouri. The Farmers were glad to be rid of their dug well with its bad-tasting water, which Mr. Farmer believed had made him ill. But Mr. McLellan, suffering from Bright's disease (glomerulonephritis—acute inflammation of the kidneys), noticed an improvement in his health with the new water source. In 1888, he began to promote the "Brosley Mineral Well" and built a two-story guesthouse, bottling works, and bathhouse.

By 1892, with a positive mineral water analysis in hand, the town of McLellan Springs had been laid out. Many patients traveled from the nearby town of Drexel. The waters became at least regionally famous for curing intractable diseases of the kidneys. But by 1897, the town and its medicinal well had begun the downhill slide toward obscurity.

CEDAR COUNTY

Arnica Springs

The Arnica Spring Park is in a shady clearing flanked by a meandering brook. The springs were once thought to mimic the medicinal properties of arnica, or mountain tobacco, a plant whose dried flowers provided a tincture for wounds. Today, the springs are little more than wet seeps. A town called Fincastle, platted here in 1882 and described as a "thriving little town," had three stores, two churches, a blacksmith shop, a mill, a school, and a post office.

Cedar Springs

The town of Cedar Springs, officially named in 1910, succeeded Balm, platted in 1884. Balm flourished by 1889. Fourth of July celebrations in the town were especially noteworthy, with bands, baseball, a horse-powered merry-go-round, and a bucking "bronco," a barrel suspended with rope that was vigorously bounced to dislodge its "riders."

Available histories mention no medicinal uses of the springs, although the name "Balm" may be a reference to their healing virtues. In 1886, Albert Peale described Cedar Springs as a health resort. A 1908 plat map shows five springs in town, one in an area set aside as a city park, complete with bandstand. Today, a traveler along U.S. Highway 54 could easily miss Cedar Springs. But a short detour north of the highway will bring him to the old park, where sandstone walls frame the orange-stained spring, now a mere seep.

El Dorado Springs

In the closing decades of the nineteenth century, southwest Missouri boasted a spa rivaling in importance Eureka Springs of Arkansas. Second in the state only to Excelsior, El Dorado Springs has a rich history entwined with its healing waters. Occasionally even today, people fill jugs or drink from the spring, swearing to the water's medicinal virtues. Medicinal or not, the spring continues to flow from the center of a neatly laid, semicircular stone basin in an attractive city park, attesting to its perceived value and the continuing care provided by the citizens of El Dorado Springs.

Local legend maintains that Indians knew of the spring's medicinal nature many years before the appearance of the first white settlers. Later, the locally important watering point provided an oft-frequented campsite on a well-worn trail. Some settlers must have suspected that the spring, named "gold" or "copperas" for the color it imparted to the rocks where it flowed, held medicinal power, because they recommended its use to a certain Mrs. Joshua Hightower of Nevada, Missouri. The Hightowers were traveling through in about 1879 on their way to Eureka Springs, Arkansas, where Mrs. Hightower hoped to be cured of a lingering illness. On the locals' advice, the family camped at the site and the old lady began sipping of the "golden" spring. The family ended up staying about two weeks, at which time the much-improved Mrs. Hightower decided to return to Nevada, as the further trip to Eureka Springs seemed unnecessary.

Not surprisingly, word of the miraculous cure spread quickly, in part through articles published in the Nevada newspaper. Someone chiseled a square catch basin from the nearby sandstone quarry and set it on stone supports to hold springwater and make it easier for travelers and campers to drink; this stone basin is now on display in the city park.

When brothers Waldo and Nathaniel Cruce, who were sheep ranching a few miles away, arrived to inspect the now-famous spring, they found hundreds of invalids camped there. Recognizing the business potential, the brothers bought the property and immediately made plans for a spa town, culminating in the platting of El Dorado Springs in 1881. Ten acres around the spring were reserved for a city park and gathering spot for health-seekers.

The business savvy of the Cruce family, which owned and operated many of the early businesses, including the first bank, helped to guarantee the town's success. Within just a few years, the permanent population had surpassed one thousand. During peak periods, eight hundred to a thousand people visited the springs at a given time. In 1890, near the height of the mineral water boom, a promotional flyer bubbled, "is it any wonder that those whose words appear in this little guide lift up their voices in a paeon of praise to the pure, sweet liquid of Nature, which performed the duty that medicine could not, eased the restless soul and made the body pure and sweet?" Dyspepsia (indigestion), scrofula (tuberculosis of the lymphatic glands), liver complaints, gravel or stone in the bladder, diabetes, syphilis, cancer, dropsy (edema—swelling of the tissues), and deafness were among the maladies reportedly cured.

Large hotels sprang up, boarding at rates of four to ten dollars a week, and several bathhouses were built. The East Bathhouse, built in 1883, featured a large central boiler and seventeen carpeted bathrooms. The West Bathhouse, built in 1888, was later remodeled and operated as the very successful Fountain Bathhouse. At the Alum Spring (actually a well), a bottling operation and a bathhouse thrived.

By 1886, the town's citizens had voted for three thousand dollars in bonds to improve the spring park, including new board sidewalks and a bandstand. When the city rebuilt this bandstand in 1905, the Cruce brothers sold the original to the park committee with the understanding that it would not be moved to the rival West El Dorado's Nine Wonders Park. A Boonville paper in 1886 spoke of local citizens who had invested in El Dorado, who could "sell out now at a large profit," reporting that property values had advanced 50 percent within the last year.

By 1887, thirteen water bottlers shipped to customers nationwide. Originally shipping in five-gallon wooden kegs, the businesses had by then switched to glass demijohns and quart bottles. Additional wells supplied the increasing demand, tapping the sulfurous subterranean reservoir. The Aperient Well, at

Rock work at El Dorado Springs, Cedar County, 1997. *Photo by author*

the corner of Jackson and Cruce, produced a mouth-pucker like eating a green persimmon. Water from the Musick Well, at Park and Thompson, sold in bulk for five cents a gallon or a penny a glass at the well. Schweitzer sampled Cruce's Well, Field's Mineral Well, and the South Forest Grove Well. By 1893, bottlers in El Dorado Springs used mineral waters in the manufacture of carbonated pop and ginger ale.

In 1892, Schweitzer described El Dorado as a flourishing little town of about fifteen hundred, located fourteen miles from Schell City, from which passengers traveled over a "beautiful and picturesque country, by a not more than two and one-half hour's pleasant drive." A daily stage arrived from Nevada, twenty miles away, "for the most part over very good roads."

With increasing public attention, improvements continued at the Park Spring. Where the spring originally issued from the hillside, townspeople fabricated a more formal setting in 1890, a curved stone grotto with steps leading down to the fountain. By 1906, the corroding iron pipe conveying water to the fountainhead had been replaced with copper, fitted with a T-arrangement to provide a double outlet—the north spout for Republicans and the south for Democrats.

Unlike many spa towns, El Dorado lived on in spite of the later decline in use of the mineral waters. Over the years, less and less of the town's budget went to promotion of the springs. But the well-established business and cultural center provided a solid platform for community survival. The 1900 population surpassed two thousand. It declined for a time after that, but growth finally resumed and today El Dorado Springs is home to about four thousand people.

Jerico Springs

It is easy to see why the Jerico spring is referred to as "chalybeate," or iron-rich. Orange stains trail from the pipe protruding from the concrete backstop of the basin in the city park. The pipe is actually the diverted outlet for two separate springs that once fed a boggy pond in the southeast corner of the park. On the rise of ground above stands the remains of the Bush Hotel.

Shortly after 1880, D. G. Stratton moved from Illinois to Cedar County. By this time, the springs fifteen miles west of Stockton had already acquired a healing reputation. As early as 1857, a Dr. Bass of St. Louis analyzed the waters and even considered building a sanitarium, but the war put his plans on hold. Stratton decided to try the water for his chronic "affection," and to his amazement achieved a complete cure. He bought the surrounding land, until then primarily a watering site for cattle, and laid out a town.

By 1883, the petition for incorporation had been filed and the town named, most local sources contend, by combining the biblical name Jericho with the surname of the land's former owner, Joseph Carico. Thus, Jerico was born. To play further on the pun, founders called the section of town across the dividing stream Jerusalem and the stream itself, the Jordan.

Stratton began donating lots to interested parties, inducing settlement in the place nicknamed the "Fountain of Youth." The United States Hotel was built in 1882, bathhouses added in 1883, and a bank in 1884. By 1899, the population had swelled to six hundred. The iron waters, bathed in or imbibed, were recommended for rheumatism and diseases of the stomach and kidneys.

Remains of Bush Hotel at Jerico Springs, Cedar County, 1997. *Photo by author*

But Jerico would not become another El Dorado Springs, its local rival. Fires destroyed most of the buildings, making it difficult to obtain insurance for hotels or bathhouses. Railroads bypassed the place. In 1891, J. D. Robertson of the Missouri Geological Survey observed that "scant accommodations and difficulty in reaching the place retard its development."

Today, about a hundred people call Jerico Springs home. But some of them may assert that the healing waters are a secret to their longevity.

Nine Wonders (West El Dorado)

The story of Nine Wonders illustrates the competitive atmosphere of health resorts at the height of the mineral water craze. El Dorado Springs was booming by 1886 when a group of investors purchased land at an iron spring just west of town. The plans made around the spring by the West El Dorado Town Company included streets, a park, and fairgrounds. The company constructed a massive stone basin around the spring and piped the water to seven separate spouts and two dripping basins—thus the "nine wonders." Promoters claimed that each fount served up a separate type of mineral water with unique healing properties.

During a series of incidents between the town company and the city of El Dorado Springs, the city attempted to annex the iron spring property and the

Nine Wonders Springs, Cedar County, ca. 1908. *State Historical Society of Missouri, Columbia*

company sued the city. Eventually, the city agreed not to annex and the company dismissed its lawsuit and promised not to incorporate as a separate town.

Nine Wonders enjoyed a thriving business for several years, but when the railroad went through the rival El Dorado Springs, its days were numbered. By 1900, the company had failed. The spring landed in the hands of private individuals who operated a tourist camp, complete with a small zoo. Today, the site is within the corporate limits of El Dorado Springs.

CHARITON COUNTY

Brunswick Mineral Well

A bathhouse and mineral well appear on the 1897 plat map of Brunswick, the well near the centerline of Kearney Street. That section of street does not exist today and there is no sign of a well. But records do exist of the bathhouse, including a handwritten lease agreement signed in 1891. A list of expenses connected with the bathhouse operation, dating from 1895, includes coal ($1.00), a pump handle ($1.00), a dozen Turkish towels ($1.20), and looking glasses ($.70). May of that year was lean, with $20.80 in expenses and only three baths sold ($.75). In June, however, the proprietor recouped some of his losses, selling thirty-six baths ($9.00).

It all began in 1887, when the city of Brunswick sunk a well in hopes of striking natural gas. After seven hundred feet, no gas was found. The city aldermen narrowly voted to continue, pumping two thousand dollars more into the project. A stock company, formed to consummate the drilling, would allow the city to receive a small percentage of the anticipated revenues. At 1,505 feet and at a cost of thirty-five hundred dollars, the drilling halted. No natural gas was found, just sulfurous mineral water. Owners developed the site as a resort and the bathhouse operated for at least ten years.

Salisbury Well

Across from the Lutheran church, near the street right-of-way, is a faint circle of sparse grass. On closer inspection, the circle can be made out to be the tops of bricks. This is about all that remains of the Salisbury Well, at one time a local landmark. Users drew water from a tile that, until fairly recent times, protruded from the center of the well. According to Edward Shepard's *Underground Waters of Missouri*, the city drilled the 825-foot well in 1895. It is shown on an 1897 plat map of the city. Apparently, the well also provided water for baths.

Triplett Well

On Wash Triplett's land, just east of the town of Triplett, a company organized in 1906 to explore for oil. Drilling stopped at fifteen hundred feet, and instead of oil, mineral water with "fine medicinal properties" flowed out. "Siloam's Pool" (presumably named after the biblical pool of Siloam) became a popular summer bathing resort.

CHRISTIAN COUNTY

Eau de Vie

The history of Eau de Vie largely parallels that of nearby Reno. Both places were established about 1880, when the mineral water boom swept the region, and both seemed to have nearly disappeared by the turn of the century. A Springfield newspaper reported in April 1881 that the new town of Eau de Vie

(French for "water of life") already had 150 residents, many of whom arrived as "walking skeletons." In addition to an official analysis of the waters, the newspaper provided a litany of testimonials. As at many spa boomtowns, the supposed powers of the healing waters were nearly universal—dyspepsia, sore eyes, old sores, dropsy, gravel, neuralgia, female disorders, paralysis, and scald head were all put right.

By the spring of 1881, eighty acres of lots had been carved out and there were thirty-eight buildings, including several boardinghouses. Records disagree on how big the town got, but by the 1890s the population had dwindled, and by 1929 the Eau de Vie post office had closed.

Reno

In May 1881, a correspondent for the *Springfield Express* reported that eight to ten buildings a week were springing up in the new town of Reno. Stores, mills, churches, blacksmith shops, a school—all were rising from the rocky Ozark soil. The smell of freshly sawed lumber must have permeated the valley.

The boom began just a year earlier, in 1880. Prior to that, Reno Spring served as a convenient watering stop on the Springfield, Missouri, to Harrison, Arkansas, haul road. In the summer, teamsters looked forward to a cold drink from Reno Spring in its shady recess along Bear Creek. And in the winter, northbound travelers paused to brace themselves for the next leg along a windy, exposed ridgeline.

With news of curative powers came the inevitable rush of invalids who camped in tents or lived out of their covered wagons. The boom that followed did not last for long. By the mid-1890s, the village was largely deserted. Orville Holt, lifelong resident of Bear Creek, in 1998 related that he could barely remember when the last of the buildings were torn down during the Depression—recycled, no doubt, on the surrounding farms.

CLAY COUNTY

Excelsior Springs

By all standards, Excelsior Springs must be considered the state's premier mineral water resort. It is the state's claim to mineral water fame, the sole competition for places like Hot Springs, Arkansas, and a host of other spas, east and west. In fact, it is the only mineral water site still operating as a resort, although it has certainly had its ups and downs over the years.

The Hall of Waters, a million-dollar project completed in 1938 using federal WPA money, is still impressive today, a sleek structure of stone and glass. The world's longest water bar, at almost fifty feet, still dispenses local as well as exotic varieties of Adam's ale. The mineral pool downstairs was damaged by the flood of 1993, and the city is working to restore it. Viewing this site, one can easily imagine 110,000 gallons of eighty-four-degree sulfo-saline mineral water, complete with teams immersed in a kind of slow dance—therapists helping patients to exercise rheumatic joints. In another corner of the basement is the abandoned polio pool and its wheelchair ramp. At one time, insurance companies paid for treatments here.

A few blocks away, the fabulous Elms Hotel remains an imposing landmark, though it, too, has fallen upon its share of hard times—bankruptcies, closings, fires—though always followed by rejuvenations, redecorations, and new paint. The Elms Hotel is a historical icon. Al Capone played all-night poker here, and Harry S. Truman celebrated his surprise 1948 election with a mineral bath.

Although it became wildly successful, Excelsior's genesis was no more spectacular than those of its counterparts. It happened near the height of the speculative mineral water boom, in the year 1880. Like many of the others, it began with an amazing healing experience. Locals advised a girl suffering from scrofula to drink from and to bathe her sores in a certain spring. Legends of Indian braves healing wounds centered here, but most settlers avoided the spring because of its yellow staining, fearing that it was "pizen." True to classic tales, the girl recovered completely. A series of other cures followed, leading to the inevitable inrush of invalids. More and more tents appeared at the site, and patrons waited to dip their cups or the community can into the receptacle, which was fashioned from a five-gallon wooden keg.

The property owner, A. W. Wyman, appreciated the value of this find. Not a greedy man, we are told, he only wanted to make the spring more accessible. He consulted with a Reverend Flack, who evidently had business savvy. The two signed an agreement wherein lots would be laid out, Wyman would hand Flack 25 percent of net proceeds, and Flack would analyze, improve, and promote the spring, producing a pamphlet to mail to his "numerous friends and acquaintances." The town of Excelsior Springs had begun (since the name Excelsior was already taken, the first post office was named Viginti, Latin for "twenty," supposedly the number of springs in the area).

Slow but steady growth occurred in those first few years. Flack outfitted the original spring, named Siloam, with a fancy pavilion. Later, there would be

Mineral water bar at Excelsior Springs, 2000. *Photo by author*

a larger pavilion, complete with benches, rows of hooks for personal cups, and a city-paid operator to pump water. Other mineral springs were discovered nearby and quickly developed. The Empire, later renamed Regent Spring, emerged from the hillside across the little Fishing River from the Elms Hotel, accessible by a footbridge. Paul Schweitzer referred to it in 1892 as the most famous chalybeate spring in the state. A year later, it received a medal at the World's Fair in Chicago, propelling itself and Excelsior Springs into the international limelight. The Superior Spring earned fame for curing kidney diseases and the Saratoga provided "sleepy water," a lighter nightcap alternative to the heavier iron waters. Eventually, over twenty of the springs in town had pagodas over them.

Later still, it was discovered that mineral waters could be obtained through wells, freeing entrepreneurs from the constraints of locating and procuring eligible springs. Wells at varying depths produced mineral waters with distinctly different chemical characteristics. Sulfo-saline waters, for example, occurred at almost fifteen hundred feet. Eventually, promoters drilled at least thirty separate wells, selling their health brews for a penny a glass in the shade of their little pagodas. People could be seen toting jugs all over town, even dragging cases of bottles on sleds specially made for the purpose.

During those early years, many other businesses located in Excelsior, often run by people who were themselves health seekers. The first hotel, the Excelsior, built in 1881, accommodated about 250 guests. Business, however, was somewhat constrained by the fact that the town's only connection to the outside world was through stage lines running from railheads at Liberty, Missouri City, and Kearney. But an event in 1887 changed that, stimulating the struggling resort town. The Chicago, Milwaukee, and St. Paul Railroad opened a line between Kansas City and Chicago, passing through Excelsior Springs. Suddenly, a new boom was on. With the rail connection, the Elms Hotel, built in 1888, stood less than two hours away from Union Station in Kansas City. The next year, an ornate Music Hall seating 1,320 patrons arose, and major conventions arrived in town.

Many civic improvements came about by the end of the nineteenth century, including a reliable new public water supply, sewerage system, electric lighting, and paved streets. The sidewalks were even heated, using excess gas produced by the city plant. Schweitzer, impressed by the modern conveniences at the Elms Hotel, noted with approval its "incandescent lights, automatic communicators and steam heaters in each room." The resort town began to cater to a variety of visitor interests, installing bowling alleys, tennis courts, parks, and drives. The city also took a more direct hand in regulating its mineral water businesses, instituting sanitary analyses in 1905 and licensing springs and wells in 1910.

During the twentieth century, Excelsior experienced a roller-coaster ride of popularity. The Elms burned in 1898. Patrons escaped in their nightclothes, and luckily there was only one injury. Rebuilt in 1908, the hotel burned again one year later, destroying sixty thousand dollars' worth of furniture. The third incarnation opened in 1912. By 1915, a journalist for the *Kansas City Star* observed that crowds were increasing, not so much because of the mineral springs that, after all, had been there all along, but because "Easterners" were finding out about the place and its "healthful recreation and restful sociability." Owners built an attractive marble and glass pavilion over the famous Siloam Spring. Bottling businesses, in full swing, used many of the therapeutic springs and wells scattered through the town. In one year, the railroad sold 370,000 tickets to Excelsior.

In the 1920s, the city reached a population of 5,000 and catered to an estimated 350,000 visitors a year. By the 1930s, there were eleven bathhouses, forty boardinghouses, and twenty clinics, but visitation had by then dropped to an estimated 250,000 per year. In about 1935, the city decided to step in to renew its image as "America's Haven of Health." Concerns about overly aggressive business tactics had increased. Patrons arriving in Excelsior were harassed by a throng of hucksters, paid by the head to snag clients. City leaders made it illegal for anyone but the city to sell mineral waters and purchased the rights to use ten springs. They secured federal funding to build the elaborate Hall of Waters with its baths, massage parlors, hydrotherapy, and "white sulphur" swimming pools. Four types of waters were piped to the building to be bottled in the city-owned plant. Doctors at the town's mineral water clinics were required to carefully examine patients and prescribe tailored mineral water regimens.

In spite of the fact that well-trained attendants scientifically administered mineral water treatments of various kinds and instructions "carefully complied with," business began to suffer after World War II. A serious blow came in the middle 1960s when the government ruled that baths and mineral water treatments would no longer be covered by medical insurance. In 1963, an article in the *Saturday Evening Post* entitled "Hucksters of Pain" cast Excelsior in an unfavorable light. Dollars for promotional campaigns shrunk drastically after that. Adding to the downturn, the Hall of Waters suffered flooding damage many times over the years and finally had to undergo major repairs. The fabulous Elms Hotel closed or sold several times.

The bottled water business also had its ups and downs. For many years, the city-owned plant produced a popular line of drinks including sparkling water, siphon water, soda pop, ginger ale, white soda, and Pepsi-Cola. These operations closed for a while in 1948, to be later resurrected. In 1967, the system took a $25,000 loss. Some city officials wanted to shut it down. In 1989, there was a new push to market Excelsior Springs water in six states, and $250,000 was invested in a retooling of the bottling plant. By the turn of the millennium, the bottling operation was again out of business. The last clinic closed in 1972, and by the late 1980s, only a handful of businesses remained open in the downtown.

Excelsior kept a good attitude throughout its trials and tribulations. The city prospered in spite of the cyclic public interest in mineral waters. In 1975, Excelsior Springs received an "All-America City" designation, built partly upon its resort legacy. More recently, there has been another awakening, as Excelsior realizes its potential as a "retreat community" for Kansas City and other urban centers. The baths now focus on relaxation, rather than cures, although some believe that the potential for real cures is there. And today, over one hundred businesses call the downtown home, capitalizing on society's new view of this "Haven of Health."

Reed Springs

At the May 24, 1895, dedication of the Liberty Odd Fellows Home, officials praised the medicinal values of the nearby Reed Springs. The springs, which supplied water to the home, would "contribute in no small degree to the general health of the occupants." Wealthy St. Louis investors originally constructed the home as a luxurious hotel in 1887. The investors, capitalizing on the well-known medicinal properties of Reed Springs, erected a pagoda over each one and connected them with gravel paths. Plans called for hundreds of homes, a half-mile racetrack, and an extensive park, but only the hotel was actually built.

The massive, three-story, 108-room hotel featured its own waterworks and steam heating plant. The pavilion in the south yard accommodated twenty-five hundred people. Health seekers came from all over the country, and one young gentleman, F. H. Matthews, upon having his health restored, married a Liberty woman and became the resident physician for twenty-three years.

Willard Winner bought the hotel in 1891, then sold it to the Odd Fellows in 1895 to satisfy bondholders. It burned in 1900, when there were 200 residents—140 elderly adults and 60 orphans—all of whom apparently escaped the blaze. Though rebuilt, the structure was eventually converted to a hospital in 1923 and then to a rest home in 1955.

CLINTON COUNTY

Peerless Spring

Peerless Spring, locally known as Walker Spring, flowed from low, rolling hills southwest of Plattsburg. Like nearby Plattsburg Spring, its site today lies under the waters of Smithville Reservoir. In 1882, the Peerless Spring Company recorded a plat, but the town never materialized, possibly due to the proximity of its competitor. However, for many years locals used the site for fishing and picnicking.

Plattsburg Mineral Spring

Gazing across the quiet upper arm of Smithville Reservoir just south of Plattsburg, it is hard to imagine the bustling, parklike setting of Plattsburg Mineral

Spring. There, beneath the quiescent waters, lies the site of the once-popular resort, on the banks of Smith's Fork Creek, where the Silver Cornet Band played and the great evangelist Sam Jones conducted his camp meetings for the multitudes in 1895.

The St. Louis laboratory of Wright and Merrill analyzed the Plattsburg mineral springs in 1881 and validated their medical properties. A local man further substantiated their worth, telling residents that Indians led him to the "great springs" sixty years earlier and tried to convey to him the fact of their healing powers. The Plattsburg Town Company certainly recognized their immediate commercial value, platting a town in 1881 bisected by the Spring Town Road. At least two hotels were built, along with a bandstand, half-mile racetrack, croquet fields, ball fields, and over a dozen residences. Horse-drawn buses ran on a regular schedule from Plattsburg to the springs. Citizens in town could reach the main spring over a footbridge spanning a ravine. Steps led down into a U-shaped, rock-walled enclosure with the tiled spring pool at the closed end. Cures were reported for dyspepsia, scrofula, rheumatism, and neuralgia.

Perched over a ravine, a bathhouse used several different springs and offered hot or cold baths. But sometime before 1900, a flood washed the bathhouse into the ravine. The town seemed to decline after that, with most of its buildings in decay by 1910. Some attribute its failure to the fact that the railroad bypassed the spot, while Excelsior Springs, about twenty miles to the southeast, prospered when it became accessible by rail from Kansas City.

COOPER COUNTY

Chouteau Springs

About a mile south of the roar of Interstate 70 is a quiet, parklike clearing that was once anything but quiet. Here lies the remains of Chouteau Springs, one of central Missouri's most successful mineral water resorts. The gravel road leading to the springs roughly aligns with the former, boulevard-like Chouteau Avenue. The main spring still flows about fifteen gallons a minute of salty, sulfurous mineral water. In the vertical tile set over the spring, the clear water welling up appears greenish black, with bubbles occasionally burping from the dark depths. Wafting in the current downstream of the tile are long, stringy filaments of algae or bacteria, pink and white tinged with green. Downstream, the flow feeds a wet, marshy area choked with cattails, home to raspy-voiced red-winged blackbirds. To the north lie the crumbling remains of a swimming pool, the springwater still discharging into it through a square orifice along one side. There are even some weathered wooden remains of the ornate pagodas that once squatted over the various spring outlets. Here, in fact, are more artifacts than at most mineral water locations in the state, rendering the site a logical candidate for historic preservation. Chouteau Springs, after all, has a long history of public use and affection.

Interest in Chouteau goes back to at least 1792, when Osage Indians bestowed the surrounding lands upon Major Pierre Chouteau, younger brother of St. Louis cofounder Auguste Chouteau. The wording of the grant, signed at Fort of the Grand Osages in what is now Vernon County, embodied a certain fondness for the Frenchman: "thou mayest remain there, and thy bones shall never be touched." The Spanish government approved the grant of 30,000 arpents (about 26,000 acres) in 1799, but when the U.S. government took control in 1803, it refused to clear the title. Years of litigation, shepherded through Congress by William Henry Ashley, finally resulted in a perfection of title in 1837. Ashley, founder of the Rocky Mountain Fur Company and father of the trappers' rendezvous, acquired a quarter of the land for helping to defend against government rejection of the claim. He named the spring on his land for Chouteau. When Ashley died in 1838, he left the land to his wife and daughters and was buried on an Indian mound overlooking the Missouri River.

A resort operated at the springs by the 1840s, when the *Boonville Bulletin* suggested a visit, especially if "your liver is torpid and you are visited with the 'blue devils.'" By the 1850s, a stock company had built a hotel and bathhouse. In 1853, the state Geological Survey prepared an official report on the mineral waters, including an analysis by Professor Litton of Washington University in St. Louis. The water, rendered "light and agreeable to the taste" by its dissolved gases, compared favorably to the Belcher water at St. Louis and the Saratoga and White Sulphur Springs of the east. A glass of Chouteau water in the morning along with an iron tonic became a very popular medical treatment.

During the Civil War, soldiers camped at the springs, and bushwhackers stole livestock and food from local residents, "even the sauerkraut," according to longtime German-born resident, Mary Day, who was quoted in a 1929 magazine. Marauders burned the resort to the ground.

Another slow rise in popularity came after the war, in the 1870s. In 1873 the *Boonville Eagle* lamented the fact that no railheads were close to the spring to enable thousands to visit rather than mere dozens. Commenting on the need

Ruins of swimming pool at Chouteau Springs, Cooper County, 1998. *Photo by author*

for an infusion of capital to improve drainage and build "commodious" hotels and bathhouses, the newspaper asked, "is it not strange that the present owner of these springs will not engage in improving them?"

By the 1880s, most of the original glory of Chouteau had been recaptured. The 1886 *Boonville Advertiser* reflected on the magnificent, eighty-foot-wide drive coursing through the center of the residential lots, which sold from fifty to a hundred dollars each. An 1888 plat shows nearly two hundred lots, the more exclusive on the higher ground above the spring. Plans were made, though never acted upon, to build a $9,500 pipeline to send the mineral water to Boonville. During this time, the locally famous Johnny Whistletrigger, with his "sad-faced horse and ramshackle wagon," delivered "Shoooo-toe watah!" to Boonville homes.

Eugene Windsor of Kansas City bought the springs with 120 acres in 1900. He expanded the operation with a swimming pool, larger bathhouses, a bowling alley, and a billiard hall. The official 1902 season flyer advertised "good, dry tenting grounds, free from annoyances," accessible by "a pleasant nine-mile drive from Boonville over good roads." Alternatively, visitors could take boats up the Missouri and Lamine rivers to within one mile of the spring, to be met there by conveyances. At the fifteen-room Edson Hotel, Grandma Day, celebrated for her midwifery and her twenty-five-cent chicken dinners, charged $4.50 per week for room and board.

In the 1920s, bootleggers worked the area and local lawmen uncovered a still in a nearby cave. Immensely popular in the 1930s and 1940s, the park hosted picnics and family reunions and the swimming pool was jammed on hot summer days. The 1941 WPA guide to Missouri listed the charge for swimming at twenty-five cents. And, of course, patrons could still imbibe a gourdful of that strong-willed water. Local authors note a decline in use by the 1940s, brought on, they speculated, by increased automobile travel and the construction of alternative attractions such as Bagnell Dam and Lake of the Ozarks. By the 1950s, interest had further waned and the park finally closed to public use in 1962.

CRAWFORD COUNTY

Saranac Springs

In 1882, author Albert Merrell predicted that "Sarnaca" Springs in Crawford County would become "the health resort of the near future." In that year, promoters laid out magnificent plans for a resort at the spring. Old buildings were torn down and a contract let for fifty thousand bricks for a new hotel. A fountain was planned that would shoot water twenty feet into the air. But within three years, business had all but ceased.

Much later, some of this history of Saranac would be covered in a brochure produced by the proprietors of Saranac Springs Campgrounds, near Leasburg, who provide camping and float services on the nearby Meramec River. The old spring still flows from its cave in the fissured limestone, through a pond, and down a watercress-choked branch to the beautiful Meramec.

DADE COUNTY

Lotus Springs

Five miles southeast of Greenfield, in the Turnback Creek drainage of Stockton Lake, is an almost forgotten mineral water location. The Rolla School of Mines analyzed the Lotus Springs, said to be four in number. Founded near the end of the Civil War, a resort boomed here for a time but probably shut down around the turn of the century. In 1899, James Crook reported that the water "at one time enjoyed a reputation as a remedy in gastric and renal disorders." Today, the only clues to the resort's existence are rock walls and steps, scattered sandstone blocks at the springs, and some surviving beds of flowers.

DAVIESS COUNTY

Crystal Springs

Crystal Springs, consisting of three mineral springs on the farm of John Gagan, five miles northwest of Pattonsburg, became, according to a local history, "one of the institutions of Benton Township." The chemists of Wright and Merrill of St. Louis performed the crucial analyses. In the late 1880s, a bathhouse and hotel operated there, with "camping parties, numbering thousands," descending upon the springs in the summer months.

Jamesport Mineral Springs

Paul Schweitzer, in his *Report on the Mineral Waters of Missouri,* included a photograph of the Jamesport Mineral Spring bathhouse, a sizable structure with a central two-story section. The spa, opened in the northern part of the town at the foot of "Vinegar Hill," used four wells, each about thirty feet deep. A Doctor Kintner ran the spa, which apparently closed in 1895 or 1896.

GENTRY COUNTY

Siloam Springs

Descending the hill into Siloam Springs, it is hard to imagine that a town of over one thousand people once thrived here. There is nothing but a small house or cabin where the large sanitarium once stood. Looking carefully in the underbrush on the south side of Highway DD, one can find the remains of an old well and an overturned bathtub, half submerged in the soil. These may or may not be relics of the mineral water days. But we know that towns called Siloam, Aerola, Gara, and Freewater were all here, riding the mineral water wave sweeping over the country at the time.

Siloam's story begins with a sad chapter. Local farmer Matt Chittim lost his wife in January 1874 and faced the prospects of raising his nine children alone. To add to the misery, as spring warmed into parched summer, the family well went dry. Chittim uncovered an old well of distasteful water that he had dug fourteen years earlier. Despite the flavor, this well produced abundantly and helped to sustain Chittim and his neighbors through the drought. One fellow remarked that the water reminded him of some he had tasted at a famous mineral water resort. As a matter of fact, Matt thought his rheumatism had improved after switching to this water. In 1880, friends persuaded him to hire the St. Louis chemists Wright and Merrill to perform an analysis. Not surprisingly, their report confirmed speculation about the water's medicinal potency.

By the winter of 1880–1881, the town of Siloam City had been platted, with twenty acres near the well set aside as a park and campground. In typical fashion, word of the healing waters rippled across the countryside and invalids began flocking in. An eyewitness described the "thickly set tents of campers in some of which were stretched the helpless victims of disease, others were parading before their tents without their crutches, showing how quickly they were healed."

The town grew quickly. Lewis Walker, a businessman from neighboring Worth County, built a two-story hotel and eight-room bathhouse in 1881. The proceeds were split fifty-fifty with Mr. Chittim. Siloam water was bottled and sold. The newly published *Mineral Avalanche,* along with sharing news tidbits, started "doing much to bring the Springs into notoriety."

Meanwhile, a man named William Childers discovered mineral springs on his own property nearby. Disgruntled about the price of Siloam water, he began advertising "free water" and laid out a village by that name on forty acres of his land. Freewater consolidated with Siloam in 1882. The name Aerola was used for the new town, but most people still referred to Siloam and Freewater. City fathers petitioned for the name "Siloam Springs," but a town in Howell County had already taken it (also at mineral springs). Finally, they settled on "Gara," after a local Baptist minister's daughter.

Sanitarium at Siloam Springs, Gentry County. Schweitzer, *Report*

A fire took the bathhouse in 1886 and the hotel closed. A man from Iowa then purchased the property and built a very large hotel and sanitarium, which he completed in 1887. The next year, Dr. J. A. Kintner, who studied hydrotherapy in Germany, took over as resident physician. Advertisements for the sanitarium and hotel shouted: "the largest building in northwest Missouri," "steam heat," and "free from malaria." Bethany newspapers in 1898 sang the praises of Siloam Springs Sanitarium, "situated in a beautiful park and provided with every appliance and facility for the restoration of health and happiness." Under the care of resident physician W. A. Thompson, the patient would find that "there is no remedy so successfully nourishes the nerves, regulates the digestive organs and beautifies the complexion as a course of these scientific treatments." The increased business must have taxed the well, for Amos Woodward observed in 1891 that "in very dry weather it gives out."

More serious problems soon arose. The hoped for, planned for, and fought over railroad spur to Siloam never materialized. When rains took the bottoms out of the dirt roads, the twelve-mile jaunt from Albany became a messy ordeal. The sanitarium still operated in 1905, but the boom was over by then.

The Gara post office closed in 1906. In 1916, the hotel sold for one thousand dollars; in its final years, raccoons roamed its once-hallowed halls.

GREENE COUNTY

Bethesda Springs

Greene County's hopeful entry into the mineral water club, the small town of Bethesda, hugged the banks of the swift, clear Little Sac River. Here a small spring issues from the limestone on the rugged valley slope. Dr. John Cochran, who moved to the county from Tennessee, "discovered" the spring in about 1850. Legend told that Indians hid the spring, jealously guarding its medicinal powers. Cochran, putting stock in other local legends, believed gold was buried in the vicinity and called the place "El Dorado." His son built a small hotel at the spring and local people came to seek relief for the usual assortment of ailments—liver complaints, sore eyes, dropsy, rheumatism, indigestion, and so on. The healing nature of the spring caused people to call the place "Bethesda," although Edward Shepard, in the *Geology of Greene County* (1899), said the spring at Bethesda could "hardly be regarded as a mineral spring."

Cochran's plans for a town proved a dismal failure. He turned the enterprise over to a Mr. Bush and Dr. Joseph McAdoo, who later served as mayor of Springfield. These men filed a plat and offered two hundred lots for sale. They did a better job of promotion than Cochran, and the town started to grow. About a dozen houses were eventually built. An icehouse at the riverbank stored huge blocks of cut river ice in sawdust for summer use. Bethesda appeared on the 1904 plat map of the county, but it was probably in decline by then.

HARRISON COUNTY

Heilbron Spring

In 1885, the citizens of Bethany attempted to cash in on the mineral boom sweeping the state. A Chicago company that was hired to drill an exploratory hole to locate minable deposits of coal found no economically extractable deposits, but at two hundred feet the drillers encountered a strong mineral water. Casing the hole with gas pipe preserved the flow.

In 1891, the Bethany Improvement Company bought the farm surrounding the well and laid out lots along either side of "Park Avenue." A "handsome, commodious and modern" four-story sanatarium, built in 1897, came under the management of the noted German hydrotherapist Dr. Jerome Kintner. Utilizing the "German Water Cure" and "Electric Medicated Baths," Kintner treated rheumatism and stomach, kidney, skin, and blood disorders.

The sanitarium, which was eventually converted into a regular hospital, burned in 1928. The fairgrounds in Bethany, dating from the early 1900s, were carved out of the original platted subdivision surrounding the medicinal well.

HENRY COUNTY

Clinton Artesian Well

The photographs at the Henry County Museum are intriguing—well-dressed ladies and gentlemen standing around the man-made geyser, cups in hand, sipping the sulfur water; the magnificent three-story hotel with its wide veranda, patrons sitting in its shade, chatting, or staring off into the wooded grounds. Such was Clinton's contribution, as "Artesian Princess of the West," to the mineral water resort boom. And it happened, at least partly, by accident.

In 1887, the Clinton Natural Gas Development Company drilled for gas on land one mile southwest of Clinton. In March, the hole reached 120 feet deep and was already "running over with sulphur" but produced no gas. The principals, undeterred, vowed: "we are bound to have gas if they have to bore through to China to get it." At 325 feet, they struck a strong vein of white sulfur water. Although the company determined to go to at least 700 feet in its search for gas, some were already thinking of ways to use all that crystal clear sulfur water, shooting up ten or twelve feet from the borehole. A local newspaper observed that "all the towns about us have been blowing about their mineral water and health resorts." The well bottomed at about 800 feet without encountering usable quantities of gas. On performing a qualitative analysis of the water, a local pharmacist found that it contained the desirable medicinal mix of minerals. Soon a steady stream of health seekers trudged toward the well, "all lugging the 'little brown jug,' forming a grand procession."

By the summer of 1888, local developer Herman P. Faris completed a twelve-room bathhouse (eight rooms for men, four for ladies) and other attractions, reached from Clinton by a line of horse-drawn cars. The overflow from the artesian well filled a small lake, where Faris took the local newspaper staffers on a moonlight boat ride. On a hill overlooking the lake, a hotel opened in 1892.

Veranda of the Artesian Hotel, Clinton, ca. 1906. *Henry County Historical Society, Clinton; photo by Ellsworth Marks*

A spacious entrance hall, thirty by one hundred feet, ended at a wide stairway to the upper rooms. The place featured modern conveniences such as "speaking tubes in each floor hall," and a "large and convenient sample room for commercial travelers." Patrons drank or bathed to cure the standard ailments—rheumatism, kidney and stomach trouble, skin diseases—but they could also seek relief from opium or whiskey addictions using the "Wherrell Bi-Chloride of Gold Treatment." An 1894 advertisement in the Clinton newspaper advertised Electric and White Sulphur Baths, and in 1899 a magnetic healer was in residence.

By 1900, Faris, who had a "genius for investigation," diverted his energies into other mineral explorations in the area. A few years later, the artesian well almost ceased flowing, a problem generally ascribed to the drilling of wells nearby. But a persistent local legend maintains that teenagers jammed bowling balls into the well. The resort declined rapidly, but Artesian Park continued to be a popular destination—featuring a racetrack and swimming in the artesian lake and, later, a municipal pool. Today, the lower end of the park, the site of the artesian well, is overgrown and neglected, consigned to the high water mark of nearby Truman Reservoir.

Ford Well

When approached for information, longtime Montrose historian Rosie Boden stated that she had never heard of Ford Well. But true to her nature, Rosie dug into the matter, producing copies of a lease agreement between Jacob Ford and the city of Montrose, signed in 1886, wherein Ford agreed to allow public use of the well for a term of ninety-nine years. The city, in turn, agreed to built a "substantial stone wall" to protect the well and install "a good and suitable pump." In 1909, a quit claim deed allowed the owner at that time to surrender the lease.

Paul Schweitzer analyzed "Ford's Spring" in 1886, and in 1890 Amos Woodward described water from the twenty-five-foot-deep well as high in sulfates and alkaline earths. He also mentioned that locals used the water extensively, but he failed to record any specific medical conditions treated.

Lewis Chalybeate (Sand Creek) Spring

In a cool, shady, picturesque sandstone canyon that unexpectedly slices through the rolling farmland of Henry County, the Sand Creek chalybeate springs flow. In 1890, Amos Woodward remarked on the brown sediment staining the spring branch, and the stain is still there, perhaps more orange, coating rocks and leaves as the iron-rich water trickles along the canyon floor. Here and there are mineralized water pools, sustaining thick stands of horsetails and adding another shade of green to this remarkably luxuriant scene.

Today, the springs are within the Conner O. Fewel Wildlife Area. A sign informs visitors that "an Osage trail once ran by the springs, connecting Kansas City to Warsaw." The area became a local gathering point and reportedly a hangout for Jesse James and the Younger Gang.

Someone has added tanks or tubs embedded in the soil to receive the flow of the springs. The tank tops are covered and the overflow outlets are screened. Possibly the water is pumped elsewhere, perhaps to homes on the ridge above.

Windsor Medical Well

On a gentle rise a few miles south of Windsor sits a handsome home surrounded by large trees. In the 1880s, the Windsor Mineral Spring Hotel stood here, a three-story, forty-two-room (or fifty-two-room, depending on the reference) structure with a porch wrapping most of the way around. The actual date of construction is unknown, but it must have been built after 1883, when a county history mentioned the nearby medicinal spring but not the hotel. In lauding the healthful overall setting of Henry County, the historian points out the "additional inducement held out to suffering humanity," the "celebrated mineral spring of crystal clear water," at that time "left to bubble and run without let or hindrance."

Southeast of the hotel, someone excavated the spring into a sort of well in the sandstone. Still visible is the indentation of a small pond that once captured the outflow. Cures were reported for kidney diseases and rheumatism. At one time, the city of Windsor owned the operation.

According to one reference, most of the hotel rooms were never completed. Sometime after 1887, the structure sold. Most of it was torn down, the materials reused for homes in Windsor, including one residence said to have been a replica of the hotel. Later, the property became a popular picnic and barbecue site, with many locals still resorting to the healing spring. At Old Settlers Reunions, for example, there were so many visiting that they would "drink the springs dry."

HOWARD COUNTY

Boone's Lick (Booneslick)

Boone's Lick is one of the state's most historically significant mineral water sites. Salt making was an industry vital to the young state, as evidenced by the saline lands provision of the federal act that allowed Missouri to form. Up to twelve salt springs, with six square miles of territory surrounding each, were to be set aside for the use of the state. The Boone's Lick area was not among those reserved, possibly because commercial production already occurred there.

The salt springs just east of the Missouri River's great bend in the center of the state were part of a four-hundred-arpent Spanish land grant to James Mackey in 1797. Some historians speculate that Daniel Boone cooked down some salt here shortly after 1800. It is known for certain that two of his sons, Nathan and Daniel Morgan, ran a salt business there. By 1806, the Boone brothers and their partners, James and Jesse Morrison, had a furnace and forty kettles working, producing twenty-five to thirty bushels of salt per day. Kettles sat over a trench dug into the soil, their edges supported by "a few handfuls of white clay," with fires burning in the pit below. Workers boiled away two hundred fifty gallons of brine to yield each fifty-pound bushel of salt. At first, they transported salt downriver in canoes fashioned from hollowed sycamore logs, their ends "closed with boards and daubs of clay." As the operation expanded, keelboats would arrive from St. Louis every two weeks with provisions and return downriver with salt. Salt making had its dangers. One young man, Joseph Morrison, was scalded to death when he fell into a boiling kettle.

Starting with six to eight workers earning forty-five dollars per month, the Boones and Morrisons soon expanded their operation to sixteen to twenty men who could turn out a hundred bushels a day, which sold at $2.00 to $2.50 a bushel. But with the expansion of major national transportation routes, Missouri salt could not compete with much larger operations elsewhere. In spite of this, salt makers worked at the Booneslick site off and on for many years. In 1819, Edwin James of Major Stephen Long's expedition described the furnace, which consisted of a "chimney-like funnel" that rose "obliquely along the side of a hill." James stated that it took three cords of wood to evaporate enough water to make eighty bushels of salt. Geologists with the Missouri survey later reported that these salt makers had denuded forests for four square miles around the saltworks.

Shortly after the Civil War, salt fever struck again. Henry Brown, a Canadian, visited his relatives, the Marshalls, who owned the salt lick property. Together, they formed the Booneslick Salt Manufacturing Company, opening with one thousand shares of hundred-dollar stock. The company began to drill near the salt springs, encountering an "inexhaustible supply of strong water" at 500 feet. Drilling continued down to 1,008 feet, with brine running out at the land surface. A ten-inch-square wooden "conductor pipe" kept the hole open down to the "bottom of the quicksand," twenty-two feet below the surface. The remains of this pipe are still visible today.

A committee assigned to investigate the venture's potential profitability compared the brine strength of Boone's Lick to successful operations in the east— with unfavorable results. Taking into consideration the costs of transporting the salt to populated areas, the brine was just too dilute. In 1879, the salt company sold for thirteen hundred dollars on the public block. Other schemes to exploit the site's economic potential were also disappointing, including a plan to raise saltwater fish and oysters in a lake formed from the dammed spring flow.

Today, the salt springs are part of the fifty-two-acre Boone's Lick State Historic Site. A trail leads down into the valley where the springs still flow (an estimated thirty-nine thousand gallons per day in 1965) and the remains of the salt well and furnace pits can be seen. A kettle on display is similar to those used by the Boones.

Mosquitoes can be bad around the springs, but around here these and other forms of life are of interest. The briny springs and adjacent Salt Creek are home to some uniquely adapted, salt-tolerant plants and animals, such as the plains killifish and saltwater mosquito. In 1890, Amos Woodward was struck by the beautiful purplish red mounds that built up around the springs, an admiration somewhat subdued by his observation that the material consisted of "clay, algae and slime."

Fayette Salt Spring

Early settlers of the Fayette area described a large buffalo lick there that was later licked and trampled by cattle. The salty spring that formed the lick, along with 2,800 acres of neighboring land, had been set aside under the Saline Lands Act when the state formed in 1821. Alphonso Wetmore, in his 1837 *Gazetteer of the State of Missouri,* mentioned the buffalo lick, the long-standing saltworks, and the potential for further salt production, advising "it is only necessary to convey fuel from the excellent coal banks in the vicinity, to make the springs at that lick productive." There are no indications, however, that large quantities of salt were ever produced there.

The site did eventually achieve notoriety as a source of medicinal waters. A 1905 publication called *Picturesque Fayette* included a photograph of the "Fayette Mineral Wells" bathhouse, a wooden structure with a pool-enclosing fence at one end and an elevated storage tank on the other. Facilities for hot and cold baths and a "deep plunge" were provided as treatments for rheumatism, skin diseases, and "blood troubles."

The well, about a hundred yards south of the old MKT railroad station, had originally been drilled to supply the city with drinking water. At 860 feet, drillers reached a strong flow of mineral water, thwarting the intended use. Owners conceived an alternative plan, building a thirty-by-sixty-foot swimming pool. They shipped bottled water, and there was "an inducement for the opening of a sanitarium," although this apparently never happened. Today, the site is a marshy area overrun with cattails.

Glasgow Mineral Spring

The old salt spring flowed from a hillside above Bear Creek, near its junction with the Missouri River. To the south, hugging the steep hills along the big river, is the historic town of Glasgow, a hub of tobacco trade before the Civil War and site of the world's first all-steel railroad bridge, spanning the Missouri River in 1879.

The mineral spring, which Amos Woodward described in 1890 as having a "very weak flow," serviced a bathhouse of six or eight rooms. For twenty-five cents, one could soak in a hot or cold mineral bath, taking the cure for sciatica or mild paralysis, or one could drink the foul-smelling water to seek relief for dyspepsia. Sunday was the busy day at the bathhouse—atonement, perhaps, for a night of revelry.

A handsome hotel, the Glen Eden, operated at the site until about 1910. There are no signs of the spring or the bathhouse today.

Well at Glasgow Mineral Spring, Howard County. Schweitzer, *Report*

HOWELL COUNTY

Dixon (Cure-All) Springs

In the rugged Ozarks of southern Missouri, about fifteen miles southwest of West Plains, is a small scattering of houses at the end of a blacktop road. This is what remains of Cure-All, another mineral water resort town that spun wildly into existence in the last quarter of the nineteenth century.

Dr. J. C. B. Dixon of West Plains, originally from Kentucky, started the boom here in 1875. He discovered the medicinal qualities of the springs, about five in number, built a hotel and bathhouse, and got a post office established. The town, named Cure-All by Dr. Dixon, soon had a sawmill, gristmill, and store.

J. D. Robertson of the Missouri Geological Survey, visiting in 1891, described a "deserted settlement" where a "flourishing place" had once been. He took samples of one of the springs, Electric Spring, but he only tasted the others, not discerning any difference between them. Not surprisingly, he soon discovered that the residents did recognize a distinction—and perhaps they still do.

Siloam Springs

Siloam Springs has the appearance of an end-of-the-road town that has boomed and faded. But as one descends the hill on the town's western flank, a massive, four-story building suddenly looms above the tree line. The Pinebrook Inn, since 1998 a bed-and-breakfast, stands on a gentle slope overlooking the valley of the once-famous medical springs.

Mr. N. O. Tate of Miami, Florida, bought the springs and surrounding land in 1921 and began construction of what he hoped would be the Ozarks' premier resort. But Tate soon got into financial trouble and sold his interests to John T. Woodruff, developer of the Kentwood Arms Hotel in Springfield. Woodruff finished the Pinebrook Inn, opening its doors in 1923. A huge fireplace dominates the main lobby. Floors and moldings are of native oak, sawed and milled at Siloam. Tall columns support verandas spreading across the front of each floor, and the exterior sports a stucco finish, applied by an Italian mason. Woodruff dammed the valley to provide storage for the springwater while also creating a lake for fishing and boating. Around the springs, he constructed a two-hundred-acre park, "well landscaped and beautified." A cement swimming pool and an exclusive nine-hole golf course, with some "unique features and natural hazards," were laid out nearby.

Access improved when a bus line reached the springs from West Plains, picking up passengers arriving by railroad from St. Louis or Memphis. People marveled at the power and endurance of the REO bus that, although loaded with passengers and luggage, managed to pull the steep hills and navigate the muddy roads. The 1941 WPA guide to Missouri mentions a golf course green fee of fifty cents and swimming in the concrete pool for twenty-five cents.

The mineral water saga of Siloam, however, began long before the Pinebrook Inn was even a dream. Origin stories include a visit by Dr. I. A. Norman of Illinois who regained his health at the springs in 1859 and a reported pilgrimage in 1817 by a Ste. Genevieve man seeking to restore the health of his ailing wife. In 1891, when the geologist Robertson visited Siloam, Johnson and Keller owned the property and were "rapidly improving it." There were bathhouses with hot or cold options, waiting and dressing rooms, and two hotels at the site. During this period, the population of the town reached at least two hundred. The springs, which had earlier been subjected to frequent flooding, were by then "walled in and protected against overflow and impurities." Robertson described seven springs, which had names like Keystone, Rheumatic, and Crooked Ash. Others recorded ten or even twelve healing springs, each with different names.

Access seems to have always been a problem for Siloam. Robertson described roads from West Plains as "very rough," covered with chert rock and nearly impassable in wet weather. The situation was no doubt improved by the time of the Pinebrook Inn, but the automobiling public eventually chose resort destinations accessible over better roads. The meager flow of the springs also created problems. One developer, in an attempt to "open" them up, dynamited the springs, which may have actually diminished flows. Today, the flows are very feeble, and one must search carefully among the briars and willow thickets to even find the curbed spring outlets.

JACKSON COUNTY

Cusenbary Spring

Cusenbary Spring, not far from the more famous Jackson Lithia Spring, provided mineral water for a bottling operation in the first few decades of the twentieth century. J. D. Cusenbary, owner of the spring, worked a three-hundred-acre farm in Jackson County but also mined and ran pack trains in the western states. Dr. D. H. Bliss analyzed the spring and demonstrated its medicinal qualities.

The water, thought to be helpful in treating rheumatism, liver, and kidney diseases and indigestion, also tasted good, according to the Independence edition of the *History of Jackson County*, which mentioned that "no medicinal properties are detected by drinking." The author further suggested that an injection of capital and enterprise could make the spring the equal of Saratoga in New York—a result never realized.

Jackson Lithia Spring

Albert Merrell's 1882 catalog of *Health Resorts and Mineral Springs of the West* introduced Lithia Spring to the outside world. It flowed on a four-hundred-acre farm owned by I. W. Duncan. Suffering from a severe ailment, Duncan had the water brought seven miles to his bedside; where drugs had failed, the water performed magic. Within a few days, Duncan was "about and attending his business." With prompting from "the leading physicians of Kansas City," he developed the spring and marketed the water, which found its way to Europe and the "islands of the ocean."

Amos Woodward in 1891 reported that the spring flowed from a steep ravine, filling a basin seven feet square and eight feet deep, from which it was pumped up to a reservoir for distribution. By this time, the Lithia Springs Improvement Company, organized in 1889, controlled the spring. Plat maps of Kansas City indicate that the company laid out lots on the ridgetops above the spring.

Vaile Spring

The Vaile Mansion, not far off of U.S. Highway 24 in Independence, is a handsome, solidly built structure. Colonel Harvey Vaile constructed the home in 1881, using hand-pressed brick that alone cost fifty thousand dollars. It has nine fireplaces, three huge chandeliers, and murals painted by Italian, French, and German artists. Vaile eventually spent a considerable portion of his wealth defending himself against charges that he embezzled government funds. West of the mansion, a spring emerged in a smooth, white, circular springhouse. The water was bottled and sold for a few years prior to 1920.

Young's Medical Well, Kansas City. Schweitzer, *Report*

Young's Medical Well

Paul Schweitzer (1892) reported that this well, at the corner of Twenty-fifth and Vine in Kansas City, reached a depth of one thousand feet. It was touted for rheumatism, old sores, and as a "blood purifier." Bathhouses and cottages served a few guests.

JEFFERSON COUNTY

Bockert (Bokert) Springs

The greatest claim to fame for Bockert Springs is that they supplied drinking water to the 1904 St. Louis World's Fair. Bockert water was hauled in by train carloads from De Soto, which was named the "Fountain City" because of its artesian wells. A Mr. Bockert, a St. Louis businessman, bought the Jefferson County property, including about a dozen springs, in the late 1890s. At that time, the place had a pall of tragedy hanging about it. A farmhand had accidentally killed himself in a booby trap set to kill a thief, and a local child had recently died in a blizzard. Bockert himself was ill when he bought the farm, but on the advice of neighbors, he drank from an iron spring on the property and began to feel better. He had the water tested, and with a positive analysis in hand, he bought additional acreage and built a bottling plant. He shipped water out in five- and ten-gallon jugs.

In 1909, the bottling plant burned, but it was soon rebuilt. Five years later, a new company took over, hatching a scheme to build a large, fine hotel. Two of the primary investors in this company, Richard Loeb and Nathan Leopold, were accused of murder in Chicago; in their sensational trial they were defended by Clarence Darrow. The hotel plans never came to fruition, and the bottling plant closed for good in 1932.

Hillsboro Mineral Spring

Edmund Flagg, traveling through Missouri in 1836, recorded that a "Mt. Vernon," which he identified as the county seat of Jefferson County, was "chiefly noted for a remarkable spring in the vicinity, said to be highly medicinal." This is a confusing statement, since the county seat of Jefferson County, Hillsboro, was originally called Monticello. As to the spring's medicinal virtues, Flagg wondered, "how this latter item may stand I know not, but I am quite sure that all of the pure element it was my own disagreeable necessity to partake of during my brief tarry savoured mightily of medicine or something akin."

This might also be the mineral spring in Jefferson County mentioned by Alphonso Wetmore in 1837, where "a company of capitalists of St. Louis are about to erect a house for the accommodations of visitors, 160 feet by forty, three-stories high, with suitable out-buildings." The developers had a view to make this a summer retreat "desirable for fashionable visitors, as well as valetudinarians." Promoting the enterprise further, Wetmore gushed, "the great salubriety of the climate here will be attractive to those who contemplate, with the natural impulse of good taste, the picturesque scenery of the surrounding hills and woodlands, and soul and body will acquire a healthful tone on the undulating surface of this fine region. Children may enact their innocent gambols here, while the flocks that surround them will give zest to the poetic pages they peruse in this sylvan retreat." If anything was ever developed here, nothing seems to be left of the resort today.

Montesano Springs

The springs at Montesano were of prehistoric as well as historic significance. Mastodons, whose remains can be viewed and contemplated at nearby Mastodon

State Park, were probably attracted to mineral springs in the area. The "medicine water" springs were also known and used by Native Americans. In about 1797, Thomas Jones made salt there, although he was driven away by Indians. At that time, the springs were known as Crystal Springs.

In 1881, the Montesano Springs Company laid out a summer resort at the springs. The company built a large, four-story hotel along with a number of houses for the use of their personnel. The hotel burned in 1886. By the early 1890s, the area had been purchased and began operating as a public resort and amusement park. Visitors reached Montesano from St. Louis by a twenty-mile ride on the Iron Mountain Railroad or by daily excursion boats, which plied the Mississippi River down to Sulphur Springs Landing. Huge iron rings where the boats tied up can still be seen fastened to the river cliffs. A round trip by boat to the park, including admission, cost twenty-five cents. During summer months, from two to ten thousand people visited the park daily.

By 1896 a theater, athletic hall, dance pavilion, "switchback" scenic railway, and boating were all available at the park. Public health was protected by a "complete sewerage system" that "drain[ed] the park and grounds into the river." Several of the fifteen springs in the valley had been walled up and fitted with seats where patrons could lounge while tasting the "very blue and slightly foul-smelling water." Or visitors could drink from a number of hydrants conveniently scattered throughout the park.

The water was rich in sulfur, as J. D. Robertson attested in 1891, noting white and pink deposits on the basin walls, even white blotches on the shells of the black snails inhabiting the springs. In 1899, James Crook mentioned that the "waters are laxative, and also possess alterative properties." He also described a "peculiar creamy substance, the natural product of one of the springs," applied to "old sores, ulcers, or raw surfaces of any kind."

At the turn of the century, St. Louis newspapers noted the success of Montesano and offered suggestions for improvements. A new hotel, though it might cost fifty thousand dollars, would "pay a dividend safely ten and probably at twenty-five percent." Or if the wealthy of St. Louis would just fund a children's home near the springs, where the "street Arabs of the city and the unfortunate babes whose parents are compelled to labor" could go to "bathe in the pool, made by the overflow from the medicinal springs, it would be a moment of more satisfaction and benefit than the same amount of money could give in any other way."

The children's home was not to be. And Montesano, though immensely popular in its heyday, began to decline after the turn of the century. Today there are few visible signs of the springs; a lake with tall cypress trees growing on the banks remains.

Sulphur Springs

The springs at Sulphur Springs, two miles south of the town of Kimmswick, were nearly destroyed when the new U.S. Highway 67 was constructed. Developers laid out the town of Sulphur Springs, a mile or so east, in 1860 on the railroad along the Mississippi River. In 1899 Sulphur Springs had two stores and a population of two hundred. Earl Taubold of Sulphur Springs remembered when the local "Magnesia Water" could be bottled and taken home, filling the house with that familiar rotten-egg aroma. Today, there are some ruins of rock buildings, walls, and a tower along the highway near the location of the springs.

JOHNSON COUNTY

Colbern (Electric) Springs

In northwestern Warrensburg, along Business Route 50, is the site of Colbern or Electric Springs. The Colbern family owned the land, with its mineral springs bubbling up in several places along a small brook, from 1836. By the early 1880s, the family had subdivided and sold the land. In 1886, however, another Colbern owned part of it, Warrensburg banker George Colbern, who purchased the ten-acre tract containing Electric Springs.

Colbern built the large Oaks Hotel, with its "double verandahs all around," perched on a hillside west of the springs and overlooking a "precipitous natural amphitheater." Through the parklike setting curved shady drives lined with stately elms. A bathhouse with forty tubs, offering hot or cold baths, straddled the ravine above the spring overflow. Colbern platted lots and shipped bottled water in five-gallon cans.

In 1889, the Electric Springs Railroad connected the springs to Warrensburg. An Irishman, hired for a dollar a day, ran the mule-drawn streetcar. A two-lane bowling alley provided recreation, and southwest of the springs a large pavilion seating twenty-five hundred was constructed. Chautauquas and other large public gatherings were common.

In 1891, a Warrensburg newspaper stated that "physicians of this city are talking of organizing a sanitarium" at Electric Springs. Although "the public is becoming incredulous about the truth of all statements made concerning the efficacy of medical water," the merits of Electric Springs made it "notorious from the personal advertisement given it by living examples, who, suffering from some affliction pronounced by the ultra medical fraternity incurable, have used the waters internally and externally and are today sound and well." In 1890, Amos Woodward observed that the springs did contain an "exceptional amount of mineral matter in solution."

The hotel burned in 1907. After that, Electric Springs seems to have declined, although the waters were marketed for several decades. In 1929, the property sold at the county courthouse. But a 1932 newspaper advertisement proclaimed that the water, analyzed by a chemistry professor at Central Missouri State Teachers College, was "unusually free from bacteria for a natural water." Apparently, locals used the water medicinally until fairly recently.

Pertle Springs

An amazing amount of memorabilia accompanied the more popular and long-lived mineral water resorts. Although most of this material has not survived, artifacts from those days of glory provide hints of the palette of promotional tools and gimmicks that were used. At a 1998 meeting of the West Central Missouri Genealogical Society, along with a program on the history of Pertle Springs delivered by a descendant of its founder, such artifacts were displayed—tokens from the trolley, bottles from the carbonated bottling works, cups and saucers painted with scenes of the springs, silver spoons engraved with *Pertle Springs*. These tangible tidbits of those nearly forgotten times bring them back to life and make them a personal experience.

Pertle Springs, a great pleasure ground, attracted large crowds from Kansas City, St. Louis, and the surrounding towns of central Missouri. The medicinal springs were known long before James Christopher acquired the property, but his promotion and boosterism launched them on their path to fame. He bought the land from a man named Zimmerman, who in turn had purchased it from William Purtle. When Christopher began platting lots at his "Purtle Springs," his surveyor suggested that "Pertle" was a more pleasant spelling of the name. All of this happened about 1883 (there are discrepancies among dates recorded).

Within a few years, Christopher built the large, three-story Minnewawa Hotel, north of the iron-rich spring. Lodging rates were kept reasonable partly because Christopher owned a large farm, complete with a forty-cow dairy, producing "nearly everything that supplies the table." From the hotel, one could cross a footbridge spanning a ravine a "dizzying height above the earth" to reach the large assembly hall. Visitors could rent cottages or bunk in tents, furnished with a board floor for an extra dollar and with straw bedding for a "nominal sum." The resort also featured a bowling alley, bottling plant, and bathhouses. During the resort's heyday, it could accommodate as many as five hundred patrons.

The spring itself, discharging about three or four gallons per minute of iron carbonate water from the sandstone, flowed over a grooved curbing. Cures for dyspepsia and kidney and liver ailments were claimed, but from the accounts of popular activities at Pertle, it seems that the spring was actually a rather minor part of the attraction.

Patrons enjoyed boating on Lake Cena, one of the resort's nine lakes, and summertime swimming and wintertime ice-skating were also very popular, especially among the students of "Old Normal," the nearby teachers' college. An 1888 flyer boasted that at Pertle a person could "expect to meet only the very best classes of people" while they escaped the "insanity and physical exhaustion" of "high pressure" society.

Cabs and coaches conveyed passengers to the springs over two miles of dusty roads until a "dummy" train line reached Pertle from Warrensburg in 1889. A small steam engine pulled a string of open cars. After the first Sunday in May, the beginning of the tourist season, the little train made eight to ten trips daily to the springs, and as many as thirty per day on holidays. Former engineer Jackson Hackley recalled the hectic work of April, cleaning and repairing the engine and painting and varnishing the cab, inside and out.

The most memorable events at Pertle—the huge summer gatherings including conventions, camp meetings, and Chautauquas—often attracted thousands. An 1891 season flyer announced the fifth season for Chautauqua, offering a "rare intellectual, moral and religious feast." Included in that bill were titles such as the Chautauqua School of Music, Summer School of New Testament, Elocution and Oratory, and the School of Methods of Church Work. Other high-profile events hosted at Pertle included meetings of the Missouri State Teachers Association, Farmers and Laborers Union, State Bar Association, State Democratic Party, and Free Silver Convention. Featured speakers at the gigantic assembly hall, which seated at least three thousand, included William Jennings Bryan and Carrie Nation. Famous camp meetings conducted by Rev. Sam Jones attracted as many as ten thousand people.

Pertle Springs, near Warrensburg. Schweitzer, *Report*

Pertle thrived well into the first decade of the twentieth century, but by the 1920s it had lost some of its momentum. In 1922, the railroad line was abandoned and dismantled, and in 1926 the famous Minnewawa Hotel burned down. In the 1930s, however, the Civilian Conservation Corps built a new camp at Pertle, the remains of which can still be found here and there. Another breath of revival occurred in 1960 when Central Missouri State College purchased the property, rebuilding the lodge and adding a golf course. It is still open for public use, and the spring can still be seen, its medicinal waters now looking rather neglected and stagnant.

KNOX COUNTY

Forest Springs

A Knox County history observed that "no well regulated county in the west is without its medical springs, with more or less of reputation for curative properties, and Knox County is no exception." The author referred to Forest Springs, earlier known simply as Sulphur Springs. As the story goes, the medicinal properties were discovered as early as 1835 by a Dr. Polonzo Conditt (variously spelled Conduett, Conduette), who inscribed his name on a nearby stone. Dr. Conditt practiced medicine as did his son, a dentist.

In 1882, William Johnson laid out the town of Forest Springs, intending to found a health resort. A post office operated there from 1886 to 1889, along with a hotel, blacksmith shop, and store. Promoters claimed the waters would benefit scrofula, dyspepsia, and sore eyes as well as "mental and physical debilities." According to the *Edina Sentinel News,* at times as many as several thousand people visited the place weekly. In spite of this, the resort failed to spawn much of a town and apparently faded even before the turn of the century. In 1948, a local landowner attempted to clean up and preserve the place as a picnic ground.

LACLEDE COUNTY

Lebanon Magnetic Well

Magnetism, like radioactivity, was once thought to confer mysterious yet profound medicinal powers upon a mineral water. Promoters claimed such powers for the Lebanon Magnetic Well. In the late 1880s, the city of Lebanon launched a waterworks program that included the drilling of a public water supply well. Drillers reached good water at 135 feet, but citizens, hoping for artesian water, pressed the drilling to 1,000 feet. A workman happened to discover that his pocketknife became magnetized when he rubbed it on iron pipes in the well. Later, when discharged from his duties, the worker claimed the magnetism was a hoax. But Paul Schweitzer reaffirmed the properties in the early 1890s, attesting to the deflection of a compass needle and the fact that a knife rubbed on the casing would pick up a nail of "eighty grains." A local worker, Erwin Ellis, offered a more graphic depiction: "Go into the engine room, make it perfectly dark and let a little steam out by the stopcock. Then put the end of your finger in the steam. Each little drop, as it forms on your finger from the condensation of the steam, will show a spark of electric light." Schweitzer gave no credence to the transfer of magnetism to the water itself, citing a study performed on this subject by the Medical Society of Michigan. Waters, the scientists concluded, either pure or containing dissolved salts, could neither "produce nor communicate" magnetism.

In spite of the scientific evidence, the Lebanon Magnetic Water Company

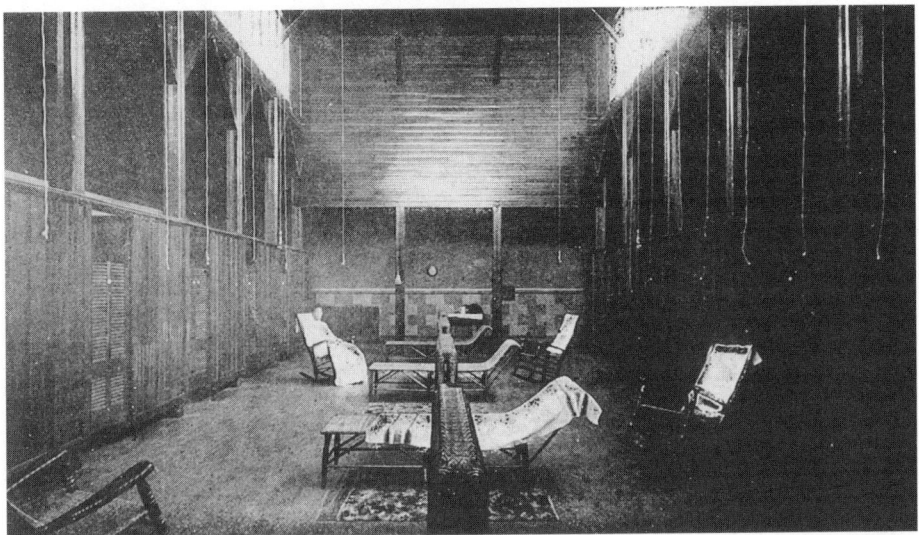

Gasconade Hotel's bathing room, Lebanon Magnetic Well, Laclede County. *State Historical Society of Missouri, Columbia*

capitalized on the well's reputed medicinal and magnetic virtues, treating rheumatism, headache, neuralgia, nervous disability, and "deranged actions of the kidneys and urinary organs." They extolled the purity of the water and the fact that "one does not have to hold his nose to drink it."

The company launched a major resort enterprise. A forty-by-sixty-foot bathhouse near the well featured a wide veranda with three round stained-glass windows above. Men and women attendants catered to the bathers' needs. In the lawn was a cast-iron drinking fountain supplied with tin cups. Down the street loomed the spacious, three-story Gasconade Hotel, a striking building of dark red color with wide verandas, ornate gingerbread trim, and lots of "nooks and crannies" for quiet repose. Guests arrived by hack or on one of the electric cars scurrying along streets lined with glass-globed lamps.

The hotel later became a sanitarium, offering a wide array of treatments under the medical supervision of a Dr. Paquin. In addition to the usual drinking of mineral water and taking hot or cold baths, patrons could sample Turkish, Russian, electric, sea-salt, and medicated vapor baths, with or without massage. Later historians observed that the sanitarium, with its more subdued clientele, was more suited to the personality of the town than a rowdy resort. Like many midwestern towns, Lebanon seems to have been suspicious of outsiders.

LAWRENCE COUNTY

Paris Springs

The 1878 *Springfield City Directory* advised, "if a watering place is wanted, the Chalybeate Springs, in Lawrence County, only twenty miles from Springfield, furnish an abundance of the finest mineral waters to be found in the U.S." By that time, many patrons took the train from Springfield to the springs.

E. G. Paris opened a hotel in 1872 at the settlement near the springs, known from 1855 as Johnson's Mill. The hotel, accommodating about a hundred guests, stood on a high ridge overlooking the spring. Paris built a bathhouse at the springs and a small pump house to supply the hotel above.

By the 1880s, tourists flocked to Paris Springs. An 1889 flyer proclaimed, "the per centage cures here are doubtless greater than that of any other water in the country." In 1899, James Crook claimed that "patients suffering from disorders of the liver, kidneys, stomach, skin and nervous system have found great benefit from a sojourn to the spring." In 1901, a bottling business and soda pop factory operated at the spring.

The resort began to decline in the first decade of the twentieth century. In 1919, the hotel burned, apparently from arson. A later reference to Paris Springs appears in the files of the state geologist when, in 1948, the owner of the land inquired about possible redevelopment. But today, very little evidence remains of the once-thriving resort.

LEWIS COUNTY

Wyaconda Water

La Grange, the "City of Mineral Springs," boasted at least two mineral water sites, with "Wyaconda Water" being the most famous. In 1887, a steel rolling mill in search of "fuel" drilled a six-hundred-foot well. The mill failed even before it began operation, but Wyaconda Well Water became known far and wide.

A 1902 edition of the *La Grange Indicator* contains an advertisement for the mineral springs, famous for curing indigestion, dyspepsia, diabetes, and kidney and bladder troubles, and for "removal of gravel and uric acid deposits." In the flowery prose of the era, the ad gushed, "as these liquid pearls spout to the surface, sparkling with carbonic acid gas, they seem to say, nature bids me come that I might befriend suffering humanity." "In fact," the ad continued, "these waters will prevent more sicknesses than all the drugs in Christiandom will cure." Wyaconda Water worked well for diseases of women "peculiar to them and directly affecting the happiness and well-being of others." And "it is a fact that sterility of long-standing has been cured by the intelligent employment of this remarkable water." The water, "kept in hospitals and sickrooms," was served in "over five-hundred locations in Chicago."

A trademark for Wyaconda Water featuring a likeness of the owner's daughter signified "purity." As to the curative properties described, "these are facts, not chimerical theories, borne out by plentiful evidence daily provided."

Although the floods of 1993 caused the artesian well to be closed for a time, the wellhead is now back in service and bears a plaque noting its history. People can still get a drink from the well that put La Grange on the mineral water map.

LIVINGSTON COUNTY

Mooresville

There is no end to the stories of miraculous cures produced by mineral springs. In the case of Mooresville, the original beneficiaries were of the four-legged variety. E. J. Moore allowed his hogs to drink and wallow in the Livingston County spring then known simply as Sulphur Spring. Moore's hogs seemed to have become immune to the hog cholera that had been common and widespread in the area for years. Quick to understand the significance of this find, Moore had the water analyzed by the St. Louis chemists Wright and Merrill. After three days of "careful testing," they pronounced the waters to be, in fact, of the medicinal variety.

In the 1880s, Dr. Theopholis Fiske built a sanitarium at the springs. He constructed a bathhouse and a sixteen-room hotel that operated for thirty years, advertising cures for dyspepsia and stomach and liver diseases. By the 1890s, the flow of the spring would not support the operation, and several shallow wells were dug nearby. In 1927, William Fitch described two wells, one of which benefited "diseases of the genito-urinary tract and in catarrhal diseases," the other helping with "neurasthenia and all depleted conditions of the blood and blood-making organs." Patrons reached the springs "via motor over the national Pike's Peak Ocean to Ocean Highway." In 1893, judges at the Chicago World's Fair awarded a prize to the Mooresville water. The hotel burned in 1925, but the spring pavilion survived until 1936.

Before Moore's hog revelation, people failed to appreciate the virtues of the spring. In 1842, a settler named Lawson observed that the water formed a crust when boiled and made cooked food "taste funny." Lawson looked elsewhere for his water supply, settling at a freshwater spring nearby.

MADISON COUNTY

White Springs

In scenic Madison County, not far from the picturesque, rocky shut-ins of the Castor River, lies the site of the once-popular White Springs. In 1891, J. D. Robertson stated that the waters earned a local reputation for curing dyspepsia and malaria. At the time of his visit, however, the place appeared neglected, with nearby cottages in a "state of dilapidation."

According to William Smallen of Fredericktown, the springs had their heyday in the 1920s. Historic Madison County president John Paul Skaggs reported that a resort hotel, bathhouse, and cottages once stood near the springs, and the place even had a "dogcatcher."

Today, the springs flow into a small lake in a very attractive valley setting. Two springs occur in close proximity, one sweet, the other sulfur. Farther up the valley, a clear spring feeds a second, smaller lake. A screened-in lodge adds to the pleasant and inviting scene.

Castor River shut-ins, near White Springs, Madison County. *Photo by author*

Spring at Vichy, Maries County. *Postcard collection of John Bradbury*

MARIES COUNTY

Vichy

Named for the famous mineral water spa of France, Vichy was platted in 1880. By the early 1900s, the resort town had become rather well known. The spring emerged into a block springhouse flanked by curving stone walls, then emptied through a small pipe into a rock-walled basin. A Maries County history maintained that after the springwater flowed through a trough for animals, it supplied the bathhouse containing two wooden tubs. Visitors from Kansas City and St. Louis stayed in the large, three-story Letterman Hotel. In 1886, a tornado nearly destroyed the town.

MARION COUNTY

Shannon Spring

An 1847 edition of the *Hannibal Gazette* mentioned Shannon Spring, southwest of Palmyra, as a watering spot. Ms. Roberta Hagood of Hannibal reported that picnics and political rallies were held there.

Vernette Mineral Well

Built as a fine brick home in the 1870s, a massive structure sits on a high knoll overlooking the west end of Hannibal. In 1890, local physician Dr. Fred Vernette bought the property and opened the Elmwood Sanitarium. He drilled two mineral wells, one reaching 1,435 feet deep, to supply patients with the "water cure." Drinking and bathing in the "lithiated magnesia" waters, patrons sought relief for gout, catarrh, and kidney and bladder diseases. Vernette bottled and sold the water for twenty-five cents a gallon. After he died in 1904, the new owner converted the sanitarium with the "commanding view" of Hannibal back into a residence.

MCDONALD COUNTY

Galbraith's Medical Well

I. D. Galbraith, a businessman of some note in southwestern Missouri, provided McDonald County residents with an early telegraph system. In 1887, Galbraith and some partners purchased property on which an oil exploration company had recently forfeited a lease. A year earlier, the oil company, hoping to obtain petroleum, sunk a well along Indian Creek. Instead of oil, they encountered at 840 feet a "strong vein of artesian sulphur water," flowing out "with a terrible force." In 1891 J. D. Robertson recorded that "its flow is very large, and its appearance clear and sparkling, with a decided odor of sulphuretted hydrogen, but with only a slight taste."

Recognizing the obvious market value, the businessmen laid out a town, calling it Sulphur Wells City. Later, a railroad depot located at the site and the town was renamed Lanagan. The 1941 Missouri WPA guide observed that the town "owes its existence to a well of gushing sulphur water that attracts visitors during summer months." Apparently, however, the mineral water business never really took off at the town, which some had thought "destined to become one of the principal health resorts of America."

Indian Springs

Tucked away in a scenic fold of northern McDonald County's Indian Creek valley is the site of the once-thriving resort town of Indian Springs. By all accounts, it became a bustling community, reaching, according to one writer, a population approaching three thousand. If that is true, the nearly complete vanishing of Indian Springs is remarkable even among the host of mineral water ghost towns.

Legends maintain that locals recognized the medicinal effects of the springs by 1840. The location was then lost, but Drury Wilkerson "re-discovered" it in 1871. The real boom began in 1880 with a reported cure for sore eyes. Surveyors laid out a town in 1881, and within seven days, the story goes, people bought two hundred lots and erected twenty dwellings. In July of that year, a printer published the first issue of the *Indian Springs Herald*.

A man named J. J. McNatt is credited with much of the town's early development. On Indian Creek, he constructed a low dam forming Lake McNatt, stretching for a few miles upstream. On the lake, a four-hundred-dollar, sidewheeled steamboat, operated by an "experienced engineer and pilot," carried seventy-five passengers paying ten cents a head. Many businesses became established, including a printing office, schools, sawmill, carding mill, and gristmill. Eventually, Dr. J. C. Petit of Joplin opened a forty-room, state-sanctioned medical and surgical sanitarium. The Segoyewatha Hotel also dispensed mineral waters.

A group of springs, reportedly very different from each other in character, flowed in close proximity at Indian Springs. One of the springs exhibited great purity in that "the most powerful glass has failed to discover the slightest trace of animalculae" (microorganisms). Nearby residents claimed that while the springs were small, the "subterranean stream can be heard for a quarter of a mile in wet weather."

By 1890, Indian Springs had begun to decline. In that year, a rail line bypassed the resort town by eight miles. And in 1930, an article in *Missouri* magazine described Indian Springs as a "phantom town."

Saratoga Springs

The use of *Saratoga* for this southwest Missouri location attests to the great national prominence of Saratoga Springs in New York. Today the spring, cascading from a low bluff, can be reached by threading along an abandoned, briar-infested roadbed near Saratoga Creek. Here, in 1880, developers laid out seven hundred lots, one hundred of which sold within the first year. The population reportedly surpassed one thousand, with churches, a school, stores, and two newspapers. The town began to wither when railroads bypassed it in the 1890s.

Twin Springs

Twin Springs Hollow appears on the U.S. Geological Survey topographic map depicting a portion of northern McDonald County. At the end of a gravel road traversing the hollow are several small springs. The Twin Springs post office opened here in 1876, and J. P. Madden platted lots in 1881. In 1892, Paul Schweitzer briefly described the site but did not mention any therapeutic uses of the springs. The town apparently survived for several years, but residents eventually abandoned the enterprise.

White Rock Sulphur Springs

Now called Jane, this village grew from a post office established in 1854 at a settlement called White Rock Prairie. After platting in 1880, the town at first called itself White Rock Sulphur Springs, but residents later renamed it for the daughter of the postmaster. At one time, there were several business houses, which enjoyed a "fair trade." Today, the spring still flows from a small park in this quiet village.

MERCER COUNTY

Bowsher Mineral Spring

Just north of Princeton, on the road to the Chloe Lowry Marsh Conservation Area, sits an out-of-place-looking brick structure with a definite institutional motif. This is, in fact, the remains of the county hospital and poor farm. But before that, Robert Bowsher operated a mineral water resort hotel here.

Born in Ohio in 1834, Bowsher moved to Princeton at an early age and became locally famous as the county coroner, proprietor of the Buck-Eye House Hotel, and the first man in the county to "put up ice." Bowsher conducted business at the resort until 1896, when the property sold to Mercer County. When Bowsher died in 1918 at the age of eighty-three, the *Princeton Post* reflected that "his life covered a stormy period with many a bitter struggle for him."

The mineral springs, analyzed by Schweitzer in 1881, could not be located during a site visit in 1998.

Lineville Mineral Well

In northern Mercer County, near the Iowa line, the Lineville Mineral Well and Hotel once operated. Paul Schweitzer's *Report on the Mineral Waters* contains

Former Bowsher Mineral Spring sanitarium, Mercer County, 1998. *Photo by author*

a picture of the imposing, two-story hotel, supplied by a mineral water well 152 feet deep. Little additional information could be located about the site, although it was apparently also called Reiger (or Reger) Spring.

MILLER COUNTY

Aurora Springs

Promoters billed the town of Aurora Springs, laid out in 1880, as the "Great Sanitarium of the West." With mineral springs effecting cures that had "baffled for twenty years the skill of the most expert physicians," the town boomed almost immediately, becoming the largest in the county by the late 1880s. Various historians estimate the population at seven to twelve hundred.

Flows of the four principal springs—the Bluff, Healing, Round, and Bath—were dammed up, and an artesian well was drilled nearby. Two bluffs overlooked the "rustic park," with its "paths and thoroughfares" leading to the "circular curb of Aurora Springs." Daily stages ran to Jefferson City. In 1899, James Crook mentioned that the springwater had a "sharp tonic effect on the economy, bracing up the digestion, promoting the appetite, and inducing healthful sleep and rest."

But as suddenly as the boom had begun, dark clouds appeared on Aurora's horizon. Developers planned a large hotel, but before construction could begin, a legal controversy swirled over the town. Governor George Anthony of Kansas claimed that he owned a critical forty-acre parcel in the center of the spring park. As the case dragged out in court, citizens began to desert the enterprise, and hotel construction stalled. Adding to the injury, a hoped-for connection on the Rock Island rail line from St. Louis to Kansas City failed to materialize. Railroad officials elected instead to pass through Eldon, a smaller town nearby. Shop owners and others began a reluctant pilgrimage to the railhead there. By 1899, Aurora Springs had a population of 421, but it had already begun its inexorable slide into obscurity.

MONROE COUNTY

Harris Springs

Thomas Harris, who owned a farm a short distance southwest of Middle Grove, noticed something peculiar about springs seeping out on his property near Milligan Creek. In 1886, he contracted for Professor Paul Schweitzer of the University of Missouri to perform the crucial tests. Sure enough, the tests revealed the medicinal potential of the springs.

By 1887, the site had a hotel, but it almost immediately fell into financial trouble, subject to a two-thousand-dollar mortgage. A Moberly man bought the property at a trustee's sale for $428. In 1889, the structure burned.

In the early 1900s, developers constructed a much larger hotel, using lumber salvaged from buildings at the St. Louis World's Fair. This venture became very successful as a self-proclaimed "Fountain of Health." Sufferers came seeking relief from "dyspepsia, scrofula, neuralgia, rheumatism, constipation, piles, poor blood, skin diseases, diabetes, dropsy, nervous prostration, paralysis and female troubles." One of the thirty-four "well ventilated, airy rooms" could be occupied for $1.50 a day. The hotel dining room was always full on Sunday, largely with people from Moberly. Cooks prepared so much food that an icehouse and smokehouse were added. Patrons bathed in tubs filled by the pull of a chain from a metal tank suspended near the ceiling. These tanks, in turn, were filled with mineral water from a pump outside.

Behind the hotel, several bathhouses provided single baths for twenty-five cents each or five for a dollar. On the grounds, campers could pitch tents for fifty cents a week, provisioning from a nearby store. Recreational diversions included a ball diamond, ice-skating rink, and dance pavilion. A large swing that arched over Milligan Creek became a popular attraction.

Sometime after 1919, the old hotel sold and was then torn down. But for years afterward, the shady grove near the creek served as an immensely popular picnic ground. Today, about all that remains of Harris Springs are a few stone foundation pillars and collapsing, brick-lined wells. The springs could not be located.

MONTGOMERY COUNTY

Mineola

The colorful history of Mineola reaches back to a time before the state of Missouri formed. Nathan Boone, son of Daniel, obtained the land containing the mineral springs as part of a Spanish grant in about 1800. Boone reportedly attempted salt manufacture at the springs, but the enterprise failed. At the time, trappers knew the place as Loutre Lick, from the French phrase for "lick of the otter."

By 1815, Boone sold the land to Isaac Van Bibber, whom Daniel Boone had raised almost as his own son from the age of three and who later served as a major in the militia under Boone's son Daniel Morgan Boone. Van Bibber constructed a rambling, two-and-a-half-story tavern and boardinghouse at Loutre Lick that would become a legendary watering hole. It served as a popular way station and roadside landmark on the newly opened Boone's Lick Road, which enabled stage service between St. Louis and Fort Osage, a distance of 273 miles. The zesty personality of Van Bibber, a man of "garrulous and speculative philosophies," contributed to local color. As Major Stephen Long's expedition to the upper Missouri made its way westward, it paused at "Van Bibber's Lick." When Van Bibber told the men a tale of "balls of fire" arising from the ground in the rainy season and attaching to the ends of riders' whips, Long's scientists dismissed the phenomenon as burning coal beds, angering the tavern keeper. Edwin James, Long's scientist, recounted the incident: "We listened with a credulity which seemed rather to disappoint and surprise our host, to his account of the phenomena that had appeared from time to time in his neighborhood." James also described the nearby lick: "There is, in the middle of the creek, a large brine spring. Over this has been placed a section of the hollow trunk of a tree, to prevent the intermixture of the fresh water of the creek."

In 1819, Daniel Morgan Boone settled at Loutre Lick. His father visited, seeking relief for a kidney ailment at the mineral springs. Two years later, as Missouri celebrated its new statehood, citizens held the first Fourth of July celebration in Montgomery County at Loutre Lick. Van Bibber laid in abundant provisions for the celebration, "including whiskey." Later, Washington Irving stopped by with his Swiss countess, remarking that if he ever got rich he would return and "build a fine home" there. And Thomas Hart Benton frequented the place, bragging on his "bethesda" in the halls of Congress in Washington, D.C.

Loutre Lick, for the most part, lost fame for several decades after the Van Bibber era. Presumably, the mineral waters continued to be used medicinally, at least locally. In 1879, Harvey Scanland laid out a town near the springs, originally calling it "Mineral Spring." But two years later, with the establishment of a post office, he petitioned for the name "Mineola," supposedly from an Indian word meaning "healing water." Historians seem to disagree about the derivation, but a 1933 account attests that Scanland later tried to adopt the spelling "Minneola," to honor his daughter Minnie and a family friend, Ola. According to the account, efforts to change the spelling were unsuccessful.

In the summer of 1880, Scanland cleaned out the spring and provided it with an overarching pavilion. He built a large home nearby in the late 1890s. The operation prospered in the first few decades of the twentieth century, with the *Montgomery County Leader* of October 6, 1916, observing: "thousands of gallons are handed out or shipped out to various parts of the state," and here you can "write, eat, sleep, swim, row, fish, hunt or chase the wily fox." For the romantically inclined, "quite a sprinkle of pure-hearted and interesting maiden ladies and handsome widows" frequented the place, but it definitely did not cater to highbrows—"the gay pleasure seekers who come with a hack load of steamer trunks filled with diaphanous gowns and other flimsy arraignment expecting to spend a season in a round of receptions, gliding through the maizy waltz, two-step, tango, fish wiggle or snake twist, had perhaps better unpack elsewhere."

Today, there is not much at Mineola for anyone to do. Just a few miles from the thundering pavement of Interstate 70, the silent spring still pumps out a

Pagoda at Mineola, 1998. *Photo by author*

few gallons of medicinal water under its weathering pagoda, perhaps waiting for the next wave of rediscovery.

MORGAN COUNTY

Versailles Medical Spring

Alum Springs Road, heading southwest from Versailles, leads toward the site of the once-valuable medicinal waters. The Versailles Medical Spring Company, headquartered in Kansas City, purchased the land containing the twenty-five-foot-deep mineral well in 1890. Promoters sent a sample of water to the University of Michigan, which confirmed its medicinal value. The water effected a "remarkable cure" for a severe case of scrofula, but it also benefited diseases of the skin, dyspepsia, sore throat, rheumatism, and catarrh. It effectively alleviated cases of hemorrhoids or "piles," the desired effect being "almost immediate."

The well or spring became locally famous long before commercial bottling began. According to an 1889 Morgan County history, teamsters discovered that "to bathe their horses' shoulders in this water would cure them of any sores."

NODAWAY COUNTY

Barnard Medical Well

At Barnard, a twenty-four-foot-deep driven well served a facility "advertised in 1882 by a joint stock company as a health resort," according to Paul Schweitzer. People who used the water found hotel accommodations in town. Barnard's Dr. Alfred Bear, who had suffered from serious health problems and had tried mineral springs in different locations, had found some relief, but in none, he claimed, "as much as in the mineral water of Barnard." Schweitzer reported that the mineral water business failed, "not possessing adequate improvements."

Burlington Junction Mineral Spring

Samuel Corken came to Nodaway County in 1860, purchasing land just southwest of Burlington Junction. On his land, near a small tributary of the Nodaway River, trickled some springs with suspected medical values. A test by the respected chemists Merrill and Wright of St. Louis quantified the springs' mineral content and confirmed their "rare virtues." Local people began carting off the springwater, and in 1881 Corken built a hotel nearby. A year later, he sold the enterprise to Dr. S. Black, who operated it as a sanitarium under the supervision of Dr. James Evans, a "practical physician." A fourteen-foot-deep well dug into the clays supplemented the small bedrock spring.

In 1900, Samuel Corken's son Elmer and some partners purchased the sanitarium. They enlarged the building, increasing the capacity from thirty-five to fifty guests. The expansive brick structure featured steam heat and a "complete water works." Patrons played croquet on the shady lawn on summer evenings, and a small lake provided fishing and boating "for invalids and pure pleasure seekers." Near the springs there were "beautiful groves for public purposes, or tenting grounds." The owners built a bathhouse with six rooms and a bottling plant producing "Nekroc" water—*Corken* spelled backwards. A case of twenty-four bottles sold for three dollars. Many diseases were supposedly cured, but a pamphlet cautioned, "we do not claim to cure all diseases, for all diseases are not curable."

The place had already declined by the time the hotel burned, sometime after 1914. Today, the area is extensively farmed and it is difficult to find the site of the once-prosperous mineral spring sanitarium, although a line of old cedars may mark the alignment of the entrance road.

OREGON COUNTY

El Dorado Springs

Mineral springs are rare in the rugged, eastern Ozarks, where "sweet," freshwater springs predominate. El Dorado Springs is the only recorded mineral water site in Oregon County, described as a resort by Peale in 1886 and mentioned in Williams's 1904 *History of Missouri*. Information about the site is difficult to find, but Grace Mainprize of Thayer, who was contacted about the site, recalled stories of people bathing in the spring as a treatment for "sore eyes." She located deeds with legal descriptions of El Dorado Springs property dated 1884, 1885, and 1891.

PERRY COUNTY

Lithium Springs

A photograph from about 1917 shows people refreshing themselves at Lithium Spring. In the background a jumble of felled trees provides evidence of a recent tornado. While the twister damaged many of the town's buildings, no one was killed. Apparently, faith in the healing waters also survived.

In 1882, developers laid out the village of Lithium around the "lithium magnetic" spring, one of two known locally for their healing waters. The town blossomed by 1883, when the *Perry County Sun* reported that "our place has taken a boom since the completion of the bath house." The structure had five rooms for baths, providing hot and cold "magnetic" water and "needle shower" baths. The same paper also observed that "every Sunday, all the rigs in town are chartered for the springs." A hotel, three boardinghouses, sawmill, gristmill, and distillery sprang up.

The water, said to be helpful for rheumatism, chronic "sore eyes," and "nervous complaints," received a positive mineral analysis from the laboratories of Washington University in St. Louis. Later, flyers printed by the Lithium Spring Company of St. Louis extolled the spring's "palatable and refreshing" nature, pointing out its desirability as a "table water." A 1925 flyer pronounced it "free from bacterial contamination."

Visiting in 1891, J. D. Robertson of the Missouri Geological Survey saw a little village with about twenty houses around the walled spring. Lacking a railroad connection, patrons could only reach Lithium via stage from St. Mary or Fredericktown, over forty miles of "hilly country." With the coming of the rail line in 1892, bottlers shipped mineral water out in one- or five-gallon jugs. Later, they trucked it to St. Louis. From the texts of various flyers, it appears that the bottled water business lasted at least into the 1930s. In 1965 and 1966, hydrologists with the Missouri Geologic Survey measured the spring's flow at 26,000 and 110,000 gallons per day. It still flows under its attractive little springhouse in the small village, free now for any takers.

Schumer Springs

A postcard from the early 1900s portrays an artist's idealized view of the Schumer Springs sanitarium, a fifty-room hotel with wide, neat promenades enveloping an imposing, symmetrical structure. According to local accounts, the venture flourished in the first decades of the twentieth century.

In 1905, six businessmen from Jackson, Missouri, formed two corporations to develop the spring site into a health sanitarium. They purchased the land from a farmer named Frank Schumer, who suffered from lingering health problems from the Civil War. By 1880, after using the springwater for three years, Schumer found his health much improved. Soon afterwards, people began to camp on his grounds and use the mineral water springs. With sixteen children, Schumer welcomed the financial boost that such a possession provided.

The investment corporations built a forty-room hotel and a sanitarium supervised by a series of doctors. They advertised the waters for dyspepsia, stomach troubles, diabetes, Bright's disease, rheumatism, malaria, and "all conditions where there is deficiency of elimination." By 1908, a post office had been established. Over a hundred cottage lots were platted, water was shipped out in five-gallon bottles, and baths were provided at seven dollars per "course."

There are indications of financial difficulties within a few years of opening. A 1913 account book for the hotel shows operations in the red in spite of respectable occupancy. By the time of the Depression, most of the town had shut down, except for one small store.

Today, only crumbling foundations and a walled spring in the underbrush mark the site of Schumer. The spring itself is interesting, of a rare variety known as ebb-and-flow, whose output varies rhythmically and independently of external moisture conditions. In 1963 through 1965, hydrologists with the Missouri Geological Survey measured the spring's flow at between 6,000 and 258,000 gallons per day.

PETTIS COUNTY

Crystal Springs

Three miles south of La Monte in Pettis County, J. H. Teague platted the town of Crystal Springs in 1887. In the center of town he created Teague's Park, containing the sulfatic mineral spring. Today, the spring issues from a neatly fitted, mossy green sandstone grotto. A 1943 history offered that its name derived from its transparent appearance. When the author visited in April 1998, two inches of rain had fallen the previous evening. Although the small creeks in the area were roiling, chocolate brown, and foamy, Crystal Spring ran clear.

Local author and historian William Claycomb of Hughesville suggested that the venture must not have been very successful, since there is no sign of the village in the 1896 Pettis County plat book.

PHELPS COUNTY

Rolla Artesian Well(s)

The *Rolla Herald* of 1888 hailed Rolla's Aqua Vitae Mineral Water, the virtues of which led one area druggist to discard "Saratoga Waters" in its favor. Promoters advertised the mineral water as "Kenklesha Water," using "beautiful hangers" in store windows and printing up fifty thousand circulars. John Bradbury of the Western Historical Manuscript Collection in Rolla suggested the mineral water business collapsed within just a few years. At least two mineral water wells operated in the Rolla area.

PIKE COUNTY

B.B. Spring

Amos Woodward, visiting B.B. Spring in 1887, found a bathhouse and bottling plant in operation. Four wells served the resort, the first dug being only fourteen feet deep. Woodward estimated the value of the property at eight thousand dollars.

Ephraim Beebee had "discovered" the mineral water the previous year—thus the name, "B.B." Spring. An early brochure for the resort stated flatly that the Epsom salts "spring" water "is not suitable as a beverage, but it is strictly a medicine." In 1899, James Crook recorded that the site did not appear to be "used extensively as a resort," but that the waters were "widely sold in the western states." Eventually, owners built a hotel at the site. A 1905 postcard shows an attractive, tree-lined drive leading up to the B.B. Spring resort. Later, the hotel converted to a hospital, then to a nursing home.

Elk Lick Springs

This spring, located near Spencer Creek in northwestern Pike County, served an early resort of frontier Missouri. Amos Woodward, visiting in 1890, saw a small hotel and "a few summer houses." The spring emerged through a rectangular, curbed basin in the floor of a stone springhouse.

Elk Lick, however, operated as a popular resort long before the Civil War. Alphonso Wetmore, in his 1837 *Gazetteer of the State of Missouri,* noted that "Elk Lick has attained some celebrity for its medical properties, and is a place of resort for persons afflicted with various infirmities. This spring, when better known, will probably become a place of resort for the gay and fashionable world, as well as the afflicted portion of the human family." The resort still thrived in the late 1840s, when the *Hannibal Journal* advertised rates of four dollars a week. Owners and managers changed many times over the next several decades. In 1901, the Elk Lick post office closed and the next year, 117 acres containing the spring, residence, and hotel were sold at public auction.

Louisiana Artesian Well

At first glance, there appears to be no evidence of the artesian well that once jutted from the ground at the corner of Fifth and Kentucky streets in Louisiana. But if one looks carefully, a tile coming from that direction can be seen in the walled bank of Town Branch, nearby. In the water flowing from that pipe, long white strands of algae or bacteria grow, and the distinct odor of hydrogen sulfide (rotten-egg smell) wafts up, both telltale signs of a mineral water (among other possibilities). Louisiana resident Robert King pointed out these facts and recalled that the well casing could still be seen in 1957, when a clinic operated at the site.

The artesian well, nicknamed the "Therapeudor," was drilled in about 1886 to a depth of 1,275 feet and contained 910 feet of casing. Amos Woodward, visiting in 1890, observed that the flow "appears inexhaustible." In 1907, Edward M. Shepard, in *The Underground Waters of Missouri,* described well water "clear and sparkling and bubbling with gas," which "corroded the rock basin into which it empties."

There is a long history of medical use for the mineral water well. Woodward wrote of the sanitarium operated by J. J. Blackwell in 1890, offering "at moderate expense" the "usual comforts for bathing" and "experienced medical treatment." In addition, a bottling plant routinely shipped water to St. Louis.

In 1931, Dr. George Bilyea opened the Mineral Spring Sanitarium, a two-story building with a swimming pool at the rear filled with "clear, icy blue" mineral water and a flowing fountain in front, where patrons filled jugs with drinking water and "the finest eye wash to be found." Maintenance of the pool and fountain proved to be a headache because the aggressive mineral water quickly corroded the pipes. Dr. Bilyea eventually opened the upstairs as a hospital and took up surgery. Finally, the building was torn down and the lot sold. Apparently, the well was capped off and the flow diverted underground into Town Branch.

Mineral Springs

The flow of this "spring" was apparently produced from an artesian well originally drilled for oil in about 1920. According to Roberta Hagood of Hannibal, the resulting Mineral Springs Park hosted picnics, camping, dances, and 4-H camps.

PLATTE COUNTY

Crystal (Tiffany) Springs

A photograph in Paul Schweitzer's *Report on the Mineral Waters* shows Crystal Springs flowing in a shady glen traversed by a narrow walkway. Promoters claimed the spring, issuing into a small, sandstone canyon, benefited rheumatism, constipation, and sore eyes.

The area was known as Artesian Springs in 1888, when Mortimer Park owned the land and springs. By 1890, the time of Amos Woodward's visit, the area had also come to be known as Crystal Springs. Woodward saw only a few private residences near the springs. Sometime later, the property sold to Dr. Flavel Tiffany of Kansas City, who intended to launch a health resort. By the middle 1890s, Tiffany had become very wealthy, living in a mansion at Twenty-fifth and Troost in Kansas City. A 1907 plat of Tiffany Springs included a large hotel depicted in the center of the town, with bathhouses and a golf course nearby. But these were never built, and the town never grew beyond a handful of homes, a store, and a blacksmith shop. Today, Tiffany Place, a planned housing development, keeps the place name alive.

POLK COUNTY

Eudora Springs

Eudora Springs, near the old town of Orleans in Polk County, was called Walula by the Osage Indians, a name meaning "medicine water." There, a Bolivar businessman attempted a health resort before the Civil War, but the war stalled his plans. After the war, locals used the Walula spring, and another nearby, named the Congress Spring, for medicinal purposes. The coming of the railroad in 1885 improved access, and four years later, C. L. Allen, a Bolivar businessman, established a resort, calling it Eudora Chalybeate Springs. After the resort's decline, the area continued to be used into the 1930s as a popular picnic and reunion site.

Graydon Springs

The mineral springs at Graydon, a whistle stop along the Frisco Railroad between Springfield and Bolivar, attracted interest from more than the usual suite of health seekers, promoters, and entrepreneurs. They captured the attention of

Springfield's Drury College professor Edward Shepard. Locally, citizens were already well acquainted with the tonic properties of the Twin, Adams, Cary, Alum, and Oil springs. Shepard was especially intrigued by the chalybeate (iron-rich) springs issuing from a massive deposit of "peculiar sandstone." Drury College, with Shepard's help, established near Graydon the Bradley Geologic Field Station, where the unusual geologic conditions and mineral waters could receive proper study. At the opening ceremony in 1903, Missouri's state geologist, Dr. E. R. Buckley, announced that "Drury College is today doing better work in geology than any other institution in the state."

By the time of the field station, health seekers had already begun to lose interest in the mineral springs at Graydon. That story begins about 1840, when George Venable homesteaded near Twin Springs. Locals swore to the medicinal properties of the two springs, discharging within a few inches of each other, yet very different in character. Venable did not develop his property, but when the railroad passed nearby in 1884, interest in the mineral springs heightened.

A man named David Rummel, living with stubborn medical problems that doctors in Ohio were unable to alleviate, moved to Bolivar seeking a change of climate. Acquaintances suggested he try the mineral springs at Graydon. Rummel visited and with a partner purchased an acre of land around the Twin Springs and built a two-story hotel in 1888 or 1889. At about the same time, two other investors, F. W. Adams and H. P. Cummings, bought land near Rummel's and also started a resort.

Prior to 1898, many visitors to Graydon made a day trip from Springfield and back, since the rail line terminated a short distance north of Graydon Springs. When the line was completed northward to Kansas City, the potential geographic base for the resort's clientele greatly expanded. In spite of this, visitation to Graydon began to decline shortly after the turn of the century. The last really big event at Graydon was the Fourth of July celebration in 1912.

Today, Graydon Springs is a ghost town on the abandoned rail line, but it is destined to become a different kind of tourist destination when the Ozark Greenways rails-to-trails project is completed. The only signs of the whistle stop, other than the sign itself, is a vine-covered ruin, once the Acuff store, along the right-of-way. Venable Spring and the Twin Springs still flow, now part of a youth camp. And some of the fieldstone buildings and walls from the Bradley Geologic Field Station remain, providing testimony to the unique geology and mineral waters in this remote corner of Polk County.

RALLS COUNTY

Spalding Springs

The colorful history of Spalding, like that of Boone's Lick, stretches back to the eighteenth century, before the area was even part of this country. Before the arrival of Europeans, animals licked salt deposits at this spring, and Indians hauled the briny crusts back to their villages. In 1792, a Frenchman named Maturin Bouvet acquired the property containing the salt lick from the Spanish government. Bouvet and his hired crew began boiling down the brine to make salt. The clarified springwater was dipped from hollow logs, or "gums," sunk into the mud. Bouvet attempted boat transportation to St. Louis, but due to the shallow water of the Salt River, he soon abandoned this route for overland travel. The saltworks operated only in summer. During the winters, Fox and Sauk Indians, resenting the intrusion, destroyed the operation. Bouvet himself may have been killed during an Indian attack on his settlement at Bay de Charles in 1805.

The saltworks ran intermittently until 1821, when Missouri achieved statehood. A "saline provision" in the legislation that allowed the state to form set aside twelve mineral springs and surrounding lands for the state's use, although the lands were usually leased to individuals. William Muldrow acquired a lease at the Bouvet lick and began drilling an artesian well for brine. Billed for the drilling work, the state required Muldrow to go deeper, to more than three hundred feet, a considerable depth in 1823. According to Edward Shepard, who wrote in 1907, workers attempted to "case this well with wooden tubing, but the pressure was too strong." Alphonso Wetmore, in his 1837 *Gazetteer of the State of Missouri,* marveled, "it is a remarkable fact that in this boring Mr. Muldrow carried his augur through sixty feet of solid rock salt, which he found on trial fit for the use of the table."

Muldrow's salt netted two dollars a bushel. He eventually sold his interests to a Mr. Trabue, who worked the salt business for ten more years. But production costs kept rising as salt prices fell, resulting in the curtailment of Trabue's salt production by about 1840.

During the 1850s the lick became a popular picnic site. In August 1852, a commentator in the *Hannibal Messenger* pronounced the water at Trabue's Lick "quite palatable," resembling the "far-famed, Blue Lick waters of Kentucky." The establishment of a health resort, the writer ventured, would "offer the seekers of health and pleasure equal inducement."

Spalding Springs development. Schweitzer, *Report*

That dream was finally realized in 1883. Robert Spalding moved to the area in 1848 and acquired the springs and four hundred surrounding acres. He almost certainly knew of the success of nearby Elk Lick Springs, which attracted thousands of guests annually by the 1850s.

In 1884, Spalding completed a three-story hotel, a "good, substantial, well-ventilated house containing twenty-three rooms, and conveniently arranged," with a veranda on two sides and furnished "from top to bottom, in the latest style," from a dealer in Paris, Missouri. Twin cisterns outside the kitchen supplied water for the hotel. A dam constructed below the mineral spring overflow created a small lake. One visitor remarked that swimming in the sulfurous waters made one "immune" to chiggers. In the center of the lake, a hexagonal pagoda provided shelter for "quiet conversation." Patrons would dip water from a tile set at the wellhead, where water bubbled up with "great force from a depth of 300 feet." Users claimed benefits for stomach and kidney ailments. In addition to their healing virtues, the waters were very corrosive. Nails in the springhouse floor rusted very quickly and white deposits accumulated on wooden surfaces.

There were several cottages, a church, a school, a dance hall, bathhouses, and a twenty-five-by-fifty-foot swimming pool. At one time two stores did business, the upstairs of one converted to a popular dance hall, requiring the ceiling downstairs to be "propped up with poles."

The resort became very popular, attracting many visitors from St. Louis and Hannibal. One of the most popular events, the "Third Sunday in June" picnic (an outgrowth of the earlier "saline days"), occurred when the "chickens and the chiggers got big enough." One such picnic in 1887 attracted a crowd estimated at three thousand, complete with brass band. The rising popularity of the automobile coincided with a gradual decline in visitation at Spalding. Picnics, however, continued to attract big crowds, and a dance hall, built in 1930, was immensely popular. The old hotel survived into the 1920s but gradually fell into disrepair and then decay. In 1963, it burned while being demolished for salvage.

Today, the town of Spalding is only a shadow of its former self, although the spring, wellhead, lake berms, and several foundations remain, along with the wooden posts that supported screening for the ladies' swimming area. Given the rich history of the site and its prominence as a regional resort, preservation and perhaps restoration would certainly seem warranted.

RANDOLPH COUNTY

Radium Spring

At the dawn of the twentieth century, the public marveled at the newly discovered, mysterious power of radioactivity. Detected in certain mineral waters, these emanations were also thought to account for previously unexplained medicinal properties. "Radium" and "radio" springs abounded across the country.

In Randolph County, visitors were invited to "bathe in the liquid sunshine" at Radium Spring, a mineral spring of "rare medical value" discovered on the outskirts of Huntsville. The state chemist confirmed the presence of "radium emanations." Luckily, a group of local businessmen with "rare judgement and commendable patriotism" formed a stock company in about 1909 and purchased the spring and surrounding land, providing a park but also protecting the "filter beds" of the spring from "drainage and other contamination."

A city "booster book" from 1910, designed to interest "foreign capital in the development of the springs," called for the construction of hotels and sanitariums. Developers did build a bathhouse with six rooms and "modern porcelain tubs," and, pending development of a hotel, guests were "delightfully entertained in private homes." Finally, in downtown Huntsville the Radium Hotel was built. Today, the springs can no longer be found, and the old hotel was long ago converted to apartments.

Randolph Spa

W. A. Skinner of Huntsville owned this mineral water well, six miles north of Huntsville in "one of the most beautiful and picturesque portions of Randolph County." A hotel, open six months of the year, treated visitors for rheumatism, indigestion, and kidney disease. In 1890 Amos Woodward observed that in August the flow of the well "almost stopped."

Randolph Springs

Sometimes called Salt Springs, Randolph Springs, a veritable mineral water smorgasbord, featured a deep sulfur well, shallow alum well, and saline and chalybeate springs, all clustered within a small area. Settlers "discovered" the site of the original salt lick in 1818 or 1819 by following an old buffalo trail. In about 1822, Dr. William Fort, Thomas Goreham, and John Honey operated a crude saltworks at the site, supplying a relatively wide market. Locals also used the springwater, it "being a fine laxative." In the 1840s, Randolph Springs became one of the state's major salt production sites.

W. T. Rutherford owned the property by 1866. He organized the Randolph Petroleum Company to explore for coal oil. A horse-powered drill, set up at the salt lick, struck nothing until reaching a depth of seven hundred feet, when the driller "smelled oil." This spurred the investors to sink another five thousand dollars into the project, and boring continued to 969 feet, when mineral water, but no oil, gushed out. The outflow, where it ran, left thick whitish deposits of sulfur. Rutherford and partners chose not to develop the site as a resort. Instead, they sold the land to John Davis, who built bathhouses and advertised saltwater baths in 1873. He changed the name to Randolph Springs.

In 1880, Davis sold the property to Bernard and Henry Horton, who altered the name to Randolph Medical Springs. The Hortons further excavated the salt spring in an attempt to increase flow to the bathhouses. They advertised the salt and sulfur water as treatments for dyspepsia and stomach and kidney conditions and the alum water for sore eyes and piles. The brothers added many appurtenances, including two hotels with a total of forty-seven rooms. An itemized

Ruins of bathhouse, Randolph Springs, Randolph County, 1998. *Photo by author*

travel bill from 1882 shows an entry for board at Randolph Springs of seven dollars for a week. Nearby were private residences, a baseball diamond, and dance pavilion.

In 1905, the Hortons sold the sixty-five-acre tract containing the springs and various structures to local businessman Charles H. Dameron, "a young man of great business tact and enterprise," who had financial interests in levees and a fine winter home in Louisiana. Dameron spent a small fortune improving the Randolph Springs hotels, building a dance hall and constructing a water and electric plant to serve the premises. He made sure the springs were again widely publicized. A 1910 circular, for example, bugled the usual suite of virtues for mineral waters—"the finest in the state or nation for drinking, bathing and medicinal purposes"—and contained the pronouncements of "eminent physicians." But things turned sour for Dameron within a few years. His own health began to decline at the same time that he suffered losses at his businesses in Louisiana. He sold the operation in 1920, but the new owners failed to make a go of it and it soon folded. The furniture and fixtures from the hotels sold in 1931 at public auction.

Today, the lakes formed as part of the resort venture remain, as do a significant number of ruins, including portions of the bathhouse and well house. Although the 1941 WPA guide to Missouri stated that "the largest spring still flows," it is difficult today to locate any spring flow.

RAY COUNTY

Mineral City

Mineral City, earlier known as Frog-eye, flourished as a sort of health resort for a few years in the early twentieth century. In 1903, Steve Mullen, an "ordinary farmer," began drilling for water on his farm northwest of Richmond. Drillers encountered deposits of coal and oil, which, though causing excitement initially, proved to be very minor. Instead, at two hundred feet, drillers hit a strong flow of mineral water, of a soda-saline variety. Neighbors began using the medicinal water and hauling it home in jugs. As word of the find spread, Mullen erected a small building over the wellhead and hired a man to pump the water.

Mullen envisioned another Excelsior Springs, which was already very successful by this time. Mullen's son drove a hack with the word *Mineral* painted on the side to pick up passengers at the railhead, making several trips a day.

By 1908, Mullen had obtained the services of a local attorney, who also became a partner in the new resort venture. They surveyed and platted the land as "Mineral City." Their plans included a bowling alley, rodeo arena, and ball diamond, which were built, and a fine hotel, which was not. Instead, people would camp in tents on the surrounding grounds. Mullen even let some patrons use his home bathtub, a rare luxury in those days. Many food concessions set up, along with amusements such as a dunk tank and a stand where people hurled rotten eggs at a man's head poking through a hole. Mineral water sold by the barrel, bringing twenty-five cents a gallon in Memphis. In 1912, near the peak of popularity, witnesses recalled that from seven to ten thousand people attended a picnic.

Mullen's dreams never came to full fruition; his legacy was instead a colossal debt. He died in 1914, and before long the "city that was not a city folded its tents and silently slipped away." Dorothy Pike, in the 1959 issue of *Ray County Reflections,* described a visit to Mineral City, wistfully lamenting, "in my mind's eye, I could see the throngs of people on the hillside, enjoying a Sunday afternoon back in 1912, and I had an empty feeling, as if a giant hand had swooped down and removed a city from the face of the earth."

St. Cloud

In about 1880, Samuel Settle "discovered" a mineral spring on his farm a few miles northwest of Richmond. The next year, he sold some of his land containing the spring to the newly established St. Cloud Springs Company, of which he was a partner, to establish and promote a health resort. The owners platted 214 lots and built a two-story hotel, a saloon, summer cottages, and a bathhouse where patrons could enjoy mineral water or mud baths. They preserved three acres of land surrounding the spring as a park. At the spring, they sunk a tile into the ground to collect and convey the clarified water into a galvanized overflow trough. They also fashioned a large stone apron around the spring, a sort of patio where health seekers could relax and sip the waters.

At the peak of St. Cloud's popularity, trains unloaded and loaded passengers four times a day at the railhead. Many visitors came from Richmond and St. Joseph, some staying in tents on the grounds for weeks. The Maple Leaf Hotel, set amid a grove of large maple trees, provided fine dining and ballroom dancing. But by the late 1880s, the resort suffered financial troubles, and then the hotel burned in 1890 "after a night of revelry which had been intended to revive the town." Even then, locals continued to use the area as a park and picnic ground. In later years, the creek at the site changed course, engulfing the spring.

ST. CLAIR COUNTY

Appleton City Well

Promoters discovered the health-giving properties of this thirteen-hundred-foot-deep well about 1900. They claimed the waters would relieve gout, rheumatism, and liver, skin, and kidney diseases. According to Paul Eye, longtime resident of Appleton City, passengers on the train running from Nevada to Sedalia

Pagoda at Appleton City Well, St. Clair County. *State Historical Society of Missouri, Columbia*

could buy a five-cent paper-cupful of water at the pagoda near the depot. The outline of the pagoda is still visible.

Iuka Spring

Schweitzer reported this spring to be "slightly chalybeate" and noted that even though it looked neglected, "considerable money has been spent on the spring and its surroundings." Locals called the area Boot's Mill, then Blakely's Mill. J. W. Wheeler, who granted land for a town in 1887, reportedly named the spring after an Indian. Today, no structures remain, but one can see evidence of a low dam downstream of the spring.

Monegaw Springs

Monegaw Springs is today a quiet village at the end of a curving St. Clair County blacktop road. When Truman Reservoir is very low, one can still see the springs welling up in the mudflats along Little Monegaw Creek, just below the town. Many years ago, on the bluff rising just to the north of the springs, stood one of the first hotels in this part of the country.

It is appropriate that a resort with the fame of Monegaw should abound with legends, and it does. Some claim that *Monegaw* derived from the name of an Osage chief and means "owner of much money." Supposedly, other Indians applied the name after the chief found a cache of Spanish silver. According to the story, a dying Spaniard—the last of a group slain by Indians—upon returning for the cached treasure, had disclosed the booty's location to Monegaw.

Monegaw was described as tall, strong, and of great intellect. It would have been difficult, according to one historian, to have found a "nobler Indian, or a better specimen of manhood than the celebrated chief." In a sad epithet to the story, Chief Monegaw, realizing the inexorable nature of the onslaught of white settlers, told his braves to depart to the west and then starved himself to death in a cave. No one knows for sure how much, if any, of this story is true, or whether Monegaw even existed.

It is known with some certainty that the first white settlers at Monegaw—the Applegate family, who arrived in 1834—built a cabin and mill. The newcomers initially referred to the place using a name given it by French trappers that meant "stinking waters." In about 1850, according to historical accounts, Congress sent out "medical experts" and "scientific men," who pronounced the Monegaw waters to be among the most medicinal in the United States. Although these sources specifically state that the men came from Washington, the author could not find corroboration for this statement. It is possible that the historians were actually referring to investigators with the state's Geological Survey, who visited the springs in the early 1850s.

There were 102 springs, the story goes, all within a small area, "each being different than the others." There were springs of "black, white and yellow sulphur, chalybeate and pure water." Neighbors claimed quick cures for rheumatism and dyspepsia "of years' standing."

By about 1852, entrepreneurs had constructed a three-and-a-half story log hotel on the bluff overlooking the springs. The resort became widely patronized and, according to one estimate, four hundred people lived in the area by 1856 or 1857. A later historian, comparing the waters to Eureka Springs, believed that Monegaw would have been patronized as much as that famous resort, "but no railroads, no telegraph, no bridges, no road, in fact," connected to the place, the people of St. Clair County not having "made the most of their opportunities."

The Civil War played havoc with Monegaw, as it did with much of St. Clair County. Ruffians pillaged and burned the town of Monegaw, as well as nearby

Log hotel at Monegaw Springs, St. Clair County, ca. 1908. *State Historical Society of Missouri, Columbia*

Warsaw, but they spared the old hotel. The spa business went idle for a number of years after the war, with public attention diverted elsewhere, such as on the marauding Younger brothers who frequented the area. Cole's younger brother John was killed near Roscoe, just south of Monegaw, in 1874.

By the late 1880s, the resort business flourished again, under the ownership of I. O. Stump of Clinton and H. Allton of Monegaw. Amos Woodward, visiting in 1890, thought Monegaw was "evidently destined to be the prominent mineral water resort of St. Clair County." He described the log hotel with twenty-seven rooms, "built many years ago," and its magnificent view of the Osage River valley. But instead of 102 springs, Woodward saw "about nine," although the valley had flooded at the time of his visit. He also estimated the flow of the most famous of the springs, "Old Black," at 240,000 gallons per day. Much later, in 1963 and 1965, personnel with the Missouri Geological Survey reported flows from that spring of 19,000 and 39,000 gallons per day.

The resort apparently remained popular through at least the first decade of the twentieth century. In 1905, men from Kansas City bought the "Monegaw Club." But the old hotel burned in 1926 and the next year some folks talked of converting the area into a state park. Today, there are no hotels or other structures near the springs, just a tinge of sulfur in the air, a faint reminder of the almost forgotten legends of Monegaw.

Salt Creek Spring

Also known as Magnolia and Looney's Spring, Salt Creek Spring was described in a St. Clair history as a "white sulphur spring of great medical quality," and "one of the most pleasant to the taste of any of the medical waters in the county." Dr. John Elliott settled near the spring in about 1850, opening a general store and attempting a health resort, which failed "simply because transportation was not to be found except on horseback and in wagons for 25 or 30 miles." In about 1911, Mrs. C. A. Mitchell coined the name Magnolia.

Taberville Spring

In 1892 Paul Schweitzer referred to a "large, fresh water spring" in Taberville that was "much resorted to during the summer." A local history, however, maintained that when Milton Heath donated five acres to the church in Taberville, there were "several fine sulphur springs upon it" and that the acreage was "reserved for a park and pleasure ground." The descriptions may or may not be of the same site. Today, Taberville Spring wells up from a tile set into low, marshy ground northwest of town. When the nearby Osage River floods, the waters back up over the spring.

ST. LOUIS COUNTY

Belcher's Artesian Well

Constructed in the 1850s, the artesian well drilled to serve the Belcher sugar refinery in St. Louis was, for its time, an engineering marvel—so much so that the St. Louis Academy of Science described the feat in detail in 1857, the author raving, "few explorations in our city, or even state, excite greater interest and furnish stronger evidence of individual enterprise and liberality." Further, a "work so expensive" (the total cost was about ten thousand dollars), "completed at the expense, not of government, but of individuals ... merits some notice."

The story begins with William Belcher, a Connecticut businessman who moved to St. Louis in 1840 and who, with a Mr. McLean, began operating a sugar refinery. Three years later, Belcher bought out his partner, and the operation soon became one of the largest and most successful refineries in the United

States, for a time cornering the market on refined sugar in the St. Louis area. Belcher, though he amassed a fortune, eventually lost most of his sugar business to eastern competitors.

By 1848 the refinery, searching for an additional, pure source of water, had dug a thirty-foot-deep well. The owners hoped that it would collect water infiltrated from the nearby Mississippi River. But the well produced disappointingly hard, basically unusable water. The next year, work began on a drilled well. A nine-inch diameter hole, bored by hand over eighteen months, reached a depth of 249 feet. Beginning in 1850, drillers engaged steam power. At 1,510 feet, they detected the strong smell of "sulphuretted hydrogen." Finally, in March 1854, at 2,199 feet, they completed the well. The Academy of Science's report contains a foldout, cross-sectional illustration of the various geologic strata penetrated by the well beneath the refinery, as well as drawings of the various drill bits, pumps, and tools used to "get broken things out of the borehole."

Though an engineering triumph, the well produced mineralized water of little use to the refinery. The artesian water continuously flowed through a twenty-inch diameter cast-iron pipe bolted to the wellhead thirty feet underground, which conducted it outside the refinery property and into a "common sewer." Here, the mineral waters, flowing "constantly from a pipe at the side of the refinery," were free for any and all to use. *Every Saturday* magazine, in 1871, described the hubbub around the great artesian well of Mr. Belcher, whose name became "connected with the bowels of the earth." At the well, "the most mixed of crowds come to drink or carry away the sulphurous liquid, known all over the city as Belcher's water." It was "served at breakfast in the hotels of the city" and some was shipped. The writer further offered, "I can imagine a sentimentalist as loving Belcher water, not so much for its own sweet sake, as for the manner in which the well perpetuates the Old World fountains, the cool waiting places where female gossip undoubtedly began."

Dr. Joseph Hennerich, an 1887 graduate of the St. Louis Medical College, organized the Belcher Water Bath Company. He built a hotel and bathhouse in 1903 on land leased from the refinery at the northwest corner of Fourth and Lucas Avenues and conveyed water to it by pipe from the artesian well.

Belcher's enjoyed great popularity as a fashionable resort during the first few decades of the twentieth century. In 1927, William Fitch described the hotel, calling it a "modern fireproof structure, with a natural mineral water Turkish bath department," containing "all appurtenances necessary for a modern hydrotherapeutic establishment—mineral water baths, vapor baths, massage, showers,

Taking the waters at Belcher's Artesian Well, St. Louis County. *Missouri Historical Society, St. Louis*

and swimming pool." For many years, he said, the bathhouse enjoyed popularity comparable to the "famous spas of Hot Springs, Arkansas," but then, "like the dowagers and gentlemen who frequented it in its heyday, the hotel began to age and decline."

In 1946, a company spent fifteen thousand dollars restoring the bathhouse. Another renewal of sorts occurred in 1950 when Dr. Leon August leased the bathhouse portion and spent a considerable sum refurbishing it for a men's health club, catering to downtown businessmen. The bathhouse stood until the 1970s, when a parking garage for the Missouri Athletic Club replaced it.

Old Orchard Spring

Ten miles west of St. Louis, "in a magnificent grove of stately trees," flowed the historic Old Orchard mineral springs. Henry Clay built his mansion in 1845 on this estate, called "Old Orchard." In 1927, William Fitch reported that the springwater "enjoyed a local reputation for relief in gastric and genito-urinary disorders." Bottled at a "modern bottling plant" to insure "sanitary handling," Old Orchard Water sold commercially for the first few decades of the twentieth century.

White Sulphur Springs

At the White Sulphur, an early resort of the St. Louis area, famous mountain man William Sublette built a hotel in the 1830s near the spring that flowed into the River des Peres. He had trouble with his managers, and although the springs were frequented by some of the well-to-do of St. Louis, Sublette's venture never achieved financial success.

Eight thousand dollars' worth of improvements made by a Mr. Hawley in 1852 rendered the place a "garden spot of the city's vicinity." A writer for the *Missouri Republican* glibly announced, "citizens who wish to recruit from the fatigues of these warm summer days must take a drive out. A fine repast and a glass of good wine for those who are merely prostrated, medicinal baths and a quantity of sulphur waters for invalids, and plenty of shade and a pure, invigorating atmosphere to all, cannot help but have the effect to draw out crowds."

But before too many years, the encroaching industrialization and urbanization of nearby St. Louis turned the River des Peres into an open sewer. In 1872, the *St. Louis Times* reported that "the cottage and spring have both fallen into bad repute and the odor of one is nearly as bad as that of the other." Three years later, the hotel burned.

The history of the White Sulphur entwined with the nearby village of Cheltenham, settled by Icarians, followers of the French communist Étienne Cabet. The Icarians moved from Texas, to Illinois, to the St. Louis area by 1855. They bought the Sulphur Springs resort and Sublette's stone home in 1857, but epidemics and fevers, blamed on the polluted River des Peres, as well as dissension and financial mismanagement caused most of the families to leave. The socialist experiment lasted only until about 1864.

Today, there is no sign of the spring; even the River des Peres is not visible, flowing in a tunnel under sections of the city. The city diverted much of it into a box to hide its foul nature from visitors to the World's Fair in 1904.

SALINE COUNTY

Blue Lick Springs

Blue Lick, named for the famous medicinal waters of Blue Lick, Kentucky, is a group of mineral springs flowing into Finney Creek just upstream of its confluence with the Blackwater River. Today, the main springs lie within the Missouri Department of Conservation's Blue Lick Conservation Area, which, according to the department's assessment, "contains the best mineralized spring complex remaining in Missouri." The large Blue Lick Spring, described in the *Springs of Missouri,* issues from a nearly circular pool forty feet in diameter. In

Blue Lick Springs, Saline County, 1998. *Photo by author*

the 1970s, the spring had a measured discharge of about six hundred gallons per hour and a dissolved mineral content of 14,600 parts per million. Schweitzer reported in 1892 that Gum Spring, the largest in the area, flowed at three thousand gallons per hour. Although the Conservation Department's map of the Blue Lick Conservation Area indicates three main springs, Schweitzer's map showed thirteen in the immediate vicinity.

According to an 1880s promotional booklet, "hundreds of thousands of bushels of very fine salt" were made at the springs between 1825 and 1850. In 1899, James Crook stated that an extensive saltworks formerly existed at Gum Spring, an "immense salt fountain." During Schweitzer's time, large ditches where salt kettles had been fired could still be seen.

In the late 1880s, Henry Strother and William Walter operated two large bathhouses at Blue Lick. Gum Spring, whose waters "fairly bristled with gases," flowed into two wooden basins, forty feet square and four or five feet deep. There were men's and women's pools, with dressing rooms and enough water circulation ("eighteen-hundred barrels per twenty-four hours") to keep the water "absolutely pure." Following the advice of the circular that "the bath is better fitted than any other means to be a remedy in most cases of curable disease," patrons had to be reminded and urged by attendants to exit the pools at the end of their allotted times.

The owners also shipped mineral waters in bottles and barrels for drinking purposes. A promotional flyer trumpeted that "babies in their second summer brought here and allowed to drink all the water they want from the Blue Lick Spring (which they soon learn to love and cry for), and consequently, as by magic, are instantly relieved of their terrible suffering, so that their mothers may see them laugh and grow fat while cutting their eye-teeth and stomach teeth." Schweitzer, in a scientist's matter-of-fact tone, stated simply that the waters were claimed to benefit kidney and bladder disease, dyspepsia, cholera infantum, diarrhea, and "other troubles."

Along with the bathhouses, a few stores and cottages sprang up in the vicinity. The little village of Blue Lick covered the ridgetop north of the spring valley, near the site of the Blue Lick Union Church, which still stands. At the height of popularity, hacks ran daily to the springs from Marshall, a "flourishing city of five-thousand." Promoters called for "some great, big-hearted, rich philanthropist to build here a $200,000 sanitarium with all the appliances, improvements and conveniences of today." But the dreams at Blue Lick, as at so many other resort hopefuls, blew away like mineral dust on a hot summer wind.

Camp Creek Springs

In 1890, Amos Woodward described these dozen or so sulfo-saline springs converging to form the Salt Branch of Camp Creek, where workers made salt "quite extensively before the war." Flowing from "alluvial clays," the springs frequently changed positions. Today, some of these springs can still be seen, depositing a sulfury white coating on the gravel where they emerge and stimulating the growth of bright green algae downstream of their mouths. Curiously, some bubble up from raised gravel bars in the center of the stream, while others rise directly into the clear water from the sands, gravels, and clays of the stream bottom.

Elk Lick Springs

At the time of Amos Woodward's visit in 1890, the waters of Elk Lick Springs, on Heath's Creek in southeastern Saline County, had been used medicinally for fifty years. By 1890, the site featured a hotel with thirty-four rooms, a dance hall, cottages, and bathhouses—development valued at twenty-five thousand dollars. The "remarkably clear, palatable water" of the main spring reportedly cured indigestion, scrofula, and rheumatism.

Elk Lick is the only site in Missouri where Julian Steyermark, the famous botanist, plant explorer, and taxonomist, in about 1938 identified a coastal plant, seashore salt grass. This "most remarkable native grass in Missouri," Steyermark marveled, "dominated several acres" of the valley below Elk Lick Spring. According to Saline County resident Mark Bellwood, this grass has now been found in other inland locations of the Midwest and may occur at additional mineral spring locations in Missouri.

Grand Pass Spring

A plat book from 1896 marks Grand Pass Spring at the foot of Gilham Road, near the railroad tracks, depot, and water tank. Trains stopped here for water from the "everlasting springs." Residents reported that the main spring, once called "Shaky Spring" because of quicksand nearby, never failed. Paul Schweitzer sampled the spring in 1890, at which time it supplied the town with drinking water. A sign at the spring read, "Ye who drink from the spring shall return to drink again."

Great Salt Spring

The Great Salt Spring must have been an impressive sight in the old days, with its deep, circular white pool, gurgling and boiling with escaping gases, its waters in a "constant state of ebulition." Today, remarkably, this once voluminous spring is difficult to find. Local farmers believe that groundwater pumping and land drainage caused the spring to dry up in the 1930s. About all that remain are some swampy areas, home to cattails, rushes, and spring peepers.

A Saline County history of 1881 maintains that the "White Spring" (the Great Salt), "an hour's drive west of Marshall," was sixty feet in diameter and twenty-five to thirty feet deep. A legend told of a team of thirsty oxen that plunged into the pool, never to be seen again. Amos Woodward, visiting in 1890, measured the spring at only twenty-five feet in diameter, flowing ten thousand gallons per hour, and depositing sulfur for "hundreds of feet along its course." He also observed that the spring's size was "gradually being reduced by the wash from the farmed lands around it." The Great Salt was one of two large springs in the immediate vicinity; the other, Blue Spring, had clear water so "strongly impregnated with sulphuretted hydrogen that it will blacken silver in a few seconds." These springs, according to Woodward, were "undoubtedly the largest of any in the county."

Prior to 1836, salt makers set up several small-scale operations at the springs. Later settlers recalled seeing abandoned tubs and vats scattered about. A man named Jones attempted to make salt commercially using solar evaporation, but he failed "only because of the very limited means of the gentleman who made the attempt." The distances that firewood had to be hauled presented a primary impediment to the ordinary form of manufacturing. Later, when the railroad passed nearby, one commentator noted that "there is no reason why salt should not be manufactured here in larger quantities than at Onandaga, New York," since coal for fuel and shipping would now be economical.

The site never became a health resort, although in 1881 an observer suggested "by a little improvement, invalids and pleasure-seekers could here have the benefits of a sea-bath."

McAllister Springs

Not far from the well-known Sweet Springs, McAllister Springs became another very popular resort. Patrons swam in the mineral water pool clear up until the 1930s. The walls of the concrete pool house remain and the springs still flow, now discharging unimpeded into the nearby Blackwater River. The only clue to the whereabouts of the defunct resort is the name of the Conservation Department river access just upstream: McAllister Springs.

Families traveling up the Lamine and Blackwater rivers by flatboat settled the area in about 1817. They boiled down the springwater to make salt for local use. John McAllister moved to the springs that now bear his name in 1838, but later owners developed the area into a resort, especially the Blair family, who initiated a real boom. They refurbished the existing hotel, constructed a power plant, and piped springwater into new bathhouses, provided with a large boiler for year-round bathing. Hot baths cost a quarter. McAllister also had summer cabins, a bowling alley and billiard hall with dance floor above, a blacksmith shop, a store, a school, and later, a sanitarium for drug addicts. The owners spanned the ravine between the hotel and bowling alley with a 250-foot-long footbridge. A quarter-mile racetrack by the river hosted informal cards or, for a

Bathhouse at McAllister Springs, Saline County. *State Historical Society of Missouri, Columbia*

slower pace, couples could enjoy rowing on the Blackwater River. People camped in tents for weeks at a time, providing the area's nickname White City. Hacks ran daily from Houstonia and Sweet Springs. A plat book from 1896 shows scores of lots laid out on the hills south of the springs.

The three or four springs were of the black sulfur, white sulfur, and salt varieties. For the most part, the water supplied the bathhouses, but a small amount was bottled and shipped. Considered helpful for skin diseases, blood poisoning, rheumatism, and liver and stomach diseases, the water serviced nearby Houstonia in five-gallon jugs, priced at $1.50 a jug and refilled for seventy-five cents.

Numerous flyers circulated to advertise the resort. In 1888, promoters emphasized healthful surroundings: "chills and fever never known to originate here," and "visitors will find here one of the largest and best ventilated ball rooms." By 1911, owners still boasted of good sanitation ("we have perfect drainage and sanitary arrangements"), but recreation was by then pushed more aggressively: "largest, finest and most complete concrete bath house and swimming pool in the west"—as was fashion—"persons wishing to enjoy a plunge in this pool will find on hand at the office the newest styles of bathing suits."

McAllister is one of those sites with something to offer the curious explorer. The old, olive green walls of the bathhouse still stand, and in the weeds lay the

Remains of bathhouse and swimming pool at McAllister Springs, Saline County, 1998. *Photo by author*

rusted remains of pumps, pipes, and other appurtenances. Considering the condition of most of the other former resort sites, the artifacts at McAllister are truly significant.

Sweet Springs

Sweet Springs, the "Saratoga of the West," became an immensely popular resort after the Civil War, catering particularly to southern tastes. This is perhaps not surprising, given that many settlers in the area came from Virginia and Kentucky and that before the war a third of Saline County's residents were slaves. In 1887, the springs gave their name to the town, which before that had been called Brownsville, and prior to that, Clayville.

Although white settlers landed in Salt Pond Township by 1818 and manufactured salt at the springs, the first real development of the water's medicinal potential is credited to Dr. John Yantis, a Presbyterian minister. Yantis was passing through in about 1836 on his way westward, founding churches along the way. His wife, an advanced pulmonary consumptive, paused by the lovely springs, sipping the water, only to find that her health soon became "perfectly and absolutely restored." Dr. Yantis vowed to buy the spring property but another man, "with an eye to the utile rather than the dulce," entered the land before him and built a mill at the spring. Yantis finally purchased the property in 1843, at the exorbitant rate of ten dollars an acre. He opened a school in 1849 where "not a single boy was ever sick enough to take medicine," presumably due to the water.

Dr. Yantis accommodated health seekers, letting people camp at the springs and use the water, even allowing a Colonel Walton of Lexington to erect a boardinghouse there in the late 1860s. Then, in 1871, the railroad arrived at nearby Brownsville, making the springs the "most easily and comfortably reached resort in the state." In about 1874, thirteen men "in private parlors" organized a joint stock company to purchase the springs. The water, analyzed by Professor Litton of St. Louis, proved to be highly medicinal. Brothers Darwin and Leslie Marmaduke invested in 1876 and within a year rebuilt the existing hotel into a fine, four-story structure with a capacity of nearly five hundred guests. They installed slat doors on each room, awnings on each sun-facing window, and "a special view to admit of escape in case of fire." They also laid out and sold lots. Some of the most influential people in the state built cottages there, including the president of the University of Missouri, a U.S. senator, and several judges. Many families spent the summer, often bringing along their servants.

The Sweet Springs resort officially opened in June 1881, with a speech by Colonel John Philips. True to its genteel roots, the resort would tolerate "no vulgar display of ostentatious living and no gambling devices." There were, however, many diversions for idle time. One could sample mineral water while relaxing on a bench under the forty-foot-tall, hexagonal pagoda at the Sweet Spring, one of several springs in the vicinity. Here, a servant in a white coat, operating a windlass, would lower trays of glasses into a spring-filled, five-foot diameter walled basin with a "cemented porcelain bottom." From this basin, the mineral water flowed into a brick bottling plant where workers packaged it in barrels and bottles, at a capacity of fifteen hundred quarts per day.

Sweet Spring itself, gushing from an orifice in the rocky ledge along the Blackwater River (an unusual situation for springs in Saline County, as Schweitzer noted, since most gently bubbled up in low areas), benefited diseases of the kidney and bladder and dyspepsia, "notably a disease of nineteenth century civilization." Further, it proved useful for cases of "nervous prostration, hysteria, paralysis," and for "treatment of the opium habit." J. M. Pelot, a doctor from Brownsville, reported in an 1878 promotional booklet that the water "nearly resembles the King's Well at Bath, England in quantity and character of ingredients."

For fifty cents, one could take a round-trip by hack from Sweet Springs to the bathhouses at salt spring, near McAllister Springs, four miles away. By 1885, there was a "huge pump" at McAllister, now drawing water from St. Mary's artesian well and pumping it four miles to the Sweet Springs through a cedar pipe bound with brass. Much later, farmers occasionally plowed up the remains of this pipeline.

Sweet Springs featured two octagonal bathing pools, each thirty-four feet in diameter and five feet deep, with cemented bottoms and sides. Mineral water flowed through at a rate of two hundred thousand gallons per day, keeping them fresh and sanitary. One pool serviced gents, the other ladies. Certain times were set aside for co-ed bathing and thus the ladies acquired "by this means the useful art of swimming."

The hotel contained a large amusement hall, bowling alley, billiard hall, and shooting gallery, and nearby there were riding stables. Patrons could take a rowboat out on the Blackwater River or, after a low dam was built on the river two miles downstream, travel by steamboat four miles upstream to McAllister Springs. Visitors could take evening strolls along paths illuminated by glass lamps and curving through the manicured grounds, where they could sniff the "refreshing breeze from the great ocean of prairie to the southwest." At the hotel, a band played on the piazza while "Robinson's big bus, drawn by four spotted horses, with its load of newcomers, came rattling around the circular driveway." Governor John Marmaduke spent so much time here during the summer that the resort came to be called the "little capital of Missouri." And the name "Sweet Springs" became so widely known that the citizens of Brownsville in 1887 petitioned to adopt it for their town. Indeed, many outsiders already thought that was its name.

Amazingly, by the late 1880s, business had already begun to decline, partly due to the general financial depressions occurring after the real estate booms of the middle 1880s. The downturn might also have been due, in part, to the rise of competing resorts, such as Excelsior Springs, that were nearer the state's major population centers. In any case, by 1891 the resort enterprise had been partially abandoned and the hotel was converted to the Marmaduke Military Academy, which began its first class in September 1891. For this use, owners upgraded the former hotel building with "appliances for steam heat and ventilation" and "water on every floor." In some ways, the conversion to an academy, with its military bands, balls, and smartly dressed cadets, created a setting "more colorful and enchanting than before." But the enterprise was short-lived. The barracks burned in 1896, in only its sixth year of operation. The academy moved to Lexington, and the Mayfield brothers of St. Louis established a sanitarium with forty rooms in one of the remaining buildings. The Mayfield Brothers Sweet Springs Sanitarium incorporated with fifty thousand dollars in capital.

Shortly before 1920, the bottling works ceased production. The city purchased the land around the springs for a park in the 1920s, and William Fitch in 1927 described a "well-arranged bathing establishment" with a "large outdoor swimming pool." Today, a replica of the Sweet Spring pagoda, built in 1982, stands near the location of the original. Signs denote the area's intriguing history. However, the springs do not flow, or at least they were not flowing at the time of the author's visit. A large pool of water surrounds the artesian well site, but there are no swimmers.

Wilton Spring

About all that remains of Wilton Spring, three miles southeast of Marshall, is a cattail-choked bog nestled in a corner between a railroad embankment and a county road. During the early 1900s, when picnics were popular and the railroad made four daily stops, people could sip sulfur waters at the spring flowing from an "open-sided" springhouse. A band pavilion, a ball diamond, and horseshoe pits added to the recreational enterprise. In 1909, the owner deeded the land and springs to ten local churches. The last big picnics occurred in the 1930s.

SHANNON COUNTY

Welch Spring

Though not strictly a mineral spring, Welch Spring once provided medicinal services. The spring discharges from a cave at the base of a rugged dolomite bluff abutting the scenic Current River. A two-story rock ruin still rises over the cave opening. This is the remains of a structure built in the 1930s by Dr. Christian Diehl of Illinois, who intended to establish a sanitarium for asthma sufferers. Diehl piped cave air, with its supposed healing properties, into patients' rooms on the second floor. The venture never really took off, at least partly because of its remote location. Diehl died in a car accident in 1940, ending the dream of a resort and medical center.

STONE COUNTY

Galena Medical Spring

The owner of this spring, which was located one mile west of Galena, attempted a resort in the 1890s through the early 1900s, but never attracted much business, according to a local history.

Ponce de Leon

Ponce de Leon, the "Fountain of Youth Town," became the largest city in Stone County at the turn of the century, boasting a population of two thousand. Today, there are about fifty residents. In a hillside cemetery a short distance east of town lies the grave of Fountain T. Welch, the man whose vision inspired the boom. His saga echoes the widespread and infectious entrepreneurial zeal evidenced in the last decades of the nineteenth century.

The story opens in about 1880, when Welch, a streetcar operator in Springfield, accepted an invitation from his uncle to come to Stone County on a hunting trip. Game was plentiful, the scenery beautiful, and Welch intended to spend the summer, perhaps already thinking of some way to make a living in this place. In dressing a rabbit, he cut his hand. Later, he washed the inflamed wound in one of the springs along Goff Creek, which he noticed had an unusual taste. By morning, according to the story, the wound had virtually healed.

Recognizing the business potential of such a find, Welch, with the help of Springfield partners, immediately began making plans for a mineral water resort town. They cleared the valley, laid off lots, and built bathhouses. From Arkansas, they hauled rough pine lumber for construction. Until houses were built, health seekers flocking to the area camped in tents or under bluffs. Rumors began to circulate that these springs were indeed the fountain of youth visited by the famous Spaniard—rumors that, if not started by the founding partners, were most likely not squelched by them either. Soon hundreds of houses, a sawmill, a dry goods store, a blacksmith shop, a candy store, and a dance hall had sprung up. Welch's partner, John T. "Peg-leg" Nelson built a hotel and a distillery that utilized mineral springwater to distill whiskey. Oil-burning lights lit the city streets. Within six years of its founding, the population of "Poncie" had reached the two thousand mark.

The downturn, though less precipitous than the boom, was equally profound. Soon after the turn of the century the flow of health seekers to the hotel and bathhouses dwindled. Some attempts were made to resurrect the town, including the opening of a new bank and a tomato cannery just before World War I. But the Depression years slowed business further, and the eventual routing of U.S. Highway 65 some miles from town ended any dreams of major renewal. Today, the sleepy little town remains picturesque in its steep, rugged valley, and the mineral springs still flow. In fact, some of the natives may still attest to their value in promoting good health and long life.

TEXAS COUNTY

Blankenship Medical Springs

A few miles north of Houston, on the road to the Mineral Springs access on the Big Piney River, is the obscure and overgrown site of Blankenship Springs, a once-popular regional resort. Legends of Indian use abound, but the real notoriety began in the 1880s with the purchase of land, including "forty-five springs," by John R. Blankenship.

Blankenship erected a hotel near the mineral springs and built some cottages. He piped the springwater to a bathhouse containing a large, round tub. Among the springs, there were "twins," one "cold" and the other "hot." No vegetation grew around the hot spring, and the mud provided a medicinal ointment. In nearby Houston, hotels were crowded, and the morning rush to the springs was initiated with an early bugle call. Today, a mural in the Houston business district depicts the early town, a bugler, and the road to the springs. But "after a few years of great success," historians tell us, the resort faded away.

The author visited the site in November 1998 with Texas County Clerk Don Troutman and Troutman's father. A small spring near the hotel site, framed with mossy stones, trickled some turbid but inodorous water. The site looked unfamiliar, not at all like the photograph we had seen in a county history book. A wider exploration, however, revealed the place where the photograph had been taken: a bluff and cave along the branch a short distance north of the spring. This may have been the place referred to in the first volume of *Texas*

County, Missouri, Heritage, where meat, milk, and butter were kept, and "superior to anything ever used for that purpose." This was certainly the very place where ladies in long dresses and bonnets and gentlemen in dark suits had posed for a camera over a hundred years ago.

Haggenbush Springs

In 1899, James Crook stated that three springs, "supposed to possess valuable medicinal properties," flowed on the farm of Lee Haggenbush, a half-mile from Cabool, but that "no analysis has yet been made."

VERNON COUNTY

Fair Haven (Conely Springs)

In northeastern Vernon County, not far from the Osage River, is the quiet village of Fair Haven. In the attractive city park, among stately trees, mineral springs issue from sunken concrete basins. Along the branch that runs through

Entrance to Fair Haven, Vernon County, 1999. *Photo by author*

the park, the springs have encouraged the growth of orange, filamentous masses. The park and its springs are about all that remain of the resort of Fair Haven.

In 1885, the landowner J. W. Conely laid out the town of Conely Springs, which "like most places of the sort grew into favor rapidly." A post office was established in 1886. Visiting in 1891, Dr. J. D. Robertson of the Missouri Geological Survey saw a twenty-four-room hotel, bathhouses, and some residences. The main spring, which flowed about one hundred gallons per hour, treated rheumatism, liver complaints, and other chronic diseases. By this time, an artesian well had been sunk nearby to supplement the mineral springs. Owners adopted the name "Fair Haven" in about 1895. A 1926 Bureau of Geology and Mines report mentioned that "the hotel is now closed and the place practically abandoned." A grocery store survived at the village until relatively recent times.

Greene Springs

At Greene Springs, a few miles southeast of Nevada "on a small branch in the prairie," George Greene of Nevada platted a village in 1886. A "good general store and a large hotel" were built, according to the 1887 *History of Vernon County*. Promoters claimed that the spring, enclosed with stonework and covered with a neat pavilion, possessed medicinal properties equaling those of El Dorado.

Nevada Artesian Well (Lake Park White Sulphur Spring; Radio Springs)

The Nevada artesian well served Lake Park Springs, a once-bustling resort and recreational area, now within the southwest part of the city of Nevada. The owner, a Mr. West of Bloomington, Illinois, was "guided by the spirit" to call the place Radio Springs when he purchased it in 1910. Perhaps he bestowed the name in recognition of the recently discovered and mysterious phenomenon of radioactivity, made famous at some of Europe's contemporary mineral water spas.

The centerpiece of the park, the artesian well, spouted from its raised casing eight or ten feet into the air, splashing into a hexagonal walled pool. Edward Shepard, in 1907, observed that in the basin grew "a deposit of white algae, the same as at Clinton." Overflow from the basin filled an "artesian lake of translucent water." In 1891, J. D. Robertson reported that the water had a distinct sulfurous odor, though "entirely palatable," the lake "inhabited by multitudes

Nevada Artesian Well, Vernon County. Schweitzer, *Report*

of excellent fish." In the middle of the lake, accessible by boat, rose a well-groomed island, complete with grandstand. A restaurant and pavilion on the grounds were reached from Nevada by electric railway or over roads "kept in good condition." The original owner of the park, Harry Moore, spent forty thousand dollars in improvements.

All of this began in 1887, when drillers bore a well to reach "oil, coal, or anything, which might be struck." At 750 feet, they found a strong flow of mineral water. In 1926 the well, which originally produced 240,000 gallons per day, ceased to flow. It then "blew itself in" and began to flow once more. In 1927, William Fitch mentioned three springs in the area—"Clear Water," "Iron," and "O-sa-ke-tah"—for which he provided a chemical analysis.

Although the mineral water boom has long passed, the city continues to maintain Radio Springs Park in an attractive condition, providing a fresh reminder of that bygone era and its entrepreneurial spirit.

Zodiac

In a 1924 Lamar newspaper appeared a headline: "Back to Zodiac after Thirty Years." "We cranked our Henry and drove over to the once noted health resort," the author began, though the roads were very rough, "even for Horse

Radio Springs Park, Nevada, Vernon County, 2000. *Photo by author*

Creek." That description holds true today, at least for the last half mile or so, which requires navigation on foot over the old, briar-infested roadbed, skirting caved-in culverts. On the hill rising above Horse Creek, some stone ruins and an assortment of rusted pipes and hardware lie in the brush, scant remains of the old bathhouse and store. At the foot of the hill, from the banks of Horse Creek, some small, oily seeps run in rivulets through the sandy soil, perhaps the last vestiges of the Zodiac springs.

Here, in 1881, Moses Hightower started a small resort. The twelve springs, which issued in a semicircle along the creek, reminded him of the signs of the zodiac. He built a hotel and a "good bath house," which were "liberally frequented during the warm season." A windmill pulled the springwater up the hill to supply the bathhouse. The property was later acquired by S. F. Taylor, portrayed in a 1917 edition of the *Kansas City Star* as a man waiting for his ship to come in, clinging to hope that "mysterious strangers from Kansas or Oklahoma" would discover oil nearby, as they had in those states.

It is easy to see how the site, in spite of its overgrown nature, might have been described as "romantic and picturesque" in 1887, and how "lovers of beautiful natural scenery," could have been "delighted with the views here presented."

WORTH COUNTY

Fairview Mineral Spring (Denver Bathhouse)

Locals "discovered" the medicinal well at Denver after once discarding it. Dug for the use of worshippers at camp meetings, the well fell into disfavor in the 1870s due to its "laxative properties" and the fact that it stained clothes and tainted washed foods. But about 1880, someone observed that the famous medicinal springs in Arkansas exhibited some of the same "peculiar properties."

Townspeople reopened the well, which had been "filled up," and sent samples to chemists in St. Louis, who pronounced the water very similar to that from the famous Eureka Springs, no "impure, useless, or incompatible substance" being found. The fifteen-foot-deep, "completely bricked" well, though productive, was subject to overflow from the neighboring Little Rock Creek but was otherwise ready for service. A Dr. Garrison opened a small bathhouse but soon Drs. W. E. Forden and B. Reagan acquired the operation. They erected a "commodious" three-story hotel and bathhouse with eight bathing rooms in the basement. This "finest bath house in the state" had at its top an observatory, providing patrons with views of the surrounding town and countryside.

In 1905, the brick bathhouse burned and was replaced with a wooden structure. Today, only a low hump of earth in the underbrush and a few scattered bricks and blocks mark the site of the Denver Bathhouse.

APPENDIX

OTHER MINERAL WATER SITES

In addition to the mineral water sites described more fully in this book, there are many more sites that have been mentioned in various historical accounts. These appear below, with the locations noted to township, range, and section, when known, or else described in wording derived from the original source. The general references for these citations are included using the following abbreviations.

C = County, local, or other histories
G = Missouri Geological Survey reports (Swallow, 1855; Broadhead, Meek, and Shumard, 1873; and Broadhead, 1875)
M = Albert Merrell, *Health Resorts and Mineral Springs in the West* (1882)
P = Albert Peale, *Lists and Analyses of the Mineral Springs of the United States* (1886)
S = Paul Schweitzer, *A Report on the Mineral Waters of Missouri* (1892)
W = Walter Williams, *The State of Missouri* (1904)

Adair County
Chalybeate Spring on Hazel Creek P, G
Chalybeate Spring on Hog Creek P, G

Andrew County
IXL Bethesda Well T59N R35W S9 M

Audrain County
Mineral Water n. of Benton City S

Barry County
Excelsior Springs T21N R28W S8 C
Seven Star Springs (Hodo Springs) 6 mi. south of Rocky Comfort S

Barton County
Alum Well	in Milford	P
Alum Well	T32N R29W S3	P
Alum Well	T33N R29W S35	P
Artesian Well	south of Lamar	S
Mineral Water	T32N R29W S3	G
Mineral Well	T33N R29W S3	G
Mineral Wells (2)	at Mr. Comstock's	G

Bates County
Alum Spring	T40N R33W S4	G
Chalybeate Spring	east of Butler	P
Mineral Spring	T40N R29W S22	P
Mineral Spring	T40N R32W S18	P
Mineral Water	T40N R29W S22	G
Mineral Water	west of Crescent Hill	G
Salt and Sulphur Well	T40N R32W S18	G

Benton County
Mineral Spring	near Cole Camp	S

Boone County
Artesian Wells (2)	near Columbia	S
Chalybeate Spring	Columbia	P
College Farm Spring	1 mi. from Columbia	S
John Harris Spring	8 mi. south of Columbia	S
Mineral Waters (3)	south of Columbia	S
Mineral Well	University Campus	S

Buchanon County
Calvin James's Mineral Well	at Easton	M
Jacob's Well	12 mi. south of St. Joseph	M

Caldwell County
Ponce de Leon Spring	10 mi. southeast of Hamilton	M
R. Hawkins Spring	at Hamilton	M

Callaway County
Deep Well	at asylum, Fulton	S

Carroll County
Artesian Well	near Carrollton	S
Mineral Springs	near Carrollton	W
Tootle Mineral Spring	at Hale	G

Cass County
Elliott's Well	Drexel	S

Cedar County
Bethesda Spring	near Stockton	P
Chalybeate Spring	T34N R28W S22	P
Sulphur Spring	near Caplinger Mills	W

Clark County
Sulphur Spring	at Luray	W
Sulphur Springs	along Mississippi River bluffs	W

Clay County
Acme Spring	T51N R32W S17	S
Evans Spring	near Harlam	S
Roger's Spring	7 mi. west of Liberty	S
Schraeder Spring	near Barry Station	S
Thornton's Chalybeate Spring	near Liberty	W

Clinton County
Frost's Spring	T55N R31W S32	S
Lathrop Spring	at Lathrop	M
O. N. Garrett's Spring	Cameron	M

Cole County
Epsom Salt Well	at Elston	G
Hickory Hill Mineral Spring	Hickory Hill	C
Mineral Spring	near Elston	M

Cooper County
Harriman's Sulphur Spring	none given	P

Dallas County
Elixer Springs	8 mi. southwest of Buffalo	C
Excelsior Springs	T35N R18W	C

Dekalb County
Acme Mineral Spring	4 mi. north of Cameron	M

Douglas County
Chalybeate Spring	T26N R14W S31	G
J. H. Elliott Mineral Well	at Ava	M
Olive Spring	Sweden	C

Gasconade County
Bland Sulphur Spring	none given	C

Gentry County
L. M. Chitton's Spring	at Stanberry	M
W. C. Hall's Spring	at Stanberry	M

Harrison County
Chalybeate Spring	near Mt. Moriah	G, S
Crystal Spring	none given	W

Henry County
Bowen Brothers Spring	near Montrose	S
Iron Spring	T40N R25W S2	S
Jordan Artesian Well	T41N R25W S19	S
Peelor Spring	1 mi. northeast Brownington	C

Howard County
Burkhart's Spring	T49N R16W S16	P
Cooley's Lick	T51N R15W S16	G
Lewis Spring	1 1/2 mi. from Glasgow	P
Salt and Sulphur Spring	T49N R15W S33	G
Salt Spring	T50N R15W S34	G

Howell County
Deep Well	Willow Springs	G
Saratoga Springs	3 mi. northwest of Willow Springs	C

Iron County
Mineral Spring	at Annapolis	W

Jackson County
Greenwood Spring	Greenwood	S, G
Hammond's Magnesia Mineral Spring	Kansas City	G
Magneso-Saline Mineral Spring	Kansas City (Kensington and Cincinnati)	S
Twin Springs	Kansas City (3500 Independence Ave.)	S
Union Spring	Kansas City (E. Sixth St.)	S
White Spring	Independence	G

Jasper County
Mineral Water	south of Carthage	S

Jefferson County
Uncle John's Health Water	Kimmswick	C

Johnson County
Chalybeate Spring	6 mi. from Knob Noster	P
Mineral Spring	2 mi. from Knob Noster	P
Mineral Spring	3 mi. northwest of Warrensburg	P
Reed's Spring	T45N R26W S29	C

Knox County
Chalybeate Spring	T62N R10W S12	G, P
Landreth's Mineral Well	Knox City	P, S

Lafayette County
Chalybeate Spring	Lexington	P

Lewis County
Aqua Vitae Mineral Spring	Canton	G
Canton Artesian Well	Canton	W
Ponce de Leon Well	La Grange	S

Lincoln County
Chalybeate Spring	on Bryant's Creek	G, P
Chalybeate Spring	near Louisville	G, P
Copperas (Sweet Sulphur Spring)	T51N R24W S31	P
Crenshaw Spring	near Winfield	S

Livingston County
Butler's Well	Chillicothe	M
Mineral Spring	near Spring Hill	P
Moss Agate Spring	none given	M
Moss's Mineral Spring	T59N R24W S31	S

Macon County
Amos Field's Spring	Macon	M
Patton Spring	near Macon	S

Madison County
John Hahn's Spring	Fredericktown	M, C
Mineral Well	1 mi. east of Fredericktown	S

Maries County
Mineral Spring	1 1/2 mi. from Lanes Prairie	P

Marion County
Artesian Well	Palmyra	S
Chalybeate Spring	west of Sharpsburg	P

Oakwood Artesian Well	at Oakwood	S
Stillwell Mineral Spring	Hannibal	C

McDonald County

Crystal Springs	none given	P
Healing Spring	none given	W
Noel Mineral Water	Noel	W
Sulphur Spring	none given	W

Mercer County

Haymaker Spring	Lineville	G
Iron Spring	T65N R24W S16	G
Walden Cooper Spring	1 1/2 mi. northwest of Half-Rock	C

Miller County

Elixer Spring	2 mi. northeast of Iberia	C
Excelsior Spring	12 mi. south of Tuscumbia	C
Vernon Spring	1/2 mi. east of DeLeon	C

Monroe County

Bowman Mineral Springs (2)	none given	S
Ragland Mineral Spring	near Madison	S

Montgomery County

Farthing Mineral Spring	near Middleton	S

Morgan County

Mineral Spring	south of Versailles	C

Newton County

Bethesda Spring	Neosho	C
Carter and Clark's Spring	north part of Neosho	C
Crystal Springs	22 mi. northwest of Pineville	C
Iron and Sulphur Springs	Neosho	W
Mertin Springs	north part Neosho	C
Mineral Spring	south of Bethesda Spring, Neosho	C
Mineral Spring	west of Neosho	C
Seneca Artesian Water	Seneca	C

Nodaway County

Anderson's Well	Burlington Junction	M
Arkoe Springs	at Arkoe	S, G
Mineral Water	C. W. Impey, at Skidmore	M

Mineral Water	E. C. Wolfers at Hopkins	M
Mineral Water	W. C. McChandliss, at Barnard	M
Red Sulphur Spring	near Quitman	

Ozark County

Chalybeate Spring	T21N R12W S3	G

Pettis County

Pettit Spring	T48N R20W S23	C
Sulphatic Spring	south of Dresden	S

Pike County

Bailey Spring	1 mi. northeast of Bowling Green	S
Buffalo Spring	near Louisiana	P
Crow Springs	near Curryville	S
Davis's Sulphur Spring	none given	P
Fike's Lick Spring	2 mi. from Elk Lick Spring	P
Fonzo Spring	Bowling Green	G
Ford's Spring	on Ramsey Creek	P
Frankford Salt Spring	Frankford	G
Hornet Spring	Bowling Green	G
Ionian Lithia Spring	Bowling Green	G
John Davis's Spring	none given	G
Kal-I-Nat Water	Bowling Green	G
Lindsay's Lick	near Big and Little Ramsey creeks	P, G
Livertone Spring	Bowling Green	G
Merriwether's Epsom Spring	none given	P, G
Mineral Springs	on Buffalo Creek	G
Mineral Water	at Bird Price's, Ramsey Creek	G
Mudlick Spring	near Louisiana/Franklin Road	G
Norton Spring	at J. D. Kinkaid's	S
Steven's Spring	near Bowling Green	S

Putnam County

Bray Mineral Well	near Newton	S

Ralls County

Buffalo Lick	T55N R7W S28	G
Freemore's Lick	T56N R5W S33	G, W
Salt Springs	none given	W
Saverton Sulphur Spring	at Saverton	G, W
Sulphur Spring	T53N R1W S6	G

Randolph County

Chalybeate Spring	at Jacksonville	G, P
Chalybeate Water	northwest of Moberly	S
Given Well	near Moberly	S
Goreham's Lick	none given	G, P
Hammett's Well	near Huntsville	S
Mineral Spring	Pearce's Mill on Moniteau Creek	G
Rucker Well	near Huntsville	S
Skinner Well	near Huntsville	S

Ray County

Mineral Water	at H. C. Garner's, Richmond	M
Mineral Water	at J. L. Faris's, Richmond	M
Mineral Water	at R. J. Clark's, Lawson	M
Sulphur Spring	near Millville	W

St. Charles County

Chalybeate Spring	near Naylor's	G, P
Chalybeate Spring	near O'Fallon	G, P

St. Clair County

Alkaline Spring	T38N R27W S14	S
Chalybeate Spring	none given	W
Chalybeate Spring	west of Osceola	P
County Line Sulphur Spring	none given	W
Crook's Spring	Roscoe township	C
Dawson's Spring	east of Osceola	P
Excelsior Spring	near Appleton City	S
White Sulphur Spring	northeast Jackson Township	C

Ste. Genevieve County

Salt Spring	on Saline Creek	C

St. Louis County

American Spring	none given	G
Manchester Spring	at Manchester Rd. and Highway 141	C
Meramec Spring	near Nasby	P
Mineral Spring	near Benton	S
St. Louis Artesian Well	at insane asylum	S
Windsor Spring	13 mi. from St. Louis	C

Scott County

Mineral Water	none given	C

Stone County
Brown Spring	T26N R24W S12	C

Sullivan County
Chalybeate Spring	T64N R21W S24	G
Chalybeate Spring	T64N R21W S34	P

Vernon County
Chalybeate Spring	T36N R31W S28	G
Ellis Well	near Nevada	P, S
Houtze's Sulphur Spring	T36N R29W S1	G, P
Hunter's Epsom Well	Nevada	P
Sulphur Springs (2)	T35N R29W S16	G

Wayne County
Lick Valley Springs	at Lick Valley	W
Mineral Water	at Brunot	W
Mineral Water	at Patterson	W

Worth County
Chalybeate Spring	near Smithton	P, G

Wright County
Mint Spring	5 mi. northeast of Hartville	P

BIBLIOGRAPHY

Adams, Frank Dawson. *The Birth and Development of Geological Sciences.* Baltimore: Williams and Wilkens, 1938.

American State Papers. *Documents, Legislative and Executive of the Congress of the United States.* Washington, D.C.: Gales and Seaton, 1836.

Back, William, Edward Landa, and Linda Meek. "Bottled Waters, Spas, and the Early Years of Water Chemistry." *Journal of Ground Water* 33, no. 4 (1995): 605–14.

Banta, R. E. *The Ohio: Rivers of America Series.* Ed. Hervey Allen and Carl Carmer. New York: Rinehart, 1949.

Baudisch, Oskar. "Magic and Science of Natural Healing Waters." *Journal of Chemical Education,* September 1939, 440–48.

Bell, John. *The Mineral and Thermal Springs of the U.S. and Canada.* Philadelphia: Parry and McMillan, 1855.

———. *On Baths and Mineral Waters.* Philadelphia: n.p., 1831.

Bennett, Mark, and Frank Parker Stonebridge, eds. *History of the Louisiana Purchase Exposition.* St. Louis: Universal Exposition Publishing, 1905.

Brackenridge, Henry Marie. *Journal of a Voyage up the Missouri River, Performed in 1811.* 1816. Reprinted in vol. 6 of *Early Western Travels, 1748–1846,* ed. Reuben Gold Thwaites. New York: AMS Press, 1966.

Bradbury, John. *Travels in the Interior of America in the Years 1809, 1810, and 1811.* 2d ed. London: Sherwood, Neely and Jones, 1819.

Bridenbaugh, Carl. "Baths and Watering Places in Colonial America." *William and Mary Quarterly* 3, no. 2 (1946): 151–81.

Broadhead, Garland C. "Mineral Springs of Missouri." In *Second Annual Report of the Missouri State Board of Agriculture.* Jefferson City: Emory S. Forster, 1867.

———. *Report of the Geological Survey of the State of Missouri, Including Field Work of 1873–1874.* Jefferson City: Bureau of Geology and Mines, 1875.

Broadhead, Garland, F. B. Meek, and B. F. Shumard. *Report of the Geological Survey of the State of Missouri, 1855–1871.* Jefferson City: Bureau of Geology and Mines, 1873.

Buchanan, Claudius. *The Healing Waters of Bethesda; a Sermon, Preached at Buxton Wells, to the Company Assembled There for the Benefit of the Medicinal Waters, on Whitsunday, June 2, 1811.* London: T. Cadell and W. Davis, 1812.

Campbell, Robert. "Letter to William Sublette" (May 30, 1842). In *Glimpses of the Past*, 8, nos. 1–6: 33, 33n. St. Louis: St. Louis Historical Society.

Carnes, Mark C., ed. *A History of American Life*. Based on a series edited by Arthur M. Schlesinger Sr. New York: Simon and Schuster, 1966.

Christensen, Lawrence O., and Gary R. Kremer. *A History of Missouri: Volume 4, 1875 to 1919*. Columbia: University of Missouri Press, 1997.

Clokey, Richard M. *William Ashley: Enterprise and Politics in the Trans-Mississippi West*. Norman: University of Oklahoma Press, 1980.

Coan, Titus. "Home Use of Mineral Waters." *Harpers New Monthly Magazine* 77, no. 461 (1888): 719–26.

Collins, W. D. "Mineral Waters." In *Mineral Resources of the U.S.: Calendar Year 1920*. Washington, D.C.: Government Printing Office, 1923.

Coombs, Jan. "Rural Medical Practice in the 1880s: A View from Central Wisconsin." *Bulletin of the History of Medicine* 64, no. 1 (1980): 35–62.

Croutier, Alev Lytle. *Taking the Waters: Spirit, Art, Sensuality*. New York: Abbeville Press, 1992.

Cuming, Fortescue. *Sketches of a Tour to the Western Country, through the States of Ohio and Kentucky*. . . . 1810. Reprinted in vol. 4 of *Early Western Travels, 1748–1846*, ed. Reuben Gold Thwaites. New York: AMS Press, 1966.

Custis, Samuel R. Personal Diary. Copy in the Missouri Historical Society, St. Louis.

Davidson, Marshall B. *Life in America*. Boston: Houghton Mifflin, 1974.

Davis, Stanley N., and Augusta Davis. "Saratoga Springs and Early Hydrogeochemistry in the United States." *Journal of Ground Water* 35, no. 2 (1997): 347–56.

de Vierville, Jonathan Paul. "American Healing Waters: A Chronology (1513–1946) and Historical Survey of America's Major Springs, Spas, and Health Resorts." Ph.D. diss., University of Texas at Austin, 1992.

Dole, R. B. "Mineral Waters." In *Mineral Resources of the U.S.: Calendar Year 1913*. Part 2. Washington, D.C.: Government Printing Office, 1914.

Dorsey, Leslie, and Janice Devine. *Fare Thee Well: A Backward Look at Two Centuries of Historical American Hostelries, Fashionable Spas, and Seaside Resorts*. New York: Crown Publishers, 1964.

Drinker, Cecil K. *Not So Long Ago: A Chronicle of Medicine and Doctors in Colonial Philadelphia*. New York: Oxford University Press, 1937.

Ellis, Arthur. "Mineral Waters." In *Mineral Resources of the U.S.* Washington, D.C.: Government Printing Office, 1920.

Featherstonhaugh, George W. *Excursion through the Slave States, from Washington on the Potomac to the Frontier of Mexico*. . . . New York: Harper and Brothers, 1844.

———. *Geologic Report of an Examination Made in 1834, of the Elevated Country between the Missouri and Red Rivers*. Washington, D.C.: Gales and Seaton, 1835.

Ferber, Edna. *Saratoga Trunk*. Garden City, N.Y.: Doubleday, 1941.

Fishwick, Marshall W. *Springlore in Virginia.* Bowling Green, Ohio: Popular Press, Bowling Green State University, 1978.

Fitch, William Edward. *Mineral Waters of the United States and American Spas.* New York: Lea and Febiger, 1927.

Flagg, Edmund. *The Far West; or, A Tour beyond the Mountains.* . . . 1838. Reprinted in vols. 26–27 of *Early Western Travels, 1748–1846,* ed. Reuben Gold Thwaites. New York: AMS Press, 1966.

Flippen, Robert G. *"Drink and Be Healed": A History of Farmville Lithia Water.* Farmville, Va.: R. G. Flippen, 1994.

Fox, Tim, ed. *Where We Live: A Guide to St. Louis Communities.* St. Louis: Missouri Historical Society Press, 1995.

Fuller, Myron. "Mineral Waters: A Review of the Trade in 1905." In *Mineral Resources of the U.S.* Washington, D.C.: Government Printing Office, 1906.

Goodwin, E. J. *A History of Medicine in Missouri.* St. Louis: W. L. Smith, 1905.

Hechtlinger, Adelaide, comp. *The Great Patent Medicine Era; or, Without Benefit of Doctor.* New York: Grosset and Dunlap, 1970.

History of Boone County, Missouri. Cape Girardeau, Mo.: Ramfre Press, 1970.

Houck, Louis. *A History of Missouri, from the Earliest Explorations and Settlements until the Admission of the State into the Union.* 3 vols. Chicago: R. R. Donnelley and Sons, 1908.

Hulme, Thomas. *Journal Made during a Tour in the Western Countries of America.* . . . 1828. Reprinted in vol. 10 of *Early Western Travels, 1748–1846,* ed. Reuben Gold Thwaites. New York: AMS Press, 1966.

Hurt, R. Douglas. *Nathan Boone and the American Frontier.* Columbia: University of Missouri Press, 1998.

Hutchinson, Woods. "Taking the Waters: The Humbug of Hot Springs." *Everybody's Magazine,* February 1913, 159–72.

James, Edwin. *Account of an Expedition from Pittsburgh to the Rocky Mountains.* . . . 1823. Reprinted in vols. 14–17 of *Early Western Travels, 1748–1846,* ed. Reuben Gold Thwaites. New York: AMS Press, 1966.

Kargau, E. D. *Mercantile and Professional St. Louis.* St. Louis: Nixon Jones Printing, 1902.

Krizek, Vladimir. "History of Balneology." In *Medical Hydrology,* ed. Sidney Licht and Herman L. Kamenetz. Baltimore: Waverly Press, 1963.

Kurlansky, Mark. *Salt: A World History.* New York: Penguin Putnam, 2002.

March, David D. *The History of Missouri.* 4 vols. New York: Lewis Historical Publishing, 1967.

McCracken, Mary. "Some Historical Aspects of Well Drilling." *Missouri Mineral Industry News* 9, no. 5 (1969): 61–67.

Merrell, Albert. *Health Resorts and Mineral Springs in the West.* St. Louis: n.p., 1882.

Michaux, François André. *Travels to the West of the Alleghany Mountains, in the States of Ohio, Kentucky, Tennessee, and back to Charleston, by the Upper Carolines.* . . . 1805. Reprinted in vol. 3 of *Early Western Travels, 1748–1846,* ed. Reuben Gold Thwaites. New York: AMS Press, 1966.

Miller, John C. *Groundwater Resources of Saline County.* Water Resources Report no. 26. Rolla: Missouri Geological Survey and Water Resources, 1971.

Missouri Department of Natural Resources. *A Brief History of the Missouri Geological Survey.* Rolla: Division of Geology and Land Survey, 1993.

Missouri World's Fair Commission. *Missouri at the World's Fair: An Official Catalogue of the Resources of the State, with Special References of the Exhibits at the World's Columbian Exposition.* Ed. James Cox. St. Louis: Woodward and Tiernan, 1893.

Moorman, J. J. *The Virginia Spas and Springs of the South and West.* Philadelphia: J. B. Lippincott, 1859.

Peale, Albert C. *Lists and Analyses of the Mineral Springs of the United States.* USGS Reports Bulletin no. 32. Washington, D.C.: Government Printing Office, 1886.

Reniers, Perceval. *The Springs of Virginia: Life, Love, and Death at the Waters, 1775–1900.* Chapel Hill: University of North Carolina Press, 1941.

Roland, Walter, Vivian Roland, J. Hurley, and Roberta Hagood. *Spalding Springs.* Hannibal, Mo.: Ruth E. Foreman, 1990.

Sanford, Samuel. "Mineral Waters." In *Mineral Resources of the U.S.: Calendar Year 1906.* Washington, D.C.: Government Printing Office, 1907.

Schweitzer, Paul A. *A Report on the Mineral Waters of Missouri.* Vol. 13. Jefferson City: Missouri Geological Survey and Water Resources, 1892.

Schworm, William B. "History of Water Supply in the St. Louis Area." 1968. Copy in the Missouri Historical Society, St. Louis.

Searle, Muriel V. *Spas and Watering Places.* Tunbridge Wells, U.K.: Midas Books, 1977.

Secretary of State. *Official Manual of the State of Missouri.* Jefferson City: Office of the Secretary of State, 1899.

Shepard, Edward M. *The Underground Waters of Missouri; Their Geology and Utilization.* Washington, D.C.: Government Printing Office, 1907.

Shoemaker, Floyd Calvin. *Missouri and Missourians.* Chicago: Lewis Publishing, 1943.

Shryock, Richard Harrison. *Medicine and Society in America, 1660–1860.* New York: New York University Press, 1960.

Sigerist, Henry E. "American Spas in Historical Perspective." *Bulletin of the History of Medicine* 11 (1942): 133–47.

Steyermark, Julian A. *Flora of Missouri.* Ames: Iowa State University Press, 1963.

Sunder, John E. *Bill Sublette, Mountain Man.* Norman: University of Oklahoma Press, 1959.

Swallow, George C. *First and Second Annual Reports of the Geological Survey.* Jefferson City: James Lusk, Printer, 1855.

Swanner, Grace Maguire. *Saratoga, Queen of Spas: A History of the Saratoga Spa and the Mineral Springs of the Saratoga and Ballston Areas.* Utica, N.Y.: North Country Books, 1988.

Szabadvary, Ferenc. *History of Analytical Chemistry.* Trans. Gyula Seuhla. New York: Pergamon Press, 1966.

Tomes, Nancy. *The Gospel of Germs: Men, Women, and the Microbe in American Life.* Cambridge: Harvard University Press, 1998.

———. "The Private Side of Public Health: Sanitary Science, Domestic Hygiene, and the Germ Theory, 1870–1900." *Bulletin of the History of Medicine* 64, no. 4 (1990): 509–39.

Trall, Russell T. *The Hydropathic Encyclopedia.* New York: Fowlers and Wells, 1853.

Unklesbay, A. G., and Jerry D. Vineyard. *Missouri Geology: Three Billion Years of Volcanoes, Seas, Sediments, and Erosion.* Columbia: University of Missouri Press, 1992.

U.S. Geological Survey. *Mineral Resources of the United States, 1923.* Part 2. Washington, D.C.: Government Printing Office, 1925.

Valenza, Janet Mace. "Places Lived, Places Lost: Taking the Waters in Texas." Ph.D. diss., University of Texas at Austin, 1992.

Viles, Jonas. *The University of Missouri: A Centennial History.* Columbia: University of Missouri, 1939.

Vineyard, Jerry D., and Gerald L. Feder. *Springs of Missouri.* Jefferson City: Missouri Department of Natural Resources, Division of Geology and Land Survey, 1982.

Walton, George E. *The Mineral Springs of the United States and Canada.* St. Louis: C. Keemle Publishers, 1873.

Weber, F. Parker, "Climatology, Health Resorts, and Mineral Springs." In *A System of Physiologic Therapeutics,* ed. Solomon Solis. Philadelphia: P. Blakiston's Son, 1901.

Wechsberg, Joseph. *The Lost World of the Great Spas.* New York: Harper and Row, 1979.

Weiss, Harry B., and Howard R. Kemble, *The Great American Water-Cure Craze: A History of Hydropathy in the United States.* Trenton, N.J.: Past Times Press, 1967.

———. *They Took to the Waters: The Forgotten Mineral Spring Resorts of New Jersey and Nearby Pennsylvania and Delaware.* Trenton, N.J.: Past Times Press, 1962.

Welby, Adlard. *A Visit to North America and the English Settlements in Illinois, with a Winter Residence at Philadelphia....* 1821. Reprinted in *Early Western Travels, 1748–1846,* ed. Reuben Gold Thwaites. New York: AMS Press, 1966.

Wetmore, Alphonso. *Gazetteer of the State of Missouri.* St. Louis: C. Keemle, 1837.

Wiley, Harvey W., and Anne Lewis Pierce. "The Mineral Water Humbug." *Good Housekeeping* 59 (1914): 107–11.

Williams, Walter. *The State of Missouri.* Columbia, Mo.: E. W. Stephens, 1904.
Works Projects Administration. *Missouri: The WPA Guide to the "Show Me" State.* 1941. Reprint, St. Louis: Missouri Historical Society Press, 1998.
Young, James Harvey. *The Medical Messiahs: A Social History of Health Quackery in Twentieth-Century America.* Princeton: Princeton University Press, 1992.

INDEX

Adair County: springs in, 117, 217; mentioned, 67
Advertising, 78–82, 95, 204; patent medicines, 62; Wyaconda Water, 166–67; mentioned, 69, 73
Akeson Springs, 59
American Medical Association: on efficacy of mineral waters, 95
"American Spas in Historical Perspective," 111
American West, 19, 20, 23
Andrew County: springs in, 217
Animals: adapting to saline conditions, 9; hog cholera, 167; remains of prehistoric, 25, 158–59; and salt licks, 24–25, 29
Appleton City Well, 192–93
Arkansas: spas in, 23, 31, 102; mentioned, 44. *See also* Hot Springs (Arkansas)
Arkansas Gazette, 31, 32
Arnica Springs, 125
Artesian Hotel, *148*
Artesian Park, *109, 148*
Artesian wells, 84–85, *85;* Belcher, 55, 197; defined, 8; "Therapeudor," 107, 183
Ashley, William, 38, 140
A System of Physiologic Therapeutics, 58
Audrain County: springs in, 217; mentioned, 59
Aurora Springs, 173–74
Automobile: and downfall of resorts, 104; and growth of resorts, 73

Baden Springs, 117
Balneology, 11*n*, 88, 109
Barnard Medical Well, 178
Barry County: springs in, 117–19, 217; mentioned, 67

Barton County: springs in, 218; mentioned, 44
Bates, Vicki, 110
Bates County: springs in, 218; mentioned, 44
Bath, England, 14; and Romans, 11
Baudisch, Oskar, 88, 109
B.B. Spring, 182
Beersheba Springs, 20
Belcher, William, 196–97
Belcher's Artesian Well, 196–98, *198;* mentioned, 55
Belcher Sugar Refinery, 42, 83, 196–97
Belcher Water Bath Company, 197
Bell, Dr. John, 12, 19, 21, 54, 77
Benton, Thomas Hart, 35, 79, 176
Benton County: springs in, 119–21, 218; mentioned, 67
Berkeley Springs, West Virginia, 17, 100
Bethesda Springs, 146
Big Bone Lick, Kentucky, 25
"Big Six" of Virginia and West Virginia: in colonial times, 77; Hot Springs, 18; Red Sulphur Springs, 18; Salt Sulphur Springs, 18; Sweet Springs, 18, 101; Warm Springs, 18, 102; White Sulphur Springs, 18, 101
Bilyea, Dr. George, 107, 183
Black Sulphur Springs, 119
Blankenship Medical Springs, 210–11
Blue Lick, 115
Blue Lick Conservation Area, 199, 200
Blue Licks, Kentucky, 19; and buffalo, 24
Blue Lick Springs, *22,* 199–201, *200;* mentioned, 59
Blue Lick Union Church, 201
Bockert Mineral Water, 93

→ 233 ←

INDEX

Bockert Springs, 157–58
Boggs, Lilburn, 41
Boling Spring, 119, *120*
Bonanza Spring, 122–23
Bond, Thomas and Phineas: survey, 16
Boone County: springs in, 122, 218; mentioned, 31
Boone family: Daniel, 27; Morgan, 27, 176; Nathan, 27–28, 175; salt-making operation, 150–51
Boone's Lick (Booneslick) 28, *29, 30,* 38, 150–52; Boone's Lick Spring, 9; salinity of, 9; mentioned, 32, 84
Booneslick Road, 28
Booneslick Salt Manufacturing Company, 151
Boone's Lick State Historic Site, *26*
Boonsborough, Kentucky, 27
Boonville Advertiser, 141
Boonville Bulletin, 140
Boonville Eagle, 140
Boston Gazette, 54
Bottled water: in Carrollton, 124–25; in El Dorado Springs, 127–28; in Excelsior Springs, 108, 137; Gum Spring, 200; as an industry, 23, 45, 60, 75, 89–98; Lithium Springs, 180; and municipal water systems, 93–94; national production of, 92; Old Orchard Water, 198; revival of, 112; at St. Louis World's Fair, 90, 91, *93*
Bouvet, Mathurin, 27, 186
Bowsher Mineral Spring, 172
Boyle, Robert, 14, 53
Brackenridge, H. M., 26
Bradbury, John, 31, 83
Bradley Geologic Field Station, 185
Bratton Spring, 122
Broadhead, Garland, 27*n*; on salt springs, 33; as state geologist, 43–44
Brunswick Mineral Well, 131–32
Buchanan, Reverend Claudius: on mineral waters, 12
Buchanon County: springs in, 218
Buffalo Lithia Water, 96
Burlington Junction Mineral Spring, 178
Bush Hotel, *130*

Cabet, Etienne, 37
Calcium magnesium carbonate, 4
Caldwell County: springs in, 122–23, 218; mentioned, 67
California: spas in, 23
Callaway County: springs in, 218
Camden County: springs in, 123–24; mentioned, 67
Campbell, Robert, 36
Camp Creek Springs, *6,* 201
Capone, Al, 134
Carroll County: springs in, 124–25, 218
Carrollton Mineral Waters, 124–25
Cass County: springs in, 125, 219
Cedar County, *2, 15, 116, 128;* springs in, 125–31, 219; mentioned, 67, 80
Cedar Springs, 125–26
Century of Progress Exposition (Chicago), *15*
Chariton County: springs in, 131–32; mentioned, 67
Chattanooga Shale, 118
Chautauqua movement, 72, 162
Cheltenham Springs (Sulphur Springs), 43
Chemical analysis of mineral waters, 14, 80–82
Chicago: Century of Progress Exposition, *15*
Chicago World's Fair: and bottled water, 90; Mooresville Water, 167
Chittum, Matt, 144
Cholera, 20, 61
Chouteau, Auguste, 140
Chouteau, Pierre, 38, 140
Chouteau Springs, *13, 39,* 39, 139–42, *141;* noted in first geological survey, 43; mentioned, 71
Christian County: springs in, 132–33; mentioned, 67, 108
Civil War: effect on resorts, 21; effect on state geologic survey, 43; troops destroying saltworks, 32
Clark, Julia, 101
Clark, William, 26, 101
Clark County: springs in, 219
Clark Sulphur Spring, 119–20
Classification of waters, 49, 54
Clay, Henry, 35

Clay County: springs in, 133–38, 219; mentioned, 46, 67
Climax Springs, 50, 123–24
Clinton, DeWitt, 79
Clinton Artesian Well, 147–49
Clinton County: springs in, 138–39, 219; mentioned, 67, 72, 104, 108
Clinton Natural Gas Development Company, 147
Cloe, Douglas, 118–19
Coan, Dr. Titus, 91
Cochran, Dr. John, 146
Colbern (Electric) Springs, 160–61
Cole County: springs in, 219
Collins, W. D., 97
Colonial America, 16–17; bathing in mineral waters, 77; and bottled water, 89; mentioned, 100
Colorado, spas in, 23
Columbia, Missouri, 47
Columbia Chalybeate Spring, 122
Common Sense and Health, 95–96
Coneley Springs, 211–12
Connate: defined, 5, 6
Conner O. Fewel Wildlife Area, 149
Cooper County: springs in, 139–42, 219; mentioned, 28, 39, 43, 67
Copeland, Senator Royal S., 87
Corken family, 178–79
Crawford County: springs in, 142; mentioned, 56, 67
Crescent Hill, Missouri, 44
Cruce family, 127
Crystal Springs, 143, 181
Crystal (Tiffany) Springs, 184
Cuming, Fortescue, 24, 25
Cure-All Springs, 154
Cusenbary Spring, 155–56
Custis, Samuel, 37
Custis, Patsy, 100

Dade County: springs in, 143; mentioned, 67, 108
Dallas County: springs in, 219
Dameron, Charles H., 190–91
Daviess County: springs in, 143; mentioned, 67

Defoe, Daniel, 69
Dekalb County: springs in, 219
De Laclede, Pierre, 38
De Lauriere, Charles, 27
Denver Bathhouse, 215
De Soto, Hernando, 19
Diehl, Dr. Christian, 208–9
Disease: cholera, 20, 61; germ theory of, 105–6; helped by Missouri's mineral waters, 57; modern theories of prevention, 56
Dixon, Dr. J. C. B., 154
Dixon (Cure-All) Springs, 154
Dole, Dr. R. B., 94
Douglas County: springs in, 219
Drennon's Lick, Kentucky, 20

Eau de Vie, 132–33
El Dorado Springs, 2, 15, 116, 126–29, *128,* 179; and advertising, *80;* and Cruce family, 127; mentioned, 7, 75, 99, 116
Electric Springs, 160–61
Elk Lick Springs, 10, 39, 182, 202
Elms Hotel, 134, 136
Erie Canal, 31, 32
Eudora Springs, 184
Eureka Springs, Arkansas, 101
European spas: American colonists buy bottled water of, 89; compared to American, 88, 97; compared to Missouri's, 50; doctors prescribe therapy at, 112; taste of water at, 76
Everybody's (magazine), 95
Every Saturday (magazine), 197
Excelsior Springs, *46, 58, 64,* 99, *100,* 133–38, *135;* attempts to control withdrawal of water, 85–86; bottled water at, 108, 137; decline of, 109–11; Elms Hotel, 134, 136; Hall of Waters, *64,* 134; revives, 111, 137; Snapp's Hotel, *111;* mentioned, 75, 83
Exploration: gas, 147; oil, 84, 213

Fair Haven, 211–12, *211*
Fairview Mineral Spring, 215
Faris, Herman P., 147–48
Fayette Salt Spring, 152

INDEX

Featherstonehaugh, George, 9, 19, 41, 101–2; and mineralization, 5
Ferber, Edna, 17
Fitch, Dr. William, 87–88
Flagg, Edmund, 36
Flora of Missouri, 10
Ford Well, 149
Forest (Sulphur) Springs, 163–64
Freemore's Lick, 27
Freewater, Missouri, 144
French Lick, Indiana, 19, 21
Freshwater/saltwater interface, 7, 8
Fuller, Myron, 89
Fur trade, 25, 35, 38

Galbraith's Medical Well, 170
Galena Medical Spring, 209
Garfield, President James, 70
Gasconade County: springs in, 219
Gasconade Hotel, 70, *165*
Gases in mineralized water, 5
Gazetteer of the State of Missouri, 24, 182, 186
Gentry County: springs in, 143–46, 220; mentioned, 67, 104
Geologic surveys of Missouri, 9, 41–42, 43, 44–47
Geology, 6; connate, 5, 6; role in mineralizing water, 4–8
Geology of Greene County, 146
Germ theory, 105
Glasgow Mineral Spring, 153
Good Housekeeping, 87, 96–97
Goreham's Lick, 44
Grand Pass Spring, 202
Graydon Springs, 184–85
Great Salt (White) Spring, 202–3; mentioned, 7
Greene County: springs in, 146; mentioned, 67, 108
Greene Springs, 212
Groundwater: biology of, 8–10; characteristics of, 4–7; origins of mineralized water, 6

Haggenbush Springs, 211
Hall of Waters (Excelsior Springs), *64,* 134
Hamilton, Alexander, 79

Hannibal Messenger, 186
Harper's, 91
Harrison County: springs in, 146–47, 220; mentioned, 67
Harris Springs, 174–75
Harrodsburg, Kentucky, 21
Health Resorts and Mineral Springs in the West, 55, 156
Heilbron Spring, 146–47
Hennerich, Dr. Joseph, 197
Henry County: springs in, 147–50, 220; mentioned, 29, 67, *85,* 108
Hereford, Dr. Thomas, 36, 37
Hillsboro Mineral Spring, 158
History of Jackson County, 156
Holmes, Dr. Wendell, 62–63
Horse racing, 21; mentioned, 36, 70–71
Hot Springs (Arkansas), 19–20, 23; mentioned, 109
Hot Springs (Virginia), 18
Houston, Sam, 21
Howard County, *26, 29, 30;* springs in, 150–53, 220; mentioned, 31, 67
Howell County: springs in, 154–55, 220; mentioned, 67, 104
Hucksterism, 55, 56. *See also* Quackery
"Hucksters of Pain," 137
Hulme, Thomas, 19
Hutchinson, Woods, 95–96
Hydrogen sulfide, 9
Hydrogeology, 85
Hydropathic Encyclopedia, 63
Hydropathy ("water cure"), 62–63
Hydrotherapy, 88, 109, 112; and Dr. Jerome Kintner, 107
Hygeia Mineral Springs Company, 94

Icarians, 37, 199
Illinois, 31
Indiana, spas in, 19, 21
Indians, American, 27; in colonial America, 16; Osage, 27, 38, 140, 194; and salt, 25; and treaties, 34
Indian Springs, 170–71
Internal Improvement Convention, 42
Iron County: springs in, 220
Iuka Spring, 193

Jackson, Andrew, 20
Jackson County: springs in, 155–57, 220; mentioned, 67
Jackson Lithia Spring, 156
James, Edwin, 5, 35, 151, 175–76
James, Jesse, 149
Jamesport Mineral Springs, 143
Jasper County: springs in, 220
Jefferson, Thomas, 77
Jefferson County: springs in, 157–60, 220; mentioned, 25, 31, 40, 67
Jerico Springs, 129, *130*
Jesuits, 25, 31
Johnson County: springs in, 160–63, 221; mentioned, 29, 67, 72, 84
Jones, Rev. Sam, 72
Journalism: and decline of resorts, 107. *See also* specific publications
Joutel, Henri, 24

Kanawha River, 32
Kansas, spas in, 23
Kansas City, 99, 111
Kansas City Star, 94
Kimmswick, Missouri, 25
King, Austin A., 41
King, Dr. Henry, 42
Kintner, Dr. Jerome, 107, 143, 144, 147
Kircher, Athanasius, 14
Knox County: springs in, 163, 221; mentioned, 67, 108

Laclede County: springs in, 163–65; mentioned, 67
Lafayette County: springs in, 221
Lake Park Springs, 212–13
Lamine River, 26, 142
Lawrence County: springs in, 166
Lead industry, 25
Lebanon Magnetic Water Company, 164–65
Lebanon Magnetic Well, 164–65, *166*
Leisure pursuits, 70–71
Leopold and Loeb, 158
Lewis, Meriwether, 26
Lewis and Clark expedition, 26, 41

Lewis Chalybeate (Sand Creek) Spring, 148–49
Lewis County: springs in, 166–67, 221
Limestone, 4
Lincoln County: springs in, 221
Lineville Mineral Well, 172–73, *173*
Lisa, Manuel, 26
Lists and Analyses of the Mineral Springs of the United States, 45
Lithium, 96–97
Lithium Spring Company, 180
Lithium Springs, *76,* 179–80
Litton, Dr. A., 42, 206
Livingston County: springs in, 167–68, 221; mentioned, 67, 73
Long, Major Stephen, 5, 26, 35, 175–76; expedition of, 5, 41. *See also* James, Edwin
Lotus Springs, 143
Louisiana, Missouri, 107
Louisiana Artesian Well, 183
Louisiana Purchase, 41
Louisiana Purchase Exposition. *See* St. Louis World's Fair
Loutre Lick, 35, 176; mentioned, 79
Lynn Springs, 16

Macon County: springs in, 221
Madison County: springs in, 168, 221; mentioned, 67
Magnetic healing, 85, 164–65
Maple Leaf Hotel, 192
Maries County: springs in, 168, 221; mentioned, 67
Marion County: springs in, 168–69, 221–22; mentioned, 68
Marmaduke, John, 207
Marmaduke Military Academy, 207
Matthews, F. H., 138
McAllister, John, 203
McAllister Springs, 203–5, *204*
McDonald County: springs in, 170–72, 222; mentioned, 68, 103
McLellan's Well (Springs), 125
McPheters, Dr. William, 61
Medical science, modern, 60–61, 105–7
Medicinal value of spring waters, 16, 39, 53–59, 58. *See also* Quackery

Medicine and Society in America, 61
Memoirs of a Natural History of Mineral Waters, 14
Mercer County: springs in, 172–73, 222; mentioned, 68
Merrell, Dr. Albert, 55–56, 156
Merrill and Wright, 143, 144, 167; mentioned, 81
Michaux, François André, 19
Miller County: springs in, 173–74, 222; mentioned, 68, 102
Mineola, *20, 36,* 175–76, *177*
Mineral Avalanche, 144
Mineral City, 190–92
Mineral Resource Reports, 97
Minerals, 96–97; chemical analysis of water, 14
Mineral springs: chalybeate, 43; in colonial America, 16–17; decline of, 114–15; Pike County, 183. *See also* Mineral water
Mineral Springs, Barry County, 117–18
Mineral Springs of the U.S. and Canada, 55
Mineral Springs Sanitarium, 107
Mineral water: 6, 16; and ancient civilizations, 11–12; bottled, 45; chemical analysis of, 80–82; classification of, 49, 55; geologic conditions relating to, 4–10; locations in Missouri, 8; taste of, 76–77; theological views on curative value, 12; therapeutic value of, 16, 39, 53–59, 58, 75–76. *See also* Mineral springs; Mineral water therapy
"Mineral Water Humbug," 96–97
Mineral Waters of the United States and American Spas, 87–88
Mineral water therapy, 167; bathing, 101; in Jerico Springs, 129; McAllister Springs, 205; medicinal use of, 16, 17, 19, 57, 60, 64, 124; and Schweitzer, 50–53; and Shepard, 53; and Sweet Springs, 206; value of, debunked, 95–97; Versailles Medical Springs, 177–78. *See also* Quackery
Minnewawa Hotel, 162, 163
Missionaries, Jesuit, 25, 31
Mississippi River: and Missouri population, 34; mentioned, 73
Missouri: early settlers of, 25; federal provisions to use salt springs, 29, 31; geology of, 4–8; growth of, 22, 34–35, 40; growth of mineral water resorts, 64, 65; location of mineral waters in, 8, 66, 67–68; mineral springs assessed by Peale, 45; state geologists, 42. *See also* individual counties
Missouri Department of Natural Resources, 115
Missouri Geological Survey, 9, 41, 56; of 1870, 43; of 1889–1892, 44–47; recommended by Lilburn Boggs, 41
Missouri Republican, 199
Missouri State Medical Association, 79
Monegaw, Chief, 194
Monegaw Club, 195
Monegaw Springs, 40, 193–96, *195*
Monroe County: springs in, 174–75, 222; mentioned, 68, 108
Montesano, 73
Montesano Springs, 158–60
Montesano Springs Company, 159
Montgomery, Dr. Thomas, 79
Montgomery County, *20;* springs in, 175–77, 222; mentioned, 35, 36, 68
Montgomery County Leader, 176
Mooresville, 167–68
Moorman, Dr. J. J., 54–55
Morgan County: springs in, 177–78, 222
Mullen, Steve, 190–92
Mundus Subterraneous, 14

Nevada, Missouri, 7
Nevada Artesian Well, *52,* 212–13
New Baden, 117
New Mexico, spas in, 23
Newspapers: and demise of mineral spas, 107. *See also* specific publications
Newton County: springs in, 222
New York state: Erie Canal, 31, 32; "Owatahox Spring," 107. *See also* Saratoga Springs (New York)
Nine Wonders, 130–31, *131*
Nodaway County: springs in, 178–79, 222–23; mentioned, 68
Notes on the State of Virginia, 77

Oil exploration, 84, 189
Oklahoma, spas in, 23
Old Orchard Spring, 198
Old Orchard Water, 198
On Baths and Mineral Waters, 19
Oregon County: springs in, 179; mentioned, 68, 108
Ozark County: springs in, 222–23

Paris Springs, 166; mentioned, 79
Patent medicine industry, 61–62. *See also* Quackery
Peale, Dr. Albert, 23, 44–45, 91–92; mentioned, 81, 90
Peerless Spring, 138
Pepys, Samuel: on bathing, 13
Perry County: springs in, 179–81; mentioned, 68, 76, 108
Perry County Sun, 179
Pertle Springs, 72–73, *73, 74,* 161–63
Petroleum, 84, 189
Pettis County: springs in, 181, 223; mentioned, 108
Phelps County: springs in, 181–82
Philadelphia Gazette, 16
Pierce, Anne, 96
Pike County: springs in, 182–84, 223; mentioned, 39, 68
Pike expedition, 41
Platte County: springs in, 184; mentioned, 43, 68
Plattsburg Mineral Spring, 138–39
Polk County: springs in, 184–85; mentioned, 68
Ponce de Leon, 209–10
Popular Science, 105
Population growth (Missouri), 22, 34–35, 40
Powell, John Wesley, 44
Pumpelly, Raphael, 43
Pure Food and Drug Act, 87, 95
Pure Food and Drug Congress, 95
Putnam County: springs in, 223

Quackery, 55, 62–63; American Medical Association exposes, 95; and Burlington Junction Mineral Springs, 101; lithium debunked, 96–97; magnetic healing, 85, 164–65; patent medicine, 61–62

Radioactivity, 86–88, 118, 188–89
Radiology, 109
Radio Springs Park, *214*
Radium Springs, 87, 118–19, 188–89
Railroads: effect on tourism, 22, 37; in Excelsior Springs, 22, 136; excursions to resorts, 73; loss of business due to routing of, 104, 122, 139, 174; Santa Fe, 23; in St. Louis, 37
Ralls County, *10;* springs in, 186, 223; mentioned, 27, 31, 68
Randolph County: springs in, 188–90, 224; mentioned, 43, 44, *68, 72*
Randolph Medical Springs, 189–90
Randolph Petroleum Company, 189
Randolph Spa, 189
Randolph Springs: and salt manufacturing, 32
Randolph Springs (Goreham's Lick), 44
Randolph Springs (Salt Springs), 189–91, *192;* mentioned, 32
Ray County: springs in, 190–92, 224; mentioned, 68, 108
Recreational and social aspects of resorts, 18; in colonial America, 16, 17; and popularity decline, 103
Red Sulphur Springs, 18
Reed Springs, 138
Religion, 72; historical significance of springs in, 12; meetings at resorts, 72
Reno, 133
Report on the Mineral Waters of Missouri, 5, 47–48, 57, 81, 119, 172–73, 184
Resorts, 124–25; "Big six" of Virginia and West Virginia, 17, 18; in colonial America, 16; decline of, 100–112; effect of automobile on, 104; effect of railroads on, 22, 37, 73, 104; effect on growth of communities, 73–74; growth in Missouri, 101–3; providing recreational pastimes, 36; Spalding Springs, 187–88; Sweet Springs, 207. *See also* individual resorts and spas

River Des Peres, 5, 35, 199; diverted for St. Louis World's Fair, 37–38; and Icarians, 37
Robertson, J. D., 49, 104, 119–20, 123
Rocheport Sulphur Spring, 122
Rolla Artesian Wells, 181–82
Rummell, David, 185
Rush, Dr. Benjamin, 105

Saline County, 4, *6, 22;* landforms and water quality in, 7; springs in, 199–208; mentioned, 10, 26, 27, 31, 32, 33, 44, 59, 68, *78, 91,* 108; mentioned, 59
Saline Creek, 25
Saline provisions, 29, 31, 186
Salisbury Well, 132
Salmagundi Papers, 18
Salt: animal licks, 24, 29, 189; importing from Europe, 32; and wells, 83–84. *See also* Saltworks
Salt Creek Spring, 196
Saltwater/freshwater interface, 6, 7, *8*
Saltworks, 25–33, 43, 189; and Boone family, 27–28, 32, 150–51; destroyed by Union troops, 32; François Vallé, 27; Great Salt (White) Spring, 203; Gum Spring, 200; "Ohio Saline," 31; Pierre Chouteau secures land for, 38; use of well water in, 83–84
Sand Creek Spring, 148
Sander, Dr. Enno, 90, 96
Sanford, Samuel, 94
Sanitariums, 107; Mayfield Brothers Sweet Springs, 208; Mineral Spring, 183; Schumer Springs, 180–81
Saranac Springs, 56, 142
Saratoga Springs (Missouri), 171
Saratoga Springs (New York), 17, 21; Simon Baruch Research Institute, 108; mentioned, 70, 79
Saratoga Trunk, 17
Saturday Evening Post, 110, 137
Schlundt, Herman, 86
Schumer Springs, 180–81
Schweitzer, Paul, 5, 47–52, *48,* 174; advises on process of drinking water, 75; and chemical analysis of water, 81–82; classifies Missouri's mineral waters, 49; on magnetism, 85; measures water flow, 114, 115; *Report on the Mineral Waters,* 124; and therapeutic value of mineral water, 57; mentioned, 65, 85
Scott County: springs in, 224
Seashore salt grass, 10, 202
Sects, medicinal, 62
Settle, Samuel, 192
Shannon County: springs in, 208; mentioned, 68
Shannon Spring, 169
Shaw, George, family, 117
Shepard, Edward, 53, 145, 183, 185
Shyrock, Richard, 61
Sigerist, Henry, 111
Siloam Spring (Clay County), *46*
Siloam Springs (Gentry County), 143–46, *145,* 154–55
Siloam Springs (Arkansas), 23
Siloam Springs Sanitarium, *145*
Simon Baruch Research Institute, 108
Smithville Reservoir, 138
Snapp's Hotel, 110, *111*
Social aspects of spas, 60, 69–74, 162; "taking the waters," 18–19
Spalding, Edward, 187
Spalding Springs, *10,* 186–88, *187*
Spas, European, 13, 14; Bath, England, 11, 14; Schweitzer compares to Missouri's, 50; Tunbridge Wells, 69
Sports, 70–71
Springfield, Missouri, 53
Springfield Republican, 90
Springs of Missouri, 121, 124, 199
Stafford Springs, 16, 17
St. Charles, Missouri, 27, 35
St. Charles County; springs in, 224
St. Clair County: springs in, 192–96, 224; mentioned, 43, 68
St. Cloud Springs Company, 192
Ste. Genevieve, Missouri, 34
Ste. Genevieve County: springs in, 224; mentioned, 24, 25
Steyermark, Julian, 10, 202
Stice's Spring, 122

INDEX

St. Louis: cholera outbreak of 1849, 61; population in 1830, 34, 35; World's Fair, 38, 90, 91, 93, 157, 174
St. Louis Academy of Science, 43; mentioned, 33
St. Louis Board of Health, 56
St. Louis County, 96–97; springs in, 196–99, 224; mentioned, 43, 68. *See also* Chouteau Springs
St. Louis Greys, 36
St. Louis World's Fair, 38, 90, 91, *93*, 157, 174; Bockert Mineral Water, 93; Missouri mineral waters exhibited at, 92
Stone County: springs in, 209–10, 225; mentioned, 68
Stratton, D. G., 129
Sublette, William, 35–37, 198–99
Sullivan County: springs in, 225
Sulphur Springs (St. Louis), 35–37, 160; mentioned, 43
Sulphur (Forest) Springs (Knox County), 163–64
Sulphur Spring tract, 35
Swallow, George, 42–43
Sweet Springs (Missouri), 205–8; and advertising, 79; bottling plant, *91;* promotional literature, 103; swimming pools, 77; mentioned, 7, 40, 43, 59, 75, 77
Sweet Springs (Virginia), 18–19
Swimming, 71; coed, 12, 77; Gum Spring, 200; mineral water used in pools, 97; remains of, *72, 141*

Taberville Spring, 196
Testimonials, 75, 79, 101
Texas, spas in, 23
Texas County: springs in, 210–11; mentioned, 68, 77, 108
Therapeutic value of mineral waters. *See* Mineral water therapy
Thurneysser, Leonhard, 12, 13–14
Tiffany, Dr. Flavel, 184
Tiffany Springs, 184
Trall, Dr. Russell, 62–63
Triplett Well, 132
Truman, Harry S., 134; mentioned, 79

Truman Dam, 121
Truman Reservoir, 119, 120, 149, 193
Twin Springs, 122, 172

Underground Waters of Missouri, 183
University of Missouri, 42, 47
U.S. Bureau of Chemistry, 96
U.S. Department of Agriculture, 95
U.S. Geological Survey (USGS), 23, 89; *Mineral Resource Reports,* 97; Montana Division, 45; mentioned, 44, 50, 86, 90, 94
U.S. Public Health Service, 87

Vaile, Col. Harvey, 156–57
Vaile Spring, 156–57
Vallé, François, 27
Van Bibber, Isaac, 35, 175
Van Bibber Tavern, *36*
Vandike, Jim, 115
Vernette Mineral Well, 170
Vernon County: springs in, 211–14, 225; mentioned, 52, 68, 106, 108
Veronica Medical Spring Water, 97
Versailles Medical Spring, 177–78
Vichy, *169*
Virginia Spas and Springs of the South and West, 54

Walker Spring, 138
Walton, Dr. George, 55, 124
Warm Springs, 17
Washington, George, 17, 18, 77; mentioned, 79, 100
Water purification plants, 93–94
Wayne County: springs in, 225
Welby, Adlard, 18
Welch, Fountain T., 209
Welch Spring, 208
Wells: artesian, 8, 84–85, *85,* 197; as source for mineral water, 83–86; water used in salt production, 83–84
West Baden, 21; mentioned, 20
West El Dorado, 130–31, *131*
Wetmore, Alphonso; 24, 28, 39, 158, 182, 186; mentioned, 29
White Rock Sulphur Springs (Jane), 172

White (Great Salt) Spring (Saline County), 202–3; mentioned, 7
White Sulphur Springs (Missouri), 40
White Sulphur Springs (Montana), 47
White Sulphur Springs (Virginia), 18, 54, 120–21; and golf, 70; and mint julep, 21; water like that of Sulphur Springs, 36; mentioned, 75
Wilcox, Mr., well of, 44
Wiley, Harvey, 95, 96, 123
Wilton Spring, 208
Windsor Medical Well, 149–50
Wisconsin Medical Society, 61
Winslow, Arthur, 44–45
Woodward, Amos, 9, 47–48; mentioned, 9
Works Progress Administration (WPA), 110, 134

World's Fair: Chicago, 90; St. Louis, 38, 90, 91, *93*, 157, 174
Worth County: springs in, 215, 225; mentioned, 68
WPA Guide to Missouri, 71
Wright and Merrill, 143, 144, 167, mentioned, 81
Wright County: springs in, 225
Wyaconda Water, 166–67
Wyman, A. W., 134

Yantis, Dr. John, 205–6
Yellowstone Park, 45, 86
Younger brothers (outlaws), 149, 195

Zodiac, 213–14

ABOUT THE AUTHOR

Loring Bullard is Executive Director of the Watershed Committee of the Ozarks. He is the author of *The Springs of Greene County,* and he lives in Springfield, Missouri.

613.122 B935h

Bullard, Loring.

Healing waters